Other Books by Dawn Potter

POETRY
Boy Land & Other Poems (2004)
How the Crimes Happened (2010)
Same Old Story (2014)

PROSE
Tracing Paradise: Two Years in Harmony with John Milton (2009)
The Vagabond's Bookshelf (2015)

ANTHOLOGY
A Poet's Sourcebook: Writings about Poetry, from the Ancient World to the Present (2013)

The Conversation

Learning to Be a Poet

Dawn Potter

DEERBROOK EDITIONS

PUBLISHED BY
Deerbrook Editions
P.O. Box 542
Cumberland, ME 04021
207.829.5038
www.deerbrookeditions.com
www.issuu.com / deerbrookeditions
distributed by spdbooks.org

FIRST EDITION
© 2015 by Dawn Potter
All rights reserved.

ISBN: 978-0-9904287-1-8

Book Design by Jeffrey Haste
Cover design & photo by Jeffrey Haste

To the teachers and the poets
of the Frost Place

This is a fire I caught from the earth.
—Robert Frost

Contents

Introduction
Fellow Feeling and Common Experience

"A poem is the act of having an idea and how it feels to have an idea."[1] Robert Frost scrawled those words in one of the more than forty notebooks he filled with thoughts, complaints, teaching ideas, and poem drafts over the course of his writing life. The sentence was his own private remark, meant for no one but himself; yet when I, nearly a half-century after his death, stumbled across the line, I recognized, with a swift conviction of wonder and completion, the shape of what he, too, had so swiftly recognized. Yes, I thought. You have said exactly what I have never said myself. You have said it, and now I have heard it.

In a later notebook entry, Frost commented, "'There you are—you've said it' is the most influencing thing you can say to a person. Or I know exactly—you get it just as I have felt it." By means of this simple interchange, the speakers share, in Frost's words, "fellow feeling and common experience."[2] At this instant, they are no longer engaged in instruction or chat, in argument or even discussion. They are participating as equals in a conversation that has crystallized around a suddenly shared perception. And that is exactly how I felt when I read his definition of a poem.

I'm sure that you, too, have been transported by a rare conversational moment when intellect and emotion and attentiveness synthesize into a "fellow feeling" of not only exquisite understanding but also exponential possibility. The participants in this conversation may be parent and child or student and teacher; they may be colleagues or lovers or accidental travel companions; they may be reader and poet, painter and viewer. They may be any two human beings in any time or place. What is necessary is the sense, whether actual or inferred, that one person has articulated some vital working of mind or heart and that the other has heard and acknowledged a shared, intense comprehension.

This spirit of conversation is at the center of poetry; and as Countee Cullen expressed in "To John Keats, Poet, at Springtime," it can thrive without regard for time or circumstance:

> "John Keats is dead," they say, but I
> Who hear your full insistent cry
> In bud and blossom, leaf and tree,
> Know John Keats still writes poetry.[3]

Yet to people immersed in their bustling present-tense affairs, this vibrating bond between people who are separated by centuries (not to mention divided by race, gender, class, religion, education, or sexual preference) may seem quaint, even suspicious. Cullen's attachment to the English Romantic poets made him an oddity among more obviously progressive figures of the Harlem Renaissance. As James Weldon Johnson noted in *The Book of American Negro Poetry,*

> Some critics have ventured to state that Cullen is not an authentic Negro poet. . . . There is in it a faint flare-up which would object to the use of "white" material by a Negro artist, or at least regard it with indulgent condescension. . . . Yet strangely, it

is because Cullen revolts against these "racial" limitations—technical and spiritual—
that the best of his poetry is motivated by race. He is always seeking to free himself
and his art from these bonds.[4]

    In other words, the conversation that Cullen sensed between himself and Keats was not
sterile scholarship. Rather, it interacted with the circumstances of his daily life, feeding
the living reader's imagination and his growth as a poet.

    An intense relationship with poetry of the past doesn't mean that a contemporary
poet must forsake the pull of her own time and place. It's natural for us to be drawn to
work that is constructed from the details of our daily concerns, and certainly this is the
world that will predominate, in one form or another, in our own writing. A closer bond
with history simply gives us more scope, both technically and imaginatively. Keats may
have loved Milton, but that doesn't mean he wrote in the idiom of a politically charged
seventeenth-century Puritan who was frighteningly well educated as well as blind and
quarrelsome. He wrote in the idiom of the man he was: a bookish, nineteenth-century,
lower-middle-class, tubercular agnostic, a loving brother who maintained a handful of
intensely sweet friendships. Likewise, no one would mistake Countee Cullen for Keats,
yet neither man would have become the poet he did had he not engaged in these century-
spanning conversations.

The Reading-Conversation-Writing Cycle

In his essay "Of Studies," first published in 1625, Francis Bacon declared, "Reading maketh
a Full Man; Conference a Ready Man; And Writing an Exact Man."[5] Certainly, all three
apply to teaching and learning about poetry. To be a writer, one must be a questing reader,
forever seeking closer intimacy with the art; and talking about its details, whether in
actual conversation or merely to oneself, can lead a reader down unexpected imaginative
paths. The three actions are entwined: one leads to the other, leads to the other, leads
to the other. Even if you think of yourself as more reader than poet, more teacher than
reader, participating in all elements of the reading-conversation-writing cycle will help
you become a more concentrated and flexible practitioner.

READING

Anyone who teaches high school or college-level English classes has wrestled with
students who are convinced that John Donne, Ben Jonson, Robert Herrick, Robert
Browning, Christina Rossetti, and the rest of the oldsters that clog the front halves of
survey anthologies are entirely irrelevant to their own lives. Even if they eventually learn
to respect such poets as historical figures, many students—even those who think of
themselves as writers—never see them as imaginative peers. This historical disconnect
doesn't just damage students creatively. It also impedes their growth as curious, questing,
complex readers. Instead of wading into the mysterious waters of the poem, they skirt
the edges, parroting the teacher's literary tour guide rather than diving after their own
treasures.

    By means of this book, I hope to coax readers into more adventurous engagements
with both canonical and contemporary poetry. Although I focus on poets from various
eras, all share modern English as a common language (as opposed to Middle English or

Anglo-Saxon), and all are accomplished and complex artists. Gender, race, religion, and other such markers have not been primary motivators in my decision about whom to include. Many other books offer such riches, and I encourage you to seek them out. But my purpose is different. My intent is to show that it is possible, even necessary, for us to converse with poets who are historically and aesthetically distinct from ourselves and that they have the power to speak to us as individual human beings and fellow artists.

There are many ways to absorb a poem: by listening, by reading silently, by reading aloud, by memorizing. But in my view, copying out a poem—letter for letter, word for word, comma for comma, line for line—is an essential tool for engaging with poetry. Although memorization is a wonderful way to absorb a poem, it leaves us open to error: for instance, we often misremember words or omit lines. It also allows us to overlook the visual power of a poem: punctuation and capitalization, stanza and line breaks. But when we write down every element of a poem, we come as close as we ever will to living inside another mind as it actively creates a poem. Moreover, copying out a poem forces a reader to slow down and take note of every single detail. This makes it an amazingly useful way to counteract writer's block, which is often simply the malaise of distraction. Copying presses us to concentrate on the entirety of the poem—not its so-called meaning but its actuality: the bits and pieces of language that accrue to form a work of art.

In the classroom I frequently dictate poems to students so that the class as a whole can experience the sensation of discovering a poem in this focused, cohesive, mesmerizing way. Master teachers Baron Wormser and David Cappella write persuasively about this approach in *A Surge of Language: Teaching Poetry Day by Day:* "By dictating the poem I can slow time down and get the words into my students' bodies. Poetry is physical and I want them to experience that physicality. By writing the words down . . . they have to grapple with the physical nature of each word."[6]

For poets, readers, and teachers who are grappling alone with a poem, copying directly from the page serves a parallel function. So I suggest that, as you read this book, you commit yourself to copying out at least some of the poems I present. If you copy the poem before you read the accompanying chapter, you will be well positioned to follow and extend my conversational gambits in your own idiosyncratic way, whether you are more interested in pursuing these discoveries as a teacher or a reader or hope to use them as impetus for your own poems.

If you are a teacher who is using this book in the classroom, you might ask your students to copy out the poems and turn them in to you. By way of this seemingly innocuous assignment, you both may discover that accurate copying requires considerable concentration and that people who create an exact facsimile of an existing poem are perforce learning a great deal about the subtle power of even the tiniest elements of the language. Not only can this discovery teach us to bring our own poems to life, but the very act of copying out a poem can be a form of homage, even a gift. Picture the look on a student's face if you were to copy out one of her poems and then return it to her, along with your admiration. In 1904 Rainer Maria Rilke offered such a gift to an aspiring young poet named Franz Kappus. In *Letters to a Young Poet,* Rilke wrote:

> You see—I have copied your sonnet, because I found that it is lovely and simple and born in the form in which it moves with such quiet decorum. . . . And now I give

you this copy because I know that it is important and full of new experience to come upon a work of one's own again written in a strange hand. Read the lines as though they were someone else's, and you will feel deep within you how much they are your own.[7]

Conversation

Most of you know how transporting a class discussion can be. There are moments when the group's verbal connection seems to lead every participant into new territory. Suddenly, students with different beliefs, ideas, skills, and backgrounds are listening and absorbing each other's words, not just for the sake of politeness but because those words are leading both the group and the individuals into complex explorations.

In 2010 I hosted an informal online reading group that centered around Shakespeare's play *The Winter's Tale*. The project began as a sudden, unplanned idea that sprang from a conversation with a friend. Although not everyone who initially expressed interest ended up taking part in the reading group, we did have a core group of participants. One was my twelve-year-old son Paul, who was thrilled about the idea of reading his first Shakespeare play. His friend Conor (also twelve) and Conor's mother Allison, a social worker, joined the group. Other participants included Donna, who was home with her young daughter and working on her associate's degree; Ruth, an elementary school teacher; Lucy, an archivist and author with a Ph.D. in history; Sheila and Scott, both high school English teachers; and an anonymous reader.

My first act as facilitator was to toss out handful of discussion questions about the first half of act 1.[8]

1. What word or phrase in this section was most beautiful, or strange, or annoying, or disturbing, or in any other way particularly noteworthy? Why?
2. What surprised you about the characters or their conversation?
3. What confused you about the characters or their conversation?
4. Who's your favorite character so far, and why?

Following are the responses to those questions, in the order in which they appeared.

Dawn

1. I love that phrase "sneaping winds" (scene 2, line 13). I don't exactly know what "sneaping" means, but it sounds like one of those chilly, pestering breezes that torment onlookers at elementary soccer games in early November.
2. I was most surprised by Hermione's conversation with Polixenes. Having read this play before, I know that her husband will become wrongly jealous of her relationship with P. But you know, she really does sound kind of flirty here. I'm not excusing Leontes' future bad behavior. But I'm beginning to see how she allowed it to happen.
3. It took me a while to figure out who Camillo and Archidamus were and how they were connected to Leontes and Polixenes and which person was king of Sicilia and which of Bohemia. I kept having to recheck the cast of characters to sort them all out. I suspect that on stage this would be less confusing than it is on the page.
4. So far my favorite character is "young prince Mamillius," and he isn't even on stage

yet. Everyone speaks of him with such affection. He is a "gallant child, one that, indeed, physics the subject, makes old hearts fresh." I have a weakness for a couple of gallant children myself, which probably accounts for this preference.

Paul

I think it started out slowly but is getting there. I don't get what the first scene was about but that's okay. It's one of those scenes that isn't rigidly connected to the story.

Lucy

Honestly, my first surprise was that that *Winter's Tale* is not *Measure for Measure*. I had mixed up the two plays in my mind. Because of that, I had to figure out if I had ever read the play and skimmed the whole play online in some early edition. As a result, I can't comment on anything in particular except for my utter surprise at how vicious the play is. As I think on that, I think about the power of jealousy especially in the face of unfaithfulness to take over your whole brain and body. I never took such dire steps as Leontes, but I sure did some pretty crazy things when caught up in those feelings. The first scene just confused me. I tried reading it out loud, but the puns and malapropisms without any context were too hard. I like it better when these kind of scenes show up later in his plays. If I was directing the play, I would have cut from that section.

Dawn

I've never researched this issue, but I've often wondered if the first scenes of many Shakespeare plays were mostly a chance for Globe audiences to finish up their fistfights, etc., and settle down to start watching the show.

Ruth

I agree with Lucy; the first scene just confused me too. By scene 2, I was getting into the language and not really worrying if I "got" everything or not and found that I had a better grip on the story. It has been way too long since I've read any Shakespeare.
1. I really like scene 2, line 47 when Hermione says, "Verily you put me off with limber vows; but I, though you would seek to unsphere the stars with oaths, Should yet say, 'Sir, no going.'"
2. Dawn, Hermione does sound flirty. Perhaps she is one of those women whom I sometimes envy: they just seem to know how to flatter their audience. I do like her and have always liked that name too. I had a doll named Hermione.
3. Paul, that's a good point about scene 1 not being rigidly connected.

Scott

"Finish up their fistfights"! lol
1. I like the line "Thou wants a rough pash and the shoots that I have" (1.2.128). I mean who doesn't want a rough pash?
2. I'm a little surprised at the extent of Hermione's efforts to keep Polixenes around. Somewhere in that exchange her requests that he stay cross the line from a polite expression of affection into something else. For his part, Polix has been gifted with a

quick wit and seems to be showing a lot of restraint, like Shakespeare doesn't want him to be held to blame for anything that happens between the happy couple later. I can't decide if that makes him dull straw man of a character or not.

3. I kept having to re-read the lines around 1.2.23–27 "were in your love a whip to me." I get the point, but I'm not sure how it gets there.

4. My favorite is Archidamus, though he doesn't really say anything to distinguish himself yet. He just strikes me as maybe one of the reasonable minds who is going to be just enough removed from the drama to be able to deliver some nice quips about it. If he doesn't, I'll be disappointed.

Sheila

Re the issue of Leontes' jealousy: Do you think that he is jealous of Hermione's ability to attract Polixenes' attention, to convince him to stay when his childhood friend Leontes cannot? I thought it was no accident that L. becomes jealous after Hermione sweet-talks P., esp. after how the two kings have been talking about how close they were when they were younger.

Anonymous

1. I had a tussle with "affection" until I realized that it meant any disposition or mood. Its repetition in the first two scenes makes me think it may be a key word for understanding the play. We shall see.

2, 3. To soon to tell. I am too busy retuning my eye and ear to Elizabethan English.

4. Without a doubt, so far, it's Archidamus. His wisecracking at the end of the first scene caught my sense of humor.

Donna

The language is very hard for me to understand although I think I am able to pick up some of the important stuff and just shrug off the rest for now.

The line that really made an impression on me was when Hermione says, "one good deed dying tongueless slaughters a thousand waiting upon that." I'm not exactly sure what the context was that she said that but it really made sense to me in that I try really hard to do good things that make a difference.

It is interesting to read what other people think of the play. Thanks for doing this. I don't think I would have attempted any more Shakespeare on my own!

Just a little funny note about the name "Hermione." When I substituted in fifth grade a long time ago the teacher was reading *Harry Potter* out loud to the class. The kids got on my case about how I pronounced Hermione. They were convinced that I was saying it wrong. When I asked how it should be pronounced, I was told that it was HER-MEE-OWN-EE-OWN. I still can't help but chuckle every time I see the name "Hermione."

Allison and Conor

Conor and I just finally got around to reading this together; we read it aloud, and Conor wanted to note that he really enjoyed the word "verily." I liked the image of Polixenes and Leontes as "twinn'd lambs that did frisk I' the sun, And bleat the one at the other." I was surprised that we both seemed to be able to follow what was going on fairly well, though we also found that the first scene seems sort of unnecessary and even unclear.

I have to jump in and defend Hermione here; I really did not feel that she was overly flirty with Polixenes. Leontes called her "tongue-tied" and asked her to intervene when he was failing to convince Polixenes to stay, and it seemed to me that there was only a short time when she was focused on addressing him alone; for most of the scene she is eliciting from him memories of his boyhood with her husband, and then teasing Leontes about his assertion that this was one of the two greatest times she ever spoke. However, I've never seen or read this play before, so I don't know if this becomes part of a pattern of Hermione flirting or behaving suspiciously with Polixenes.

Lucy
If anyone else is interested in Shakespeare as a live drama, I just found an interesting version of *Winter's Tale* called the Viola Allen Acting Version from 1905 on Google Books. It splits up the play differently and has some nice "production notes" and pretty pictures of Viola Allen (I don't know who she was except I bet a famous actress).

It's been almost four years since this exchange about *The Winter's Tale* first appeared on my blog. Nonetheless, I still shiver with pleasure at the accidental, improvisational beauty of this conversation. It combines so many different kinds of reactions—wonder, worry, curiosity, opinion, delight, memory—and all work to expand confidence, emotional connection, intellectual growth, and civil engagement. One person's thoughts jumpstart another person's thoughts. Readers agree and disagree. They draw connections from their personal lives. They branch into further research. They puzzle over crabbed bits of language. They consider the complexities of character. They honestly admit confusion.

At the same time, no one out-talks anyone else. No one behaves as if she has privileged, superior knowledge. No one imposes a viewpoint or hijacks the topic under discussion. Older readers do not patronize younger readers. Younger readers do not sneer at older readers.

Finally, no one loses focus, gets flippant, or digresses into vagaries. This is an intellectual conversation. People are thinking hard. They are taking risks when they articulate their perceptions and ideas. They force themselves to stay concentrated on the work at hand.

Most of you know that this kind of intense civil engagement is not an everyday event. A teacher may weaken the discussion by focusing too much on her own preconceived answers. Conversely, she may not offer enough structural guidance so that participant remarks become scattered and irrelevant. Self-confident chatterboxes may squelch diffident participants. Small groups may align themselves according to gender, age, or experience. Debates may descend into quarreling.

Despite these challenges, productive conversation is a crucial element of collegial growth and discovery. Too often, we develop the habit of distrusting our own curiosity about a work of literature because, long ago, a teacher or a classmate dismissed or ignored our observations. Such injuries can fester for a lifetime. But the opposite is also true: a challenging, stimulating group discussion can give us the courage to continue our own private conversation with a work of literature.

Even though writing is a solitary business, the driving force behind it is a longing to communicate with our own kind. Writers and readers play both sides of the street. They move back and forth, demanding at one moment isolation, at another connection. As Gretel Ehrlich writes, "A writer makes a pact with loneliness. It is her, or his, beach on which waves of desire, wild mind, speculation break. In my work, in my life, I am always moving toward and away from aloneness. To write is to refuse to cover up the rawness of being alive, of facing death."[9] Within that aloneness comes, now and again, the grace of a conversation—with a poem, with a forest, with a circle of readers, with another burning, lonely mind.

WRITING

In *The Life of Poetry,* Muriel Rukeyser prefers to use the word *witness* rather than *reader* or *listener* because it "includes the act of seeing or knowing by personal experience, as well as the act of giving evidence."

> The overtone of responsibility in this word is not present in the others; and the tension of the law makes a climate here which is that climate of excitement and revelation giving air to the work of art, announcing with the poem that we are about to change, that work is being done on the self.
>
> These three terms of relationship—poet, poem, and witness—are none of them static. We are changing, living beings experiencing the inner change of poetry.[10]

Reading, conversation, and writing are bound to one another. What we read not only changes us but presses us, in Rukeyser's terms, to take "responsibility" for "giving evidence" of that change. For an analogy, think of how listening intensely to music can press a songwriter to create her own work. Yes, the listener is acquiring information about song craft and construction. But she's also drawing the sounds and emotional resonance into her inner self. Her subsequent need to write her own music is driven by the "climate of excitement and revelation" that creates her "inner change."

Philip Levine describes this sensation in his essay "The Poet in New York in Detroit":

> I had known García Lorca only as the author of the "gypsy poems," a writer of lovely, exotic poems that meant little to me. But now one Saturday afternoon became a miracle as I stood in the stacks of the Wayne University library, my hands trembling, and read my life in his words. How had this strange young Andalusian, later murdered by his countrymen, come to understand my life, how had he mastered the language of my rage? This poet of grace and "deep song" had somehow caught my emotions in a way I never had, and suddenly he opened a door for me to a way of speaking about my life. I accepted his gift. That's what they give us, the humble workers in the field of poetry, these amazingly inspired geniuses, gifts that change our lives.[11]

So it's important, whether you're in the classroom or working alone at home, to make sure that your forays into writing aren't limited to detached poetry prompts. By linking creative writing directly to creative yet focused reading, you and your students may be lucky enough to discover that "suddenly [a poet] opened a door for me to a way of speaking about my life."

I'm sure you've met more than one would-be poet who writes reams of verse but never bothers to read books. Often these writers seem to believe that a poem is nothing more than a blurt of undigested feeling, a hysterical diary entry broken randomly into lines. Detached poetry prompts do nothing to solve this attitude. Merely they offer a formula. Many, for instance, function as templates ("Write a four-syllable first line, a five-syllable second line, a six-syllable third line"). Others are simply story starters ("Imagine you've found a locket in a leaf pile"). Even though they induce writing, they don't draw the writer into the larger conversation of poetry—what Jorge Luis Borges calls "the tale wherein all the voices of mankind might be found."[12]

Just as importantly, detached writing prompts don't inspire revision. When you've fulfilled the instructions of the prompt, you've finished the poem. Revision becomes a chore, an imposition, not a natural stage of writing. But when you write within the reading-conversation-writing cycle, you're always returning to poetry: perhaps rereading a poem, perhaps engaging with a very different one. The cycle ignites fresh conversations, and the poet strives to capture her quickened emotions and ideas in new approaches to a draft. Like Borges, she aspires: "Sometimes I am courageous and hopeful enough to think that it may be true—that though all men write in time, are involved in circumstances and accidents and failures of time, somehow things of eternal beauty may be achieved."[13]

Thinking Critically about Poetry

"Criticism," according to M. H. Abrams, "is the study concerned with defining, classifying, analyzing, and evaluating works of literature."[14] Many of us tend to think of criticism as a scholarly or academic endeavor rather than an active element of our creative growth. But for writers such as Woolf, Auden, Miłosz, and many others, personal essays were a way for them to sort out the historical, intellectual, and emotional threads that bound them to their art.

Even writers without a formal commitment to criticism have sought outlets for this kind of thought. In his personal letters, Keats discussed books, reactions, epiphanies, and fears. As much as anything, those letters were messages to himself—a means to stand back from his work and take stock of what he had and hadn't learned.

If you're a teacher, you're already working hard to promote your students' critical-thinking skills. Often these assignments involve literary research and analysis. But do you ask students to think critically about their own creative work? About their own subjective reactions to what they have read? If you're a poet working independently, do you push yourself to record your own intellectual quests and confusions?

In *The Life of Poetry,* Rukeyser asks, "What does [a poem] invite? A poem invites you to feel. More than that: it invites you to respond. And better than that: a poem invites a total response."[15] That total response, she argues, includes both the emotions and the intellect, which are not separate routes but lead naturally from one to the other.

In this book, I've tried to demonstrate the organic relationship between emotional and intellectual reactions to poetry. To do so, I've organized the chapters into three sections, all of which take into account the reading-conversation-writing cycle while also pushing you to think critically about your own place in poetry. The first section, "Watching a Poet

Make a Poem," addresses specific elements of poetic language or structure. The second, "Writing about Poets and Poetry," centers on writing personal literary essays about poetry. Finally, the third, "Meeting a Poem in Its Context," focuses on the way in which poets choose to combine individual poems into a larger work of art. The book concludes with an afterword that takes up the subject of publication, always a fraught question for writers. I also offer a brief list of books that, over the years, have become important personal resources. My hope is that both the details and the structure of *The Conversation* will be useful guides as you, too, forge your own path into teaching or writing.

But most of all I hope you commit yourself to reading poems. As Rukeyser reminds us,

> It is a great thing to hear the words of those who are worthy to speak them. It is a great thing to learn this in oneself. . . . It is a great thing to laugh with pleasure and delight, as children laugh; it is a great thing to say to our wordless, we will speak, in self-knowledge, in faith, at a beginning-place of many beginnings, in which none of these means is enough in itself, since each is an index to a beginning of the single spirit or of the world; it is a great thing to come to the unbegun places of our living and to say: Now we will find the words.[16]

Acknowledgments

I am grateful to the many people who supported the writing of this book. Jeffrey Haste at Deerbrook Editions was firmly committed to bringing the manuscript into the world. Without the encouragement of Michael Simms, I would never have undertaken the project in the first place. The readers of my blog offered useful responses to the excerpts I posted, and I thank the editors of the *Coal Hill Review* for reprinting a number of those posts. Featured poet Gray Jacobik was extraordinarily generous, as were members of *The Winter's Tale* reading group: Lucy G. Barber, Paul Birtwistle, Sheila Byrne, Conor Eliot, Scott Hill, Ruth Harlow, Donna Miller, Allison Nelson-Eliot, and an anonymous reader. Much of what I say in this book is directly indebted to conversations among the brilliant teachers and poets who participate in the annual Frost Place Conference on Poetry and Teaching. Christopher Woodman offered thoughtful and helpful comments on several early chapters. Above all, I thank Carlene Gadapee, who not only proofread and commented on the entire manuscript but also put many of these reading, teaching, and writing strategies into direct practice.

Watching a Poet Make a Poem

1

William Shakespeare
Sonnet 81

But all these preferences and partialities, all these adjustments and attempts of the mind to relate itself harmoniously with another, pale, as the flirtations of a summer compared with the consuming passions of a lifetime, when we consider the great devotions which one, or at the most two, names in the whole of literature inspire. Of Shakespeare we need not speak. The nimble little birds of field and hedge, lizards, shrews and dormice, do not pause in their dallyings and sportings to thank the sun for warming them.

—Virginia Woolf

About the Poet and the Poem

The son of a glove maker, William Shakespeare (1564–1616) grew up to become the most influential writer in the history of English literature. Even people with no interest in books have heard his name, and most can list the titles of a few of his plays. Yet Shakespeare was as much a poet as he was a dramatist. Indeed, the two pursuits are so entwined that his poems, which demonstrate so much physicality and psychological movement, feel like tiny, intense dramas. Likewise, his plays, with their rich, precise language and their unmatched delineation of the complexities of emotion and motivation, can be seen as enormous poems. As Samuel Taylor Coleridge said in "Shakespeare's Poetry":

> Had no *Lear,* no *Othello,* no *Henry the Fourth,* no *Twelfth Night* appeared, we must have admitted that Shakespeare possessed the chief if not all the requisites of the poet—namely deep feeling and exquisite sense of beauty, both as exhibited to the eye in combinations of form, and to the ear in sweet and appropriate melody; . . . [and] that these feelings were under the command of *his own will*—that in his very first productions he projected his mind out of his own particular being, and felt and made others feel.[1]

Shakespeare's collection of 154 sonnets was first published in 1609, but some of the individual poems had been available in manuscript for at least ten years before that printing. No one knows if Shakespeare dictated their order of appearance in the collection or if the publisher made that decision. Nor does anyone know definitively to whom, if anyone, these love poems were directed, though historians will never cease speculating about those behind-the-scenes shadows, and critics will never cease bickering about the sonnets' esoteric meanings and intent.

Sonnet 81
William Shakespeare

Or I shall live your epitaph to make,
Or you survive when I in earth am rotten;
From hence your memory death cannot take,
Although in me each part will be forgotten.
Your name from hence immortal life shall have,
Though I (once gone) to all the world must die;
The earth can yield me but a common grave,
When you entombed in men's eyes shall lie;
Your monument shall be my gentle verse,
Which eyes not yet created shall o'er-read,
And tongues to be your being shall rehearse,
When all the breathers of this world are dead;
        You still shall live (such virtue hath my pen)
        Where breath most breathes, even in the mouths of men.

What's the Most Important Word?

On the surface, this is one of the simplest questions a reader can ask about any poem. Words are words: any English reader, however innocent or sophisticated, can identify them, react to them, and talk to each other about them.

Words are also a poet's solid artisan materials, which she grasps and throws down and grasps again as she struggles to construct a poem out of silence. In this way, making a poem is very much like building a stone wall. Poets create something out of nothing; they use words to shape what has, till now, been wordless. "How should this grief be properly put into words?" is how Roman poet Horace chose to open his ode "To Virgil."[2] The way in which he wrestled with that question is the way in which he created the poem.

So when a reader asks, "What's the most important word?" she's starting to think about a poem as a poet thinks about it. She's also starting to realize that her answer is impermanent. Great art, unlike so much else in our daily lives, requires us to come to terms with our own fluidity. As a reader becomes more familiar with the poem, her choice may change. As she grows older, her choice may change. As she experiences some momentous event in her own life, her choice may change. These shifts are themselves part of the ongoing poetic conversation; in some sense, they become part of the poem itself. A reader with a long, intense relationship with a particular poem might even agree with Adrienne Rich, who wrote in "Images for Godard" that "the moment of change is the only poem."[3]

During my most recent rereading of Shakespeare's sonnet 81, my answer to "What's the most important word?" changed several times within the space of five or ten minutes. I'll take you through a few of those changes, beginning with my attraction to the simple, almost throwaway word that launches the poem.

Or

I felt, when I began copying out the poem, as if the poet had fallen through a window into his own sonnet. Or perhaps he'd been carrying on a conversation with someone outside the frame of the poem before he suddenly began to realize that he was writing it. Or perhaps this sonnet was the articulated half of a half-silent internal quarrel. Or perhaps what he wanted was for me to suddenly feel the need to write sentences that begin with *or*.

This is not a scholarly response by any means. But neither is it frivolous. Art makes artists want to make art; and as readers of poetry, we need to be sensitive to words that trigger our desire to become writers. For me, at this first rereading of sonnet 81, the word *or* was that trigger.

Notably, *or* isn't just the first word in the poem; it's the first word of the first two lines. Moreover, its sound resurfaces again in line 10, as *o'er*. "Somewhere else. / Somewhere else. / How these little words ring," wrote Wisława Szymborska in "The Railroad Station."[4] In sonnet 81, Shakespeare's little word *or* rings with simple yet ambiguous clarity; and when a poet starts to repeat a word, he may, consciously or not, be pressing a reader to pay attention to it.

Simply by taking curious notice of this unassuming word I began a private conversation with the sonnet. I also immediately made an error. According to the notes that accompany my edition, Shakespeare was using *or* as a synonym for *whether,* not in the sense that we use *or* today. Yet even though such dictionary information adds precision to the poem's opening sentence, it doesn't negate my first reaction. The power of sonic repetition, of imaginative suggestion—my feeling that the poet had just fallen through a window into his own sonnet: these reactions initiated my relationship with the poem. Moreover, they were *my* discoveries, not something I'd read in a concordance or a teacher's guide. Just ask Keats how miraculous it is to read a poem and suddenly feel "like some watcher out of the skies / When a new planet swims into his ken."[5]

But my dalliance with *or* also gave me a technical lesson in the power of English sentence structure, and in this case my newfound awareness of its etymology extended that lesson. By choosing this particular grammatical formula, Shakespeare set his argument in motion, swiftly, economically, irrevocably. *Or* drives this sonnet into being. It is proof that a rhyme scheme does not a sonnet make. And if you happen to be the teacher of facile rhymers, or a facile rhymer yourself, discovering that the first word of a line might be more crucial than the last is an invaluable though possibly crushing tutorial in sonnet composition.

ROTTEN

Rotten is one of those words that automatically makes my skin crawl—which is to say: unlike *or,* whose connotations are fairly bland, *rotten* is a word with baggage. And thanks to *Hamlet*'s "something is rotten in the state of Denmark," it's also a word that I think of as peculiarly Shakespearean.[6] So because I already have a strong personal connection to *rotten,* the word is charged with intensity even before I begin to sense how it might link to other words in this particular poem.

In her poem "Words," Sylvia Plath compared words to "Axes / After whose stroke the wood rings, / And the echoes!"[7] It's notable that both she and Szymborska's translators turned to *ring* as a way to describe these linguistic reverberations. Sometimes I feel as if I'm a conduit for such echoes; everywhere I look, there's that word again, ringing its changes, seducing or mocking or mystifying me.

Thus, when I encountered *rotten* in line 2 of the sonnet, I felt (as I had already felt with *or*) as if the frame of the poem had opened. But *rotten* worked as a connotative rather than a grammatical trigger—as if it were somehow echoing within both the poem and my linguistic memory. Even as the word was reverberating outside the poem, it was also reverberating within it.

I began to hunt for other words in the sonnet that I might tie to *rotten,* and my basket quickly overflowed with connections. Some of the words shared similar connotations (*death, earth, grave, entombed*); some shared sounds (*forgotten, cannot, common*); some were refutations (*survive, immortal, being, live*). My list could have gone on and on until I had tracked a relationship between *rotten* and every other word in the poem.

Clearly, then, the answer to "What's the most important word?" could be "every word." By tracking such connections, what I am really doing is following the coils of Shakespeare's mind at work. This is a powerful realization, and also a liberating one. Shakespeare, as a writer in process, was simply doing the same thing that we present-day writers are also doing when we are engaged in creating a poem. We choose words that speak to other words. Our poem is finished when each of those chosen words is exactly right in the context of all the other words that surround it.

Once again, I picture a wall in which each stone is essential to holding every other stone in place. *Exactly right* takes many, many elements into account: definition, connotation, sound, cadence, visual appearance, even the poet's private associations with the word. For instance, if you were to note the words *dawn* or *sunrise* or *rosy-fingered* in my poems, you would not be wrong to suspect a personal resonance, any more than I am wrong to suspect a parallel resonance in Robert Frost's many references to snow and ice. Our names, after all, are among the oldest echoes in our own minds. "Where was the child I was, / still inside me or gone?" asked Pablo Neruda in *The Book of Questions*.[8] The words that call forth these deep reverberations are the conversation of poetry.

BREATHERS, BREATH, BREATHES

Like *or, or, o'er* (as well as other words that I lingered over, such as *death, die, dead*), these words stand out because they reappear, with variations, more than once in the sonnet. But the *breath* trio also drew my attention because of the words' placement in the poem and their shifting function within a single sentence.

In his notebook Frost once wrote, "A poem should be a set of sentences."[9] That is, the words in a poem do more than build a web of echoes. As sentence elements, they also syntactically propel the poet into undiscovered thought. In other words, a poet doesn't begin writing a poem because she already knows what she wants to say. Rather, the act of writing itself allows her to begin piecing together what has lurked, unarticulated, in the back corners of her mind.

When I go back to look at sonnet 81, I see that Shakespeare constructed it using only two sentences: one is the exact length of the first quatrain (lines 1 through 4), while the other finishes out the poem (lines 5 through 14). He managed to thread his way through this massive ten-line sentence, which encompasses two quatrains and a couplet, by following the guidance of his sentence structure. Subjects led him into predicates; dependent clauses led him into independent clauses. The grammatical patterns of the English language drove his pen down the page.

Which brings me back to the *breath* trio. Shakespeare might have chosen to spread that repetition throughout the poem, as he does with the *death* variants, but he instead packs all three words into the tail end of the final sentence. In line 12 he introduces the noun *breathers*. Then, in line 14, he reprises that word, first as the root noun *breath* and finally, two words later, as the verb *breathes*. These final variants work grammatically in tandem: "Where breath most breathes, even in the mouths of men."

Among those of us addicted to the thesaurus, that treasure chest of paraphrase, a sonnet is often the poem that calls forth our most florid verbal instincts. We feverishly count syllables and shuffle rhymes; we burrow into the thesaurus as if it's a synonym grab bag. What Shakespeare demonstrates in sonnet 81 is a much more precise and economical approach that allows him to balance the complexities of a long sentence with a simplicity of word choice. It also allows him to take advantage of visual unity while playing up sonic variation. *Breath* looks a lot like *breathers* and *breathes,* but it sounds very different. *Breathers* and *breathes* share a similar pronunciation, but the difference in syllable count means that they have a different cadence. *Breath* and *breathes* are both one-syllable words, but each distinctly embodies the physicality of what it represents. Say *breath* and you discover that the word is a breath. Say *breathe* and you discover that the word imitates the action of exhaling. Within the thundering roll of his complex sentence, Shakespeare places these three poised, delicate, modest words.

Jorge Luis Borges spoke of Shakespeare's sonnets in his lecture "Of Thought and Poetry": "I know for a fact that we *feel* the beauty of a poem before we even begin to think of the meaning."[10] This beauty exists because the poet, "under the command of *his own will*" (to recall Coleridge's Napoleonic phrasing), chose specific words to frame and articulate it. He didn't sprawl on the grassy riverbank and say to himself, "I'm going to write a sonnet that means *sadness* or *loss* or *desire*." Those abstract meanings are revealed only by way of a reader's interactions with the solid materials of the sonnet.

As I hope you're beginning to see, a question such as "What's the most important word?" narrows a reader's focus while broadening her possibilities for discovery. There's no single correct answer. In fact, the more answers you come up with, the more intensely you participate in the life of the poem. As a classroom discussion starter, this question and others like it are prime ways to light an intellectual fire among your students: one person's chosen word links to another person's chosen word, a third person begins explaining why, a fourth person disagrees, and the room becomes charged with the excitement that arises when curious, concentrated people overflow with opinions and ideas.

If you're a reader alone with a poem, a structured yet open question such as "What's the most important word?" can help you sidestep distraction and develop your own conscious connections to details of a poem. But it can also help you relax. Too often, especially when faced with a canonical bigwig such as Shakespeare, our instinct is to hunch up in a corner like some sort of lesser being. Yet one day, several centuries ago, he was no better off than we are at this moment. He was faced with a blank sheet of paper. He knew he wanted to write something, but where were the words? He snatched an *or* out of the air. And so he began. By coming face to face with those bare words he chose, we become, in a way, his peer and his partner. We begin to understand what it felt like to be Shakespeare writing a poem.

Ideas for Writing

Sonnets can be dangerous writing prompts because they tend to lure poets into rhyme-scheme obsession. Those fourteen come-hither line endings often become so distracting that the poet allows the rest of her draft to fade into undifferentiated filler. Yes, a sonnet is a poem that follows a predictable pattern of rhymes. But as a glance at sonnet 81's two sentences will remind you, that pattern is not the principal propulsion of the poem. Sonnets should be active dramas, moving both the writer and the reader from one state of mind to another. By starting with rhyme rather than content, you risk a mire.

I suggest you take the opposite tack. Concentrate on the first words. To get yourself started, you might even borrow Shakespeare's first words in sonnet 81:

Or
Or
From
Although

Your
Though
The
When
Your
Which
And
When
You
Where

Now that I've erased the rest of Shakespeare's sonnet, his first words stand out as remarkably colorless—at least connotatively. With the exception of the bland personal pronouns *your, your,* and *you* and a single article, *the,* all of the words function as sentence drivers. *Or* what? *Although* what? *From* where? *Where* to? Every one of them requires a writer to push herself to choose a next word.

When I'm teaching a class, I sometimes throw out a poem's opening words as prompts. "The first word is *Or!*" I shout, and the students write feverishly. "Next line!" I shout. "The first word is *Or!*" I don't give them time to analyze but push them to write quickly. The results of these rapid first drafts are always varied, but they are consistently active and dramatic, making full use of the propulsive sentence logic that fluent English speakers internalize over the course of their lives. The bland opening words force the students to keep moving down the page, yet each writer retains control of her subject matter. Simply she's responding to an arrangement of grammatical sign posts.

If you're working alone on a poem, press yourself to write a fast first draft using each of these words as a line prompt. Don't slow down and start fiddling with end rhymes. If you decide to add them, you can figure them out later. At that point, if you find that you need to replace some or all of the opening words, you'll already have an active, muscular draft in hand. Conversely, if you discover that what you need to write requires more or less than fourteen lines, you now have a flexible framework that you can expand or contract as you revise.

Thinking about Words: An Anthology

Robert Frost: Range-Finding
Catherine Doty: The Hungry Child
Ben Jonson: On My First Son
Hayden Carruth: Adolf Eichmann
William Wordsworth: Composed upon Westminster Bridge, September 3, 1802

A sluggish, listless time here. This is what I was thinking this morning, so I had to go look up "list" in the big dictionary, having in mind that the wind "bloweth where it listeth," my guess being that the root meaning had to do with will, probably because that's what I feel I lack these days. Close but no cigar. It has more to do with wish, desire, velleity. I guess that's close enough. . . .

I don't know if it has anything to do with being a writer, but I have to look up words pretty often—just to be sure. In the same way I have to look up places in the atlas. . . . It's a madness.
—Hayden Carruth

Range-Finding
Robert Frost

The battle rent a cobweb diamond-strung
And cut a flower beside a groundbird's nest
Before it stained a single human breast.
The stricken flower bent double and so hung.
And still the bird revisited her young.
A butterfly its fall had dispossessed,
A moment sought in air his flower of rest,
Then lightly stooped to it and fluttering clung.
On the bare upland pasture there had spread
O'ernight 'twixt mullein stalks a wheel of thread
And straining cables wet with silver dew.
A sudden passing bullet shook it dry.
The indwelling spider ran to greet the fly,
But finding nothing, sullenly withdrew.

The Hungry Child
Catherine Doty

The child sleeps, her arm over the side of the bed,
trawling, the hand cupped, knuckles knocking wood.
Into her dreams swings the man from the TV show.
In his checkered coat, his polka-dot bowtie,
he scoops her from the cold and salty sheets,
flies her to his hideout, where she sees
a table just her size, and two red chairs
so small that when he sits with her his knees
bob before his smiling, wide-eyed face.
He serves her tiny, buttered red potatoes,
midget hotdogs that come from a little can.
There's rain, the sound of rain, the scratch of orange records
on the Mickey Mouse Victrola. "Tomorrow we'll eat the fishes
in the tin. We'll have a can of beer, and a bowl of white frosting."
This last sweet launches a sleep within her sleep,
deeper than dog sleep, a thick rug, a furry sleeve.
Morning comes, the cold walk to school, bells, prayers and milk.
The child opens books, waves her arm in the classroom air.
Then a walk home, and homework, and supper, and TV,
and sleep, that well of fulfillment, that deep warm pail of ocean
squirming with stars.

On My First Son
Ben Jonson

Farewell, thou child of my right hand, and joy;
My sin was too much hope of thee, loved boy,
Seven years thou wert lent to me, and I thee pay,
Exacted by thy fate, on the just day.
O, could I lose all father, now. For why
Will man lament the state he should envy?
To have so soon 'scaped world's, and flesh's rage,
And, if no other misery, yet age!
Rest in soft peace, and, asked, say here doth lie
Ben Jonson his best piece of poetry.
For whose sake, henceforth, all his vows be such,
As what he loves may never like too much.

Adolf Eichmann
Hayden Carruth

I want no tricks in speaking of this man.
My friends deplore my metaphysical mind,
But now I am a plain and plain-spoken man.

In my life only two men have turned my mind
To vengefulness, and one was this man's chief,
Who was, I now think, probably out of his mind.

But this one is rational. Naturally a mad chief
Needs sane lieutenants. Both were named Adolf,
An ugly Teutonic word which means the chief,

And earlier, in the cold north forest, this Adolf
Meant the wolf, a favorite totem. Let disgrace,
I say, fall for all time to come upon Adolf,

And let no child hereafter bear the disgrace
Of that dirty name. Sometimes in my bed
I study my feet, noticing their disgrace,

For the human foot is an ugly thing. But my bed
Is nothing like the bed that I have seen
Where hundreds of unclothed bodies lay. That bed

Was for dead people, deeply dug, and whoever has seen
Their feet knows the real ugliness and in their voice
Has heard the only true language. I have seen

And I have heard, but my feet live and my voice
Is beautiful and strong, and I say let the dung
Be heaped on that man until it chokes his voice,

Let him be made leprous so that the dung
May snuggle to his bone, let his eyes be shut
With slow blinding, let him be fed his own dung,

But let his ears never, never be shut,
And let young voices read to him, name by name,
From the rolls of all those people whom he has shut

Into the horrible beds, and let his name
Forever and ever be the word for hate,
Eichmann, cast out of the race, a loathsome name

For another kind, a sport spawned in hate
That can never be joined, never, in the world of man.
Lord, forgive me, I can't keep down my hate.

Composed upon Westminster Bridge, September 3, 1802
William Wordsworth

Earth has not any thing to show more fair:
Dull would he be of soul who could pass by
A sight so touching in its majesty:
This City now doth, like a garment, wear
The beauty of the morning: silent, bare,
Ships, towers, domes, theatres, and temples lie
Open unto the fields, and to the sky;
All bright and glittering in the smokeless air.
Never did sun more beautifully steep
In his first splendour, valley, rock, or hill;
Ne'er saw I, never felt, a calm so deep!
The river glideth at his own sweet will:
Dear God! the very houses seem asleep;
And all that mighty heart is lying still!

2

Emily Dickinson
"He put the Belt around my life"

It was odd to think as my voice rang out through the big silent house that Miss Emily in her weird white dress was outside in the shadow hearing every word.
                                             —*Mabel Loomis Todd*

About the Poet and the Poem

Emily Dickinson (1830–86)—reclusive, shy, nearly invisible to many of her neighbors—
passed most of her life inside a single house in a small Massachusetts town. Yet she was
one of the first great American voices, a ferociously ambitious poet, a linguistic radical
embedded in the region's ascetic Protestant culture. Certain fellow New Englanders
were immediately drawn to what they recognized as a vision of their own familiar world.
Dickinson scholar Christopher Benfey writes, "From the beginning [her] poetry strongly
appealed to traditionalists, . . . especially to those who felt that she captured perfectly a
certain lost New England world, an austere landscape of the spirit all but eliminated by
Gilded Age excesses." Samuel Ward, a writer for the Transcendentalist journal *The Dial,*
told her first editor, Thomas Wentworth Higginson,

> She may become world famous, or she may never get out of New England. She is
> the quintessence of that element we all have who are of the Puritan descent *pur sang.*
> We came to this country to think our own thoughts with nobody to hinder. . . .
> We conversed with our own souls till we lost the art of communicating with other
> people. The typical family grew up strangers to each other, as in this case. It was
> *awfully* high, but awfully lonesome.[1]

Yet as Benfey notes, there was always a tension between Dickinson's "austere landscape
of the spirit" and her strange idiosyncrasies of language:

> When Emily Dickinson's poems began appearing in slim volumes during the
> 1890s, many readers viewed her as an avant-garde writer. Her innovations and
> transgressions in subject and style were occasion for either censure or celebration.
> "'Alcohol' does not rhyme to 'pearl,' sniffed one English reviewer, scowling at the
> first stanza of "I taste a liquor never brewed"—while implying that the intoxicating
> experiment did not go well with aesthetic, "pearly" permanence. "She reminds
> us," he added, "of no sane or educated writer." Alice James, the brilliant sister of
> William and Henry James, noted with patriotic delight that British critics were deaf
> to Dickinson's peculiar, and peculiarly American, excellence. "It is reassuring to
> hear the English pronouncement that Emily Dickinson is fifth-rate," she reflected in
> January 1892, "they have such a capacity for missing quality; the robust evades them
> equally with the subtle."[2]

Dickinson wrote "He put the Belt around my life" in about 1861, a year before she
diffidently sent Higginson a sheaf of her work. She would have been in her early thirties,
with nearly three hundred poems already finished and docketed in her drawer, including
the far more famous "There's a certain Slant of light" and "Hope is the thing with
feathers." Both of those poems are also dated circa 1861, an indication that this was an
intensely productive period in the poet's development.

"He put the Belt around my life"

Emily Dickinson

He put the Belt around my life—
I heard the Buckle snap—
And turned away, imperial,
My Lifetime folding up—
Deliberate, as a Duke would do
A Kingdom's Title Deed—
Henceforth, a Dedicated sort—
A Member of the Cloud.

Yet not too far to come at call—
And do the little Toils
That make the Circuit of the Rest—
And deal occasional smiles
To lives that stoop to notice mine—
And kindly ask it in—
Whose invitation, know you not
For Whom I must decline?

What's the Most Important Line?

Line is, at its most obvious level, a visual cue on the page: it announces, "This is a poem you're about to read!" But historically it is more closely tied to sound than to sight. Line is poetry's direct link to song. In *Teaching the Art of Poetry: The Moves,* Baron Wormser and David Capella call it "the bearer of rhythm" in which "accents, sounds and pauses all consort."[3] While this musical heritage is clearest in formal poems, with their steady metrical pulse and their often-predictable rhyme schemes, it remains fundamentally important in the speech-driven cadences of much contemporary free verse.

In *Walt Whitman's America,* David S. Reynolds notes that Whitman, the great stylistic innovator of the nineteenth century, "recognized that the loose structure of his poetry had precedent in a wide variety of cultural styles between which he was trying to negotiate"—sermons, everyday conversation, dime novels, minstrel shows, newspaper articles, as well as the eloquence of poets such as Shakespeare, many of whose plays he knew by heart.[4] His long, flexible lines incorporate the crowded immediacy of his century yet retain a dense rhythmic power that recalls the bardic incantations of the world's most ancient poetry.

Whitman's contemporary, Emily Dickinson, was in certain ways his mirror opposite: small where he was large, secretive where he was expansive. Yet her poems, like his, forever changed our understanding of line. In the poem "Amherst," Amy Clampitt sought to pinpoint Dickinson's idiosyncratic, hinting manipulations; the clutching grip of her ironies:

> such
> stoppered prodigies, compressions and
> devastations within the atom—*all this*
> *world contains: his face*—the civil
> wars of just one stanza.[5]

"Behind these poems lurks a terrible question that has no answer," wrote Federico García Lorca in his essay-lecture "Deep Song."[6] Though his subject was Andalusian traditional music, he might have been speaking of Dickinson's work. What is it about her lines that makes them both so compelling and so difficult? There is something essentially unpredictable about their syntax; their cadence; their prim, implacable, often ghoulish word choice; their stuttering gaps of silence. When I ask myself, "What's the most important line?" in a Dickinson poem, I feel I am attempting to untangle a mystery, not by teasing out the poem's meanings but by looking at the way in which it was constructed. Why is this poem so simple yet so strange? Which lines seem most crucial to the poet's transmission of pervading, unnerving, sly peculiarity? "What's the most important line?" could be rephrased as "What's the weirdest line?"

A sense of puzzlement is often hard for us to admit. If we're teachers, we feel vulnerable about revealing our ignorance to our students. If we're students, we worry that the teacher is mocking our stupidity. If we're alone with a poem, we imagine that we're the only reader in the world who's ever been confused and bewildered by it. But you should always feel entitled to announce that you're mystified. As Lorca's remark reminds us, great art doesn't have answers. What it does is push us to ask questions—to examine a piece curiously, to measure it against our own evolving emotions and experiences. If the poem were a mysterious piece of wood, you'd turn it end over end between your hands; you'd rub its roughness with your fingers; you'd let your eyes track the shifting stripes of the grain. You'd make your sense of puzzlement the centerpiece of your exploration. That approach works just as well with poetry.

I chose to focus on Dickinson's "He put the Belt around my life" specifically because I have never read anything anyone else has ever said about it. Nor, before writing this chapter, had I spent any significant time with it myself. Naturally, given Dickinson's fame, I had preconceptions about her work, but I didn't have foreknowledge about this particular poem. I wanted mystery, and the piece, to me, was a tiny map into an unknown wilderness.

I think this map analogy offers one pertinent way for a reader to begin approaching the concept of poetic line. Like a mapmaker's delineations of roads, rivers, and mountain ranges, lines offer us a track into the wilderness of the poem. "What's the most important line?" could be rephrased as "What's the most important road into the forest?" I chose three roads.

I HEARD THE BUCKLE SNAP—

In her poem "Lines," Ruth Stone speaks of "the self longing to cross the barrier," of the "angst of brevity."[7] Lines embody these metaphors. Unlike sentences, they are discrete, end-stopped, capped at beginning and end with the white silence of the margins, even as grammar and syntax press a reader forward into the poem. This "angst of brevity" is particularly acute in a Dickinson poem: the very sound of her lines can be like a wail cut short.

"I heard the Buckle snap—" is a line that, to me, encapsulates the "angst of brevity." To begin with, it accomplishes in sound exactly what it accomplishes in sense. "I heard" stands alone at the opening of the line, anticipating, even dreading, "the Buckle snap." The capitalized *Buckle* is clumsy, oversized, in this narrow space; *snap* is a bite. It is a terrifying line: tight-lipped, inexorable, ugly, yet exquisitely constructed. As it happens, it is also a complete sentence—barring the famous Dickinsonian dash, which slashes open the simple subject-predicate construction and makes the line far more ambiguous than it might otherwise have been.

Metrically, the line is constructed of three cadenced pairs of syllables, following a stress pattern that you might summarize as *soft-**loud**, soft-**loud**, soft-**loud**.* In *The Sounds of Poetry,* Robert Pinsky explains, "The technical name for the pattern . . . is an 'iambic foot' or 'iamb.' The stressed syllable is determined only in relation to the other syllables within the foot. Thus, a stressed syllable within one foot may be less stressed than the unstressed syllable in another."[8] In other words, even a line with a predictable meter can incorporate delicate differences in emphasis.

That delicacy is not apparent in Dickinson's line, which advances across the page like hard-soled boots striding down a dark hall—"I ***heard*** the ***Buc****-kle **snap**—" with the weight of the final stress dropping powerfully onto the final word. *Snap* also offers the first hint at a rhyme scheme, introducing a sharp *p* sound that "My Lifetime folding up—" picks up two lines later. Though the word is remarkable in itself, it is closely bound not only to the rest of its own line but also to the lines around it.

William Blake once wrote, "Nature & Art in this together Suit / What is Most Grand is always most Minute."⁹ His remark is pertinent to this line. Dickinson chose plain words, a plain grammatical construction, a plain cadence. Nonetheless, the line makes me wince. She shares with Blake an eerie directness of purpose, as if her language exactly reflects the movement of her mind. Both poets are difficult to imitate, difficult to pigeonhole, yet their lines can be as simple as speech. "I heard the Buckle snap—": What could be more innocuous? Or more frightening?

AND DEAL OCCASIONAL SMILES

This line is different from my previous choice in several ways. To begin with, "And deal occasional smiles" is not a grammatically complete thought but a phrase that appears in the middle of a stanza that itself never quite resolves its sentence status. Is it one long awkward question? Is it a six-line fragment followed by a separate query? Whatever the case, the line lacks the sharp clarity of "I heard the Buckle snap—," a contrast that is both attractive and perplexing.

In her poem "Reading," Betsy Sholl writes of the way in which the fragments of language can become a sort of sea, or perhaps a windy hill—a place outside of meaning in which the mind can rest and linger:

> On my lap an essay explaining
> Dickinson's deft ironies, elusive
> dashes and slants, so dense I have to stop
> wanting to get to the end, the bottom
> of anything, and just live in the drift
> of phrase and clause.¹⁰

I think it's important, as a reader, to allow oneself to linger in this "drift of phrase and clause"—not pressing to make logical sense of the language but letting the phrases "lean and loafe at [their] ease" in the imagination.¹¹ Those words, from Whitman's *Song of Myself,* seem in context to describe the poet-narrator, but they could just as easily refer to the fluid interaction between poet and poem, reader and poet, reader and poem. Art such as Dickinson's requires patience—and not just with the convolutions of the poem. It also requires us to be patient with the workings of our own minds.

As I ponder "And deal occasional smiles"—allowing my eyes to travel the shape of the line, my lips to repeat the words, my mind to relax away from the anxiety of "What am I going to write to fool the readers of this book into thinking I know what I'm talking about?"—I note that only the first word is capitalized and that the line contains no dashes. These absences differentiate the line from most of the others in the poem, the majority of which contain one or the other of these tics. As I continue to reread the line, I become aware that I am lingering on the word *deal.* It's a quiet word yet contextually an odd one. I note that the image of *dealing smiles* as opposed to, say, *dealing cards* adds a tinge of irony and detachment that a phrase such as *sharing smiles* would not. Also, there's the issue of the missing word: if Dickinson had written "deal out smiles," the more typical construction, she would have preserved the flavor of irony but would have lost the iambic cadence: "And *deal*" would have become "And *deal out.*" But as I look more closely at the meter, I see that, with *occasional,* she's already compromised that cadence: "And *deal* oc-*ca*-sional

smiles."Although the stress variations are somewhat more subtle than my typographical rendering indicates, the sound of the line remains vastly different from the sound of "*I heard the Buc-kle snap*—.""

Thus, within the space of the previous paragraph, my thoughts slipped from my own separate concerns into visual comparisons, then to undifferentiated attention to a word, then to connotation and context, then to grammatical construction, then to meter, and then to sound comparisons. In other words, by allowing myself to "lean and loafe" with a single line, I learned a great deal about the details of Dickinson's craft, information that is precisely relevant to my own work as a poet.

It's also relevant to students. If you are a high school English teacher, you've probably broken down each of those language elements into separate class assignments. But as you can see, one line from a small poem can efficiently guide your students through all of those language-arts hoops. Simultaneously, by focusing on the language itself, you honor the poem's mysteries. Discovering a poem shouldn't feel like solving a crossword puzzle. Rather, it should open both our students and ourselves to the possibility that we, too, can stand awestruck on Keats's "peak in Darien." We can glimpse the "undiscover'd country" of Shakespeare's *Hamlet* and the "stately pleasure-dome" of Coleridge's "Kubla Khan." We can collect for ourselves what in "Dream Dust" Langston Hughes called "One handful of dream-dust / Not for sale."[12]

FOR WHOM I MUST DECLINE?
As the final line of the poem, "For Whom I must decline?" seems to bear the weight of all the lines that come before it. We might read it as the poet's last words on the subject or the final twist of her ironic knife. We might see it as a sudden revelation or a sudden concealment. Merely because of its position in the poem, the line is uniquely potent. If Dickinson had chosen to make it the first line or the fifth or even the fifteenth, all of our assumptions about it would be different, even if every word had remained the same.

Lines frame and structure a poem. They create visual and sonic boundaries, which, like "For Whom I must decline?," also become dramatic boundaries. In addition to demarcating the beginning and end of stanzas and poems, their length determines the width of margins, which can have significant influence on a reader's interaction with the page. For instance, many of the lines of Allen Ginsberg's "Transcription of Organ Music" are too long to fit compactly into the design of the printed page. The result is visual overflow, an abundance of type.

> The flower in the glass peanut bottle formerly in the kitchen crooked to take a place in the light,
> the closet door opened, because I had used it before, it kindly stayed open waiting for me, its owner.[13]

In contrast, the lines of Linda Pastan's "snow shower" are often only as long as a single word. As a result, the page is dominated by white space rather than print.

the size of doilies
of porcelain
cups[14]

In "Deuce: 12:23 a.m.," Barbara Anderson takes a third visual tack, injecting ragged left-margin indents into what is otherwise a relatively compact column of lines. That decision not only adds visual variation but also becomes a way to indicate dynamic shifts in her narrator's insistent voice.

> SO HEY,
> I'm a rehabbed convict, recovering addict,
> someone you would walk THE OTHER WAY
> from on the street, but I'm also
>   into broadcasting LIKE YOU.
> When I was in the joint, I was the HEAD HONCH,
>   TOP-NOTCH DEEJAY, the main voice
> over the caged waves, but once you've had
> a tracheotomy, it's NEVER REALLY the same.[15]

Line is often one of the most recognizable elements of a poet's style, and Dickinson's approach to line in "He put the Belt around my life" is characteristic of much of her work. Peppered with dashes and internal capitalization, the lines vary between two lengths, short and shorter, which always fall in pairs. The three lines I've discussed in this chapter are all in the *shorter* category and thus are always the second lines in their particular set.

Though I did not consciously decide to discuss only lines in this position, I'm guessing that I was drawn to the way in which they seem to elaborate on the previous line or speak as dramatic asides or, in the case of "For Whom I must decline?," subvert and misdirect. When I read this line in tandem with its longer partner, I find myself struggling among snags and stumps. The syntactical awkwardness of "know you not / For Whom I must decline?" reinforces the confusion of my discovery that suddenly three characters are involved in this unclear situation—*you, Whom,* and *I.* It seems that *I* is responsible for declining *Whom*'s invitation, that *you*'s advice is being sought. Is *Whom* the same character as *He* in the first line? The poem seems to be rife with unsubstantiated pronouns, and the fact that this final line also contains the only question in the poem just adds to the complications.

Suddenly, our central question, "What's the most important line?," has leaped back to "What's the most important word?" as well as forward to "Who's the most important character?" and "What's the most important punctuation?" (questions I'll focus on later in the book). One query leads to the others because the elements of language are interdependent. As Octavio Paz writes in his essay "The Other Voice":

> The operative mode of poetic thought is imagining, and imagination consists, essentially, of the ability to place contrary or divergent realities in relationship. All poetic forms and all linguistic figures have one thing in common: they seek, and often find, hidden resemblances. In the most extreme cases, they unite

opposites. . . . In language, the unions and the divisions, the love affairs and the separation of stars, cells, atoms, and men are reproduced. Each poem, whatever its subject and form and the ideas that shape it, is first and foremost a miniature cosmos. The poem unites the "ten thousand things that make up the universe," as the ancient Chinese put it.[16]

In "He put the Belt around my life," Dickinson isn't interested in solving a mystery but in delineating its existence, and her art lies in how she uses a poet's plain and solid tools—words, lines, punctuation—to weave and tangle the threads of her imagination.

Ideas for Writing

Lines are movable elements in a poem under revision. As a poet writes, she often shifts her lines around, and each new position offers her new imaginative options. A line that begins the poem may now end a poem, or it may start a new stanza, or it may suddenly break into two lines.

Dickinson herself offers an example in two versions of a poem numbered "494" in *The Complete Poems of Emily Dickinson* (both dated circa 1862), in which she demonstrates that even subtle revisions greatly influence the impact of a poem. Here's a section of version 1's final stanza:

> What could it hinder so—to say?
> Tell Him—just how she sealed you—Cautious!
> But—if He ask where you are hid
> Until tomorrow—Happy letter!
> Gesture Coquette—and shake your Head!

Compare it with the same section in version 2:

> What could—it hinder so—to say?
> Tell Her—just how she sealed—you—Cautious!
> But—if she ask "where you are hid"—until the evening—
> Ah! Be bashful!
> Gesture Coquette—
> And shake your Head![17]

The revisions in the lines don't, at a quick glance, seem earth-shattering. The poet has swapped one pronoun for another, added a dash and some quotation marks, broken one line into two, deleted some words, added a short new line. Yet something has happened. Even though the second poem looks rather similar to the first, it now sounds significantly different—not to mention that the pronoun switch has entirely reconfigured the piece's impact on the reader.

One of the simplest ways to experience the power of line in your own writing is to push yourself to experiment with line placement. Find a poem you've already written—perhaps a draft of the exercise I suggested in chapter 1, in which each line begins with the first word of Shakespeare's sonnet 81. Then try out some or all of these revision exercises.

1. Take the last line of your first draft and use it as the first line of an entirely new poem.

2. Turn the first draft inside out: now the original last line is the first line, and the original first line is the last line. Rewrite the middle lines to link the new beginning to the new ending.

3. Turn the middle line of your first draft into a question. Rewrite the other lines as necessary so that they lead toward and then away from that new central question.

4. Break every line of your first draft into two lines, rewriting as necessary.

5. Delete three lines entirely from your first draft, rewriting as necessary.

6. Make each of your original lines twice as long, either by adding new words or white space or by combining existing lines.

7. Choose your favorite line from the original poem. Now rewrite it, adding a syllable to one of the words. Now rewrite it again, taking away a different syllable. Keep repeating and experimenting, adding and subtracting syllables throughout the line.

These suggestions are akin to an athlete's stretches or a musician's scale practice. Even if the result of the activity isn't a finished poem, you'll be pressed as a writer to think more flexibly about line. For instance, you may find yourself asking specific questions about the kinds of words that begin and end your new lines. Are they transitions? Descriptors? Actions? Do they break, or enjamb, the syntactic flow of the sentence, or do they preserve the phrases in natural groupings? Which of these new words seems particularly compelling to you? Which ones seem almost invisible? How does the sense of a line change when you add and subtract syllables? What new cadence patterns are you noticing?

All of these experiments and discussions work equally well as student assignments, and they are a good way to help students break the stigma of the word *revision*. For most of us, the term probably still conjures up the excruciating boredom of the high school research paper. Yet for a poet—for any creative writer—revision is the center of the endeavor. We try something out; then we try it in different ways; then we try it yet again. The task is not only necessary: it's also *interesting*.

So if you're a teacher, you will only gain from leading your students through revision exercises that emphasize experimentation and independence (rather than tedious research protocols) but that also offer structural parameters that are easy for both you and the class to assess. Did X add a syllable or didn't he? Did Y turn the sentence into a question or didn't she? You want your students to express their inner lives, but you also want them to understand that poetry is an intellectual activity, not just words thrown onto a page.

Just as importantly, these exercises give you and your students some ways to talk productively about a poem in process. It can be scary to proffer a personal remark about another human being's creative work. It can be even more terrifying to wait for comments on a new raw piece you've just produced. These kinds of revision activities circumvent that fear because they give both you and your students specific tasks and assessment criteria, even as they allow for bottomless freedom of expression.

Thinking about Lines: An Anthology

Lawrence Ferlinghetti: "See it was like this when"
George Gordon Byron: "So we'll go no more a roving"
Baron Wormser: Jerry Lee Lewis at Nuremberg
John Keats: To Autumn
Michael Casey: break room

Here as elsewhere the language is so simple and open, so plausible, that one scarcely notices the artfulness of the compression, the understatement, the nice distortion, . . . the rightness of the unpunctuated linear structure based (but not slavishly) on the short span of the breath units.
                    —Stanley Kunitz on the poetry of Michael Casey

"See it was like this when"

Lawrence Ferlinghetti

See

   it was like this when

      we waltz into this place

a couple of Papish cats

      is doing an Aztec two-step

And I says

   Dad let's cut

but then this dame

     comes up behind me see

      and says

    You and me could really exist

Wow I says

   Only the next day

    she has bad teeth

     and really hates

        poetry

"So, we'll go no more a roving"
George Gordon Byron

So, we'll go no more a roving
        So late into the night,
Though the heart be still as loving,
        And the moon be still as bright.

For the sword outwears the sheath,
        And the soul outwears the breast,
And the heart must pause to breathe,
        and Love itself have rest.

Though the night was made for loving,
        And the day returns too soon,
Yet we'll go no more a roving
        By the light of the moon.

Jerry Lee Lewis at Nuremberg
Baron Wormser

In unreal time, as when a head dices up decades
Centuries and millennia
While slowly sluicing into the nether bog of sleep,
Jerry Lee Lewis, also titled "The Killer,"
For among other things, his pianistic prowess,
Appears at Nuremberg in a stiff, wide-lapel suit
He could have bought at Lansky's in Memphis
If he was from Memphis but he wasn't,
Standing there with that too-cool hairdo
To confront the modest panoply of Nazis who
Are standing in for many Nazis
Who are there to take the rap and glad in their
We-are-the-superior-race way
To do that because
It was no evil to do what they did,
It was a service to Aryans to cleanse the earth of scum
Which by implication included musicians
Humping pianos and their thirteen-year-olds
While braying like country-western-boogie-woogie banshees
A category Jerry Lee has no intention of discussing
Because he doesn't care about some stuck-up *ism* crap
That is just so much goose-stepping viciousness.

What matters is what's shaking in his love-exercised mind—
A naked female and a pair of intuitive hands
Dismantling a keyboard, which is what a mind should hold,
So that when Göring starts in with his witty repartee
Jerry Lee says, "You are one sad motherfucker"
And the world, for once, gets what it is to be American
And unafraid of what anyone thinks, especially some
Nazi slime ball who believes he's better than anyone else
Because he's from Europe and has a lot of unhappy history
Up his hateful asshole that got made into more history that
People like my uncle Nathan paid for with his life
On the beach at Anzio, his precious blood vanishing
Into the grievous sands of oblivion.

Göring says something smug but Jerry Lee is busy
Waggling his eyes around the courtroom.
No chicks or pianos.
Being serious is fucking boring.
Being serious has killed a lot more people than not being serious.

The dream ends here.
In Hollywood time, Spencer Tracy is talking about
"The real complaining party in this courtroom," which is "civilization."
Everyone nods at this large last word.
It sounds good like maybe you could use it in a song,
Each syllable taut yet sibilant in its brief articulate leap,
Though it doesn't rhyme with much,
Though it feels like some wish, something badly out of touch.

To Autumn

John Keats

I

Season of mists and mellow fruitfulness,
    Close bosom-friend of the maturing sun;
Conspiring with him how to load and bless
    With fruit the vines that round the thatch-eves run;
To bend with apples the moss'd cottage-trees,
    And fill all fruit with ripeness to the core;
        To swell the gourd, and plump the hazel shells
With a sweet kernel; to set budding more,
    And still more, later flowers for the bees,
    Until they think warm days will never cease,
        For summer has o'er-brimm'd their clammy cells.

II

Who hath not seen thee oft amid thy store?
    Sometimes whoever seeks abroad may find
Thee sitting careless on a granary floor,
    Thy hair soft-lifted by the winnowing wind;
Or on a half-reap'd furrow sound asleep,
    Drows'd with the fume of poppies, while thy hook
        Spares the next swath and all its twined flowers:
And sometimes like a gleaner thou dost keep
    Steady thy laden head across a brook;
    Or by a cyder-press, with patient look,
        Thou watchest the last oozings hours by hours.

III

Where are the songs of Spring? Ay, where are they?
    Think not of them, thou hast thy music too,--
While barred clouds bloom the soft-dying day,
    And touch the stubble plains with rosy hue;
Then in a wailful choir the small gnats mourn
    Among the river sallows, borne aloft
        Or sinking as the light wind lives or dies;
And full-grown lambs loud bleat from hilly bourn;
    Hedge-crickets sing; and now with treble soft
    The red-breast whistles from a garden-croft;
        And gathering swallows twitter in the skies.

break room
Michael Casey

coffee break yesterday
one of the office girls
stops by the coke machine
and she is wearin a dress
and looks really fine
something like wrapped
in a pink towel with sparkling tights
and Mo is lookin at her
all the time she is there
and she's leavin
he goes
        hey you
and she turns around
and I am hiding my head in my arms
for what he's about to say
and he goes
        what a pretty dress

3

Percy Bysshe Shelley
To a Skylark

The bodies of Shelley, Edward Williams, and Charles Vivian were eventually washed up along the beach between Massa and Viareggio ten days after the storm. The exposed flesh of Shelley's arms and face had been entirely eaten away, but he was identifiable by the nankeen trousers, the white silk socks beneath the boots and [Leigh] Hunt's copy of Keats's poems doubled back in the jacket pocket.

—Richard Holmes

About the Poet and the Poem

The artistic reputation of Percy Bysshe Shelley (1792–1822) has probably changed more drastically than that of any other poet in the English canon. During his lifetime, the literary establishment reviled his poetry, which many saw as not only politically radical but dangerously immoral. After the young poet's sudden death in a sailing accident, his widow, novelist Mary Shelley, made a concerted effort to repair this public image. In the preface to her 1839 edition of *The Poetical Works of Percy Bysshe Shelley,* she wrote, "He loved to idealize reality; and this is a taste shared by few. We are willing to have our passing whims exalted into passions, for this gratifies our vanity; but few of us understand or sympathize with the endeavour to ally the love of abstract beauty . . . with our sympathies with our kind. In this, Shelley resembled Plato."[1]

Mary Shelley's efforts paid off. Shelley's poetry—in particular, his late lyrical work—rapidly increased in popularity, and he became a favorite among the Victorians. Elizabeth Barrett Browning, Robert Browning, and Alfred Tennyson were all devoted to his poems. Even that famously misanthropic couple, Thomas Carlyle and Jane Welsh Carlyle, gloried in the bust of the poet (a gift from Shelley's close friend Leigh Hunt) that "ornamented" their drawing room.[2]

Shelley's poetry had a significant influence on twentieth-century poets such as William Butler Yeats and Robert Frost. But with modernism in the ascendant, his star fell. In 1932 T. S. Eliot declared, "I was intoxicated by Shelley's poetry at the age of fifteen, and now find it almost unreadable," and thirty years later W. H. Auden flatly stated, "I cannot enjoy one poem by Shelley."[3] Today the poet's reputation remains musty and muted. Unlike his contemporary, John Keats, who is still widely adored, Shelley has become stereotyped as flowery, high-toned, and old-fashioned. Few contemporary readers think of him as a radical writer.

Shelley wrote "To a Skylark" in July 1820. At the time, he was living in Pisa, Italy, and was immersed in family turmoil. Dogged with depression and anxiety, he went for an evening walk with his wife. Mary Shelley recalled, "It was on a beautiful summer evening, while wandering among the lanes whose myrtle-hedges were the bowers of the fireflies, that we heard the caroling of the skylark which inspired one of the most beautiful of his poems."[4]

To a Skylark
Percy Bysshe Shelley

I

Hail to thee, blithe Spirit!
  Bird thou never wert,
That from Heaven, or near it,
  Pourest thy full heart
In profuse strains of unpremeditated art.

II

Higher still and higher,
  From the earth thou springest
Like a cloud of fire;
  The blue deep thou wingest,
And singing still dost soar, and soaring ever singest.

III

In the golden lightning
  Of the sunken sun,
O'er which clouds are brightening,
  Thou dost float and run;
Like an unbodied joy whose race is just begun.

IV

The pale purple even
  Melts around thy flight;
Like a star of heaven,
  In the broad day-light
Thou art unseen, but yet I hear thy shrill delight.

V

Keen as are the arrows
  Of that silver sphere,
Whose intense lamp narrows
  In the white dawn clear
Until we hardly see, we feel that it is there.

VI

All the earth and air
  With the voice is loud,
As, when night is bare,
  From one lonely cloud
The moon rains out her beams, and heaven is overflowed.

VII

What thou art we know not;
  What is most like thee?
From rainbow clouds there flow not
  Drops so bright to see,
As from thy presence showers a rain of melody.

VIII

Like a poet hidden
  In the light of thought,
Singing hymns unbidden,
  Till the world is wrought
To sympathy with hopes and fears it heeded not:

IX

Like a high-born maiden
  In a palace-tower,
Soothing her love-laden
  Soul in secret hour
With music sweet as love, which overflows her bower:

X

Like a glowworm golden
  In a dell of dew,
Scattering unbeholden
  Its aërial hue
Among the flowers and grass, which screen it from the view.

XI

Like a rose embowered
  In its own green leaves,
By warm winds deflowered,
  Till the scent it gives
Makes faint with too much sweet those heavy-winged thieves.

XII

Sound of vernal showers
  On the twinkling grass,
Rain-awakened flowers,
  All that ever was
Joyous, and clear, and fresh, thy music doth surpass.

XIII

Teach us, sprite or bird,
  What sweet thoughts are thine:

I have never heard
   Praise of love or wine
That panted forth a flood of rapture so divine.

     XIV
Chorus hymeneal,
   Or triumphal chant,
Matched with thine would be all
   But an empty vaunt—
A thing wherein we feel there is some hidden want.

     XV
What objects are the fountains
   Of thy happy strain?
What fields, or waves, or mountains?
   What shapes of sky or plain?
What love of thine own kind? what ignorance of pain?

     XVI
With thy clear keen joyance
   Languor cannot be:
Shadow of annoyance
   Never came near thee:
Thou lovest: but ne'er knew love's sad satiety.

     XVII
Waking or asleep,
   Thou of death must deem
Things more true and deep
   Than we mortals dream,
Or how could thy notes flow in such a crystal stream?

     XVIII
We look before and after,
   And pine for what is not:
Our sincerest laughter
   With some pain is fraught;
Our sweetest songs are those that tell of saddest thought.

     XIX
Yet if we could scorn
   Hate, and pride, and fear;
If we were things born
   Not to shed a tear,
I know not how thy joy we ever should come near.

XX

Better than all measures
  Of delightful sound,
Better than all treasures
  That in books are found,
Thy skill to poet were, thou scorner of the ground!

XXI

Teach me half the gladness
  That thy brain must know,
Such harmonious madness
  From my lips would flow
The world should listen then, as I am listening now.

What's the Most Important Stanza?

In Italian the word *stanza* means "room." For a poet who is working out the structure of a poem, that image is a compelling one. *Room* implies both enclosure and space, and stanzas in poetry entail a similar commitment to constriction and freedom. This is particularly evident in formal poems, where stanzas often frame the pattern of the form—for instance, rhymed couplets or rhymed quatrains. Even as these rigid patterns restrict a poet's word choice, they may also push her to invent images or details that radically alter the trajectory of the poem.

Like the verse of a song, a stanza controls cadence, sound, and pacing. When revising a poem, a poet often clusters and reclusters lines, searching for the combination that will propel the work into completion. As he wrote the 117 poems that make up his *Sonnets for Chris,* John Berryman shifted among stanza styles, most often settling on two per poem but frequently choosing one and occasionally even four. His choices had a significant effect on the dramatic movement of the individual poems, even though they all share the same form and subject matter.

Consider Gwendolyn Brooks's sonnet "The Rites for Cousin Vit," which she chose to arrange as a single stanza rather than break into multiple sections. The accumulating density of the last five lines seems to mirror the crowded, vigorous details of the character's life:

> Even now she does the snake-hips with a hiss,
> Slops the bad wine across her shantung, talks
> Of pregnancy, guitars and bridgework, walks
> In parks or alleys, comes haply on the verge
> Of happiness, haply hysterics. Is.[5]

In contrast, the final five lines of Berryman's sonnet 54 convey a barrenness, which the stanza break enhances and illuminates:

> Sprinting my ribbon down the world of green . .
> Shadow to shadow, under tropical day . .
>
> Flat country, slow, alone. So in my pocket
> Your snapshot nightmares where (cloth, flesh between)
> My heart was, before I gave it away.[6]

The tension between constriction and freedom is equally important in free verse, where stanzas are not bound by form. In "The Grass on the Mountain," Mary Austin demonstrates that carefully designed free-verse stanzas wield visual as well as sonic power. By varying the length of both her stanzas and the lines within them, she replicates the physical impact of silence and spaciousness:

> Oh, long, long
> The snow has possessed the mountains.

The deer have come down and the big-horn,
They have followed the Sun to the south
To feed on the mesquite pods and the bunch grass.
Loud are the thunder drums
In the tents of the mountains.[7]

According to W. H. Auden, "the poet who writes 'free' verse is like Robinson Crusoe on his desert island: he must do all his cooking, laundry and darning for himself." That is, a free-verse poet must invent her own version of structural coherence. The aim (in Auden's acid terms) is to create "something original and impressive" instead of "squalor—dirty sheets on the unmade bed and empty bottles on the unswept floor."

Yet Auden knew that formal poetry also carries risks. "In verse, as the Alka-Seltzer advertisements testify, the didactic message loses half its immodesty." Without "the exposition of ideas," even the most perfectly tuned terza rima ode becomes a radio jingle.[8] Thus, like paragraphs of prose, stanzas must also function as units of thought.

Whether they are working in form or in free verse, poets frequently use stanzas to outline an argument or advance a dramatic situation. For instance, in Aphra Behn's three-stanza poem "The Willing Mistress," the stanzas control the pace of a basic narrative trajectory. The first stanza creates the setting:

Amyntas led me to a grove
  Where all the trees did shade us;
The sun itself though it had strove
  It could not have betrayed us.
The place secured from human eyes
  No other fear allows,
But when the winds that gently rise
  Do kiss the yielding boughs.

The second stanza introduces the action of the situation:

Down there we sat upon the moss,
  And did begin to play
A thousand amorous tricks, to pass
  The heat of all the day.
A many kisses he did give,
  And I returned the same,
Which made me willing to receive
  That which I dare not name.

Finally, the third stanza leads the reader to an inevitable conclusion:

His charming eyes no aid required
  To tell their softening tale;
On her that was already fired

'Twas easy to prevail.
He did but kiss and clasp me round,
  Whilst those his thoughts exprest;
And laid me gently on the ground:
  Ah, who can guess the rest?[9]

Although Shelley's formal control was masterful, intellect was always the vital underpinning of his poetry; and he was apt to speak dismissively of his briefer, lighter poems. According to biographer Richard Holmes,

> Those celebrated late Italian lyrics—"To a Skylark," "The Cloud," "To Jane," "When the Lamp Is Shattered,"—which subsequently established his reputation among a sentimental Victorian reading public, and among generation after generation of schoolchildren, were never of serious concern to Shelley. For the most part they were products of periods of depression and inactivity, haphazard acts of inattention when the main work could not be pushed forward. Throughout his life, Shelley's major creative effort was concentrated on producing a series of long poems and poetic dramas aimed at the main political and spiritual problems of his age and society. . . . He was moreover a writer who moved everywhere with a sense of ulterior motive, a sense of greater design, an acute feeling for the historical moment and an overwhelming consciousness of his duty as an *artist* in the immense and fiery process of social change of which he knew himself to be a part.[10]

Why does this explanation disturb me? It's not that I disbelieve Holmes's biographical conclusions. But there's something embarrassing about being lumped into the category of "sentimental Victorian reading public" and "generation after generation of schoolchildren." It's disarming, as a reader, to feel that something you treasure is worthless in another reader's eyes . . . especially when that reader is the poet himself.

Still, we have a right to love what we love—which is why I've chosen to feature "To a Skylark" in this chapter. Unlike Shakespeare's sonnet 81 and Dickinson's "He put the Belt around my life," both of which are relatively obscure, this poem is one of Shelley's most famous. These days, he isn't a particularly fashionable poet, so "To a Skylark" is less heavily anthologized than it used to be. Nonetheless, it's gotten a good deal of press over the years, and most of you will at least recognize the first line.

I chose three answers to the question "What's the most important stanza?" As I reread the poem, studying my choices, I reminded myself to keep rephrasing the question as "What's the most important stanza *to me?*" When working with a very famous poem, I'm always tempted to defer to other people's opinions and reactions. But if I want to learn from a poem, I need to press myself to meet the piece as its curious equal. I cannot let myself be cowed by its fame, but neither can I let myself be swayed by remarks such as "Who bothers to read Shelley anymore?" or "Why waste time with that old romantic saw?" I can't even let Shelley's own assumptions sway me. The conversation must start between the poem and myself. Otherwise, I'll never truly get the chance to discover what it holds for me.

STANZA III

Though a poet must be committed to her vision, that commitment doesn't mean she's always the most reliable reader of her own work. Because she lives inside it, she cannot easily cast a dispassionate eye on it or position it within a larger context. We struggle with this difficulty when we revise our poems, when we listen to others speak critically about our work, when we suffer over rejection letters. Is it better to cling to our own preconceptions about a piece? Or is it better to accept and learn from the valuation of others? The answer varies, depending on the poem, the reader, and the poet's state of mind.

As I reread "To a Skylark," I wondered which stanzas would rise to the surface and beg for attention. At the same time I was recalling Holmes's description of Shelley as "a writer who moved everywhere with a sense of ulterior motive, a sense of greater design, an acute feeling for the historical moment and an overwhelming consciousness of his duty as an *artist* in the immense and fiery process of social change of which he knew himself to be a part." What stanzas in this poem, which Shelley himself dismissed as lightweight, might reflect the mind of such a poet? Would they be the same as the stanzas that were most important to me?

As I pondered this conundrum—the poem itself versus the poet's conception of himself as a poet—my eyes lingered on stanza III:

> In the golden lightning
> Of the sunken sun,
> O'er which clouds are brightening,
> Thou dost float and run;
> Like an unbodied joy whose race is just begun.

What is it about this stanza that drew my attention? Like all the others, it contains a set of five lines that follows a regular rhyme scheme: *a, b, a, b, b*. The lines, like those in the other stanzas, are indented in a standardized arrangement that reflects the length of each individual line. The shortest lines have the deepest indents, while the longest line hugs the left margin.

This careful design gives the poem great visual and sonic unity, but it also adds a gloss of sameness to the poem as a whole. And because Shelley is not telling a tale (as Aphra Behn does in "The Willing Mistress") but is striving to capture feelings and reactions, I can't grasp at dramatic threads such as rising action or suspense. In another poem those narrative elements might give me a way to measure "What's the most important stanza?" But they're no help in "To a Skylark."

Nonetheless, something was happening to me as I reread stanza III. I was beginning to understand that the skylark might not be the central subject of the poem. Instead, it might be what Richard Hugo calls a "triggering subject":

> In [a] news article the relation of the words to the subject . . . is a strong one. The relation of the words to the writer is so weak that for our purpose it isn't worth consideration. Since the majority of your reading has been newspapers, you are used to seeing language function this way. When you write a poem

these relations must reverse themselves. That is, the relation of the words to the subject must weaken and the relation of the words to the writer (you) must take on strength.

This is probably the hardest thing about writing poems.[11]

In the final line of stanza III, Shelley gives me the first hint that his physical reaction to the skylark has, in Hugo's words, "switch[ed his] allegiance from the triggering subject to the words."[12] When I read, "Like an unbodied joy whose race is just begun," I suddenly feel Shelley's imagination uniting with his ambition. I'm convinced, in a single rushing moment, that he has just found words for that inarticulate knot in his heart.

When I go back to reread the poem up to this point, I also realize that the line is Shelley's first use of simile. Later in the poem he devotes four complete stanzas in a row to his elaborate similes. But here, very early in the poem, he limits himself to a single line. So the leap feels not only sudden but very powerful: an intake of breath, a discovery. The simile's position in the stanza—introduced at the very end, just before the pause of an empty space; composed as a single complete line that is also the longest line of the set—reinforces that grandeur.

André Breton once declared, "The most exalting word is the word LIKE, whether it is pronounced or implied."[13] In Shelley's line, the word is the link between the physical image of a soaring bird and the abstraction "unbodied joy." That phrase strikes me as immensely beautiful but also immensely vague. It pulls me away from nature into pure imagination. Yet Shelley doesn't choose to leave me unanchored in the firmament. He finishes the comparison with "whose race is just begun."

Now "unbodied joy" is sandwiched between the solidity of a living creature and the active connotations of "race," which itself links back to the previous line, "Thou dost float and run." These two lines, in turn, float smoothly out of the first three, which create both a physical setting for the skylark and an atmosphere of anticipation for "unbodied joy." To quote Browning: "This I call his simultaneous perception of Power and Love in the absolute, and of Beauty and Good in the concrete."[14]

STANZA XV
I also found myself lingering over stanza XV, which appears in the last quarter of the poem. The stanza is notably different from all the others because it is entirely composed of questions.

> What objects are the fountains
> Of thy happy strain?
> What fields, or waves, or mountains?
> What shapes of sky or plain?
> What love of thine own kind? what ignorance of pain?

In his introduction to Pablo Neruda's collection *The Book of Questions,* William O'Daly writes: "Neruda is interested in inquiring about the nature of things, a process initiated by asking questions rooted in experience, offering us what he intuits as true and does not understand. Rather than remain in control, he submerges himself in not-knowing, in the unknowable questions that enter the imagination."[15]

Gjertrud Schnackenberg ventures into similar terrain in her long poem "Darwin in 1881," which opens with a comparison between Charles Darwin and Prospero, the magician of Shakespeare's play *The Tempest:*

> His voyage around the cape of middle age
> Comes, with a feat of insight, to a close,
> The same way Prospero's
> Ended before he left the stage
> To be led home across the blue-white sea,
> When he had spoken of the clouds and globe,
> Breaking his wand, and taking off his robe:
> Knowledge increases unreality.[16]

As a counterbalance to Neruda, who "submerges himself in not-knowing," both Darwin and Prospero come to recognize that "knowledge increases unreality." In this same questing vein, Shelley devotes stanza XV to unanswerable questions about the skylark, as if what he "does not understand" is a way to advance more fully into imaginative partnership with the bird of the air and the bird of the poem.

If you're a teacher, you know all too well how emotional your students can be. No doubt, as you've watched them work to express those emotions in writing, you've also noticed how often they feel obliged to sum up their emotional chaos with a pat conclusion—sometimes a moral epigram, sometimes a cynical shrug. In essence, they swerve away, using words to slam the door on chaos rather than allowing it to rule the poem. I think many of us succumb to a similar urge whenever we feel ourselves struggling to come to terms with, or simply articulate, the enormous, engulfing, unavoidable losses and desires that define the human condition. We want to find answers even as we run away from the questions.

Rainer Maria Rilke touched gently on this point in one of his *Letters to a Young Poet:*

> You are so young, so before all beginning, and I want to beg you, as much as I can, dear sir, to be patient toward all that is unsolved in your heart and to try to love the *questions themselves* like locked rooms and like books that are written in a very foreign tongue. Do not now seek the answers, which cannot be given you because you would not be able to live them. And the point is, to live everything. *Live* the questions now. Perhaps you will then gradually, without noticing it, live along some distant day into the answer.[17]

It is tempting to try to manipulate a poem into simulating an open-and-shut answer—perhaps a sentimental one, perhaps an ironic one—to this painful state of "not-knowing." But Shelley refused to let himself fall into that trap. Instead, the questions in stanza XV pushed him, in the subsequent two stanzas, to imagine a skylark that does not simply reflect the human concerns embodied in the questions but is a far more complex synthesis of emotion and action:

Waking or asleep,
>   Thou of death must deem
Things more true and deep
>   Than we mortals dream,
Or how could thy notes flow in such a crystal stream?

Stanza XVIII

My third stanza-for-discussion appears just down the page from my second:

We look before and after,
>   And pine for what is not:
Our sincerest laughter
>   With some pain is fraught;
Our sweetest songs are those that tell of saddest thought.

Both position-wise and as a unit of thought, stanza XVIII is closely tied to the questions in stanza XV. Yet even though it follows directly after the imaginative speculations that arose from the questions, something about this stanza feels different. For one thing, the tone changes starkly. In the previous stanza, Shelley constructed what I have called "a complex synthesis of emotion and action." To do so, he relied on a similarly complex sentence structure: a brief dependent clause (in line 1), followed by a long and syntactically contorted independent clause (in lines 2, 3, and 4), followed by a second independent clause arranged as a question (line 5).

Then, in stanza XVIII, he completely reconfigured his style. Although this stanza, too, is composed of a single sentence, the clauses are much more straightforward, both grammatically and syntactically. It begins with an independent clause (lines 1 and 2), which is followed by a second independent clause with a slight syntactic contortion (lines 3 and 4), which is followed by an independent clause (line 5).

If you're a grammar teacher, you might choose to deconstruct these sentences more fully with your students. But even my quick overview demonstrates that Shelley took very different grammatical approaches to the two contiguous stanzas. If we think of each one as a unit of thought, we start to see the stanzas as an unfolding reflection of the thought process itself. "What am I thinking about?" asks the poet. The grammar—straightforward or convoluted—pushes him toward an answer.

Compared with much of the rest of "To a Skylark," the language in stanza XVIII is restrained, even stark. Not only is the sentence structure plainer, but the cadence of the lines feels slower. There are fewer adjectives, and the nouns are less vivid. Whereas stanza XVII embraced the skylark's "crystal stream," this stanza returns us to the bleakness of the human condition. Even when we are happy, we are sad.

Frost wrote, "There is a residue of extreme sorrow that nothing can be done about and over it poetry lingers to brood with sympathy. I have heard poetry charged with having a vested interest in sorrow."[18] The joyousness of "To a Skylark" is freighted with this "residue of extreme sorrow," and the stanzas, as units of thought, are constructed to pull both the poet and the reader back and forth between parallel emotional states. The history of popular music, which overflows with murder ballads and he-done-me-wrong laments, is proof enough that humans are drawn to such brooding. For as Shelley himself explained in *A Defence of Poetry,* "tragedy delights by affording a shadow of that pleasure which exists in pain. This is the source also of the melancholy which is inseparable from the sweetest melody. The pleasure that is in sorrow is sweeter than the pleasure of pleasure itself."[19]

Ideas for Writing

Stanzas frame units of thought, but what does this mean in practice? On the simplest level framing a unit of thought means using language to both mirror and intensify your concentration. This framing ability is important when you're working to capture a first draft as well as when you're revising that rough piece into a finished poem.

For instance, think back to something that happened to you yesterday. Spend a few moments immersing yourself into the memory of that particular experience. Now set a timer for five minutes and quickly write a four-stanza poem. Each stanza should respond to the following statements about the experience:

> *Stanza 1.* Say what you are doing.
> *Stanza 2.* Say what you see.
> *Stanza 3.* Say what you remember.
> *Stanza 4.* Ask a question.

Although it may seem counterintuitive, pushing yourself to write very quickly often gives you a much richer first draft. For one thing, you have no time to erase or delete. Everything gets thrown onto the page; and the more material you have to work with, the more options you have for revision. Even more important, fast writing seems to allow many of us to bypass our brain's usual channels of logic, analysis, assumption, and self-protection. It rushes us directly to the poetic source—our emotions, reactions, observations, memories—and requires us to snatch words to describe them.

So now you have a four-stanza first draft. It's likely, given the controlling focus of my prompt, that the sentences inside each stanza are relatively cohesive units of thought. But what about the stanzas as a larger interactive element? They, too, must be arranged to create a unified whole.

When revising, a poet takes note of stanzas that seem lead to dead ends, ones that shout or whisper without cause, ones that coil back on themselves into a swollen muddle of detail. One approach may be to add or delete stanzas. Another may be to reorder the existing stanzas. As we saw in chapter 2, lines are movable elements. By changing their position, we can change the entire trajectory of the poem. Likewise, by reordering stanzas, we reorder our thoughts, which can open us up to new opportunities.

Keeping this in mind, go back to your first draft and, without rewriting anything, reorder it as follows:

> *Stanza 1.* Say what you are doing.
> *Stanza 2.* Say what you see.
> *Stanza 3.* Ask a question.
> *Stanza 4.* Say what you remember.

What happened to your poem when you made this single shift? When I've used this prompt in the classroom, students are uniformly stunned. Simply by switching the order of their thoughts, they feel as if they've slipped into a parallel universe. The poem has become familiar yet unfamiliar. They're unnerved; they're also excited. They're not accustomed to imagining their perceptions as movable building blocks. Yet this is one of the great intellectual pleasures of writing a poem: the work of discovering a structure that is also a surprise. As Margaret Atwood says, "Some of your writing, at least, should be as evanescent as play."[20]

Thinking about Stanzas: An Anthology

Thomas Hardy: The Self-Unseeing
Sara Teasdale: Summer Night, Riverside
Christina Rossetti: Twice
Jane Kenyon: Having It Out with Melancholy
Tim Seibles: Trying for Fire

When I think about a poem, I think about it being analogous to a song. I think about the songs I love the most. For example, let's take a song by Jimi Hendrix from his Band of Gypsies *album, "Power to Love."... I ask myself, "Why?" When he did the guitar work on that song, he was not out to lunch, thinking about something else. He gave that piece all he had.*
                                                        —Tim Seibles

The Self-Unseeing
Thomas Hardy

Here is the ancient floor,
Footworn and hollowed and thin,
Here was the former door
Where the dead feet walked in.

She sat here in her chair,
Smiling into the fire;
He who played stood there,
Bowing it higher and higher.

Childlike, I danced in a dream;
Blessings emblazoned that day;
Everything glowed with a gleam;
Yet we were looking away!

Summer Night, Riverside
Sara Teasdale

In the wild soft summer darkness
How many and many a night we two together
Sat in the park and watched the Hudson
Wearing her lights like golden spangles
Glinting on black satin.
The rail along the curving pathway
Was low in a happy place to let us cross,
And down the hill a tree that dripped with bloom
Sheltered us
While your kisses and the flowers,
Falling, falling,
Tangled my hair. . . .

The frail white stars moved slowly over the sky.

And now, far off
In the fragrant darkness
The tree is tremulous again with bloom
For June comes back.

To-night what girl
When she goes home,
Dreamily before her mirror shakes from her hair
This year's blossoms, clinging in its coils?

Twice
Christina Rossetti

I took my heart in my hand,
  (O my love, O my love),
I said: Let me fall or stand,
  Let me live or die,
But this once hear me speak—
  (O my love, O my love)—
Yet a woman's words are weak;
  You should speak, not I.

You took my heart in your hand
  With a friendly smile,
With a critical eye you scanned,
  Then set it down,
And said: It is still unripe
  Better wait awhile;
Wait while the skylarks pipe,
  Till the corn grows brown.

As you set it down it broke—
  Broke, but did not wince;
I smiled at the speech you spoke,
  At your judgment that I heard:
But I have not often smiled
  Since then, nor questioned since,
Nor cared for corn-flowers wild,
  Nor sung with the singing bird.

I take my heart in my hand,
  O my God, O my God,
My broken heart in my hand:
  Thou hast seen, judge Thou.
My hope was written on sand,
  O my God, O my God:
Now let thy judgment stand—
  Yea, judge me now.

This contemned of a man,
  This marred one heedless day,
This heart take Thou to scan
  Both within and without:
Refine with fire its gold,
  Purge Thou its dross away—

Yea hold it in Thy hold,
    Whence none can pluck it out.

I take my heart in my hand—
    I shall not die, but live—
Before Thy face I stand;
    I, for Thou callest such:
All that I have I bring,
    All that I am I give;
Smile Thou and I shall sing,
    But shall not question much.

Having It Out with Melancholy
Jane Kenyon

> If many remedies are prescribed for an illness, you may be certain that the
> illness has no cure.
>
> —A. P. Chekhov, *The Cherry Orchard*

1 From the Nursery

When I was born, you waited
behind a pile of linen in the nursery,
and when we were alone, you lay down
on top of me, pressing
the bile of desolation into every pore.

And from that day on
everything under the sun and moon
made me sad—even the yellow
wooden beads that slid and spun
along a spindle on my crib.

You taught me to exist without gratitude.
You ruined my manners toward God:
"We're here simply to wait for death;
the pleasures of earth are overrated."

I only appeared to belong to my mother,
to live among blocks and cotton undershirts
with snaps; among red tin lunch boxes

and report cards in ugly brown slipcases.
I was already yours—the anti-urge,
the mutilator of souls.

2 Bottles

Elavil, Ludiomil, Doxepin,
Norpramin, Prozac, Lithium, Xanax,
Wellbutrin, Parnate, Nardil, Zoloft.
The coated ones smell sweet or have
no smell; the powdery ones smell
like the chemistry lab at school
that made me hold my breath.

3 Suggestion from a Friend

You wouldn't be so depressed
if you really believed in God.

4 Often

Often I go to bed as soon after dinner
as seems adult
(I mean I try to wait for dark)

in order to push away
from the massive pain in sleep's
frail wicker coracle.

5 Once There Was Light

Once, in my early thirties, I saw
that I was a speck of light in the great
river of light that undulates through time.

I was floating with the whole
human family. We were all colors—those
who are living now, those who have died,
those who are not yet born. For a few

moments I floated, completely calm,
and I no longer hated having to exist.

Like a crow who smells hot blood
you came flying to pull me out
of the glowing stream.
"I'll hold you up. I never let my dear
ones drown!" After that, I wept for days.

6 In and Out

The dog searches until he finds me
upstairs, lies down with a clatter
of elbows, puts his head on my foot.

Sometimes the sound of his breathing

saves my life—in and out, in
and out; a pause, a long sigh. . . .

7 Pardon

A piece of burned meat
wears my clothes, speaks
in my voice, dispatches obligations
haltingly, or not at all.
It is tired of trying
to be stouthearted, tired
beyond measure.

We move on to the monoamine
oxidase inhibitors. Day and night
I feel as if I had drunk six cups
of coffee, but the pain stops

abruptly. With the wonder
and bitterness of someone pardoned
for a crime she did not commit
I come back to marriage and friends,
to pink fringed hollyhocks; come back
to my desk, books, and chair.

8 Credo

Pharmaceutical wonders are at work
but I believe only in this moment
of well-being. Unholy ghost,
you are certain to come again.

Coarse, mean, you'll put your feet
on the coffee table, lean back,
and turn me into someone who can't
take the trouble to speak; someone
who can't sleep, or who does nothing
but sleep; can't read, or call
for an appointment for help.

There is nothing I can do
against your coming.
When I awake, I am still with thee.

9 Wood Thrush

High on Nardil and June light
I wake at four,
waiting greedily for the first
note of the wood thrush. Easeful air
presses through the screen
with the wild, complex song
of the bird, and I am overcome

by ordinary contentment.
What hurt me so terribly
all my life until this moment?
How I love the small, swiftly
beating heart of the bird
singing in the great maples;
its bright, unequivocal eye.

Trying for Fire

Tim Seibles

Right now, even if a muscular woman wanted
to teach me the power of her skin
I'd probably just stand here with my hands
jammed in my pockets. Tonight
I'm feeling weak as water, watching the wind
bandage the moon. That's how it is tonight:
sky like tar, thin gauzy clouds,
a couple lame stars. A car rips by—
the driver's cigarette pinwheels past
the dog I saw hit this afternoon.
One second he was trotting along
with his wet nose tasting the air,
the next thing I know he's off the curb,
a car swerves and, bam, it's over. For an instant,
he didn't seem to understand he was dying—
he lifted his head as if he might still reach
the dark-green trash bags half-open
on the other side of the street.

I wish someone could tell me
how to live in the city. My friends
just shake their heads and shrug. I
can't go to church—I'm embarrassed by the things
preachers say we should believe.
I would talk to my wife, but she's worried
about the house. Whenever she listens
she hears the shingles giving in
to the rain. If I read the paper
I start believing some stranger
has got my name in his pocket—
on a matchbook next to his knife.
When I was twelve I'd take out the trash—
the garage would open like some ogre's cave
while just above my head the Monday Night Movie
stepped out of the television, and my parents
leaned back in their chairs. I can still hear
my father's voice coming through the floor,
"Boy, make sure you don't make a mess down there."
I remember the red-brick caterpillar of row houses
on Belfield Avenue and, not much higher than the rooftops,
the moon, soft and pale as a nun's thigh.

I had a plan back then—my feet were made
for football: each toe had the heart
of a different animal, so I ran
ten ways at once. I knew I'd play pro
and live with my best friend, and
when Vanessa let us pull up her sweater
those deep-brown balloony mounds made me believe
in a world where eventually you could touch
whatever you didn't understand.

If I was afraid of anything it was
my bedroom when my parents made me
turn out the light: that knocking noise
that kept coming from the walls,
the shadow shapes by the bookshelf,
the feeling that something was always there
just waiting for me to close my eyes.
But only sleep would get me, and I'd
wake up running for my bike, my life
jingling like a little bell on the breeze.
I understood so little that I
understood it all, and I still know
what it meant to be one of the boys
who had never kissed a girl.

I never did play pro football.
I never got to do my mad-horse,
mountain goat, happy-wolf dance
for the blaring fans in the Astro Dome.
I never snagged a one-hander over the middle
against Green Bay and stole my snaky way
down the sideline for the game-breaking six.

And now, the city is crouched like a mugger
behind me—right outside, in the alley behind my door,
a man stabbed this guy for his wallet, and
up the block a four-year-old disappeared. When I
turn on the radio the music is just like the news.
So, what should I do?—close my eyes and hope
whatever's out there will just let me sleep?
I won't sleep tonight. I'll stay near my TV
and watch the police get everybody.

Across the street a woman is letting
her phone ring. I see her in the kitchen

stirring something on the stove. Farther off
a small dog chips the quiet with his bark.
Above the moon looks like a nickel
in a murky-little creek. This
is the same moon that saw me twelve,
without a single bill to pay, zinging
soup can tops into the dark—I called them
flying saucers. This is the same
white light that touched dinosaurs, that
found the first people trying for fire.

It must have been very good, that moment
when wood smoke turned to flickering, when
they believed night was broken
once and for all—I wonder what almost-words
were spoken. I wonder how long
before that first flame went out.

4

Gerard Manley Hopkins
The Soldier

[Hopkins's] poetry comes up from the pages like sudden storms. A single short stanza can be as full of, aflame with, motion as one of Van Gogh's cedar trees.
                                                              —*Elizabeth Bishop*

About the Poet and the Poem

Gerard Manley Hopkins (1844–99) was a poet, a Jesuit priest, and a naturalist. He grew up in a prosperous and artistic family, and he was already writing poems when he entered Oxford. But after his conversion to Catholicism, he gave up writing. In a letter he explained how he came back to poetry:

> What I had written I burnt before I became a Jesuit and resolved to write no more, as not belonging to my profession, unless it were by the wish of my superiors; so for seven years I wrote nothing but two or three little presentation pieces which occasion called for. But when in the winter of [18]75 the Deutschland was wrecked in the mouth of the Thames and five Franciscan nuns, exiles from Germany by the [anti-Catholic] Falck Laws, aboard of her were drowned I was affected by the account and happening to say so to my rector he said that he wished someone would write a poem on the subject. On this hint I set to work and, though my hand was out at first, produced one. I had long had haunting my ear the echo of a new rhythm which I now realised on paper.[1]

Although Hopkins was chronologically a Victorian poet, his work was not published until 1918, when his friend Robert Bridges released a posthumous volume of his poems, including "The Soldier" (1885). In the editor's preface to that collection, Bridges fretted over Hopkins's peculiarities, searching for ways to excuse "the rude shocks of [the poet's] purely artistic wantonness."[2] Clearly, even three decades after his death, Hopkins was ahead of his time.

The Soldier
Gerard Manley Hopkins

Yes. Why do we all, seeing of a soldier, bless him? bless
Our redcoats, our tars? Both these being, the greater part,
But frail clay, nay but foul clay. Here it is: the heart,
Since, proud, it calls the calling manly, gives a guess
That, hopes that, makesbelieve, the men must be no less;
It fancies, feigns, deems, dears the artist after his art;
And fain will find as sterling all as all is smart,
And scarlet wear the spirit of war there express.
Mark Christ our King. He knows war served this soldiering through;
He of all can reeve a rope best. There he bides in bliss
Now, and seeing somewhere some man do all that man can do,
For love he leans forth, needs his neck must fall on, kiss,
And cry "O Christ-done deed! So God-made-flesh does too:
Were I come o'er again" cries Christ "it should be this."

What's the Most Important Punctuation?

It's so easy to overlook punctuation. Our eyes are trained to glide past it, automatically registering the marks as pauses or sentence endings but not otherwise lingering over them. Baron Wormser and David Cappella note in *Teaching the Art of Poetry,* "Punctuation makes necessary distinctions so that things don't blur and tangle and confuse," and this is why its absence often distresses us. "Punctuation seems ironclad. There had better be a period at the end of each sentence. It's the law—and poets flout it."[3]

Well, some poets flout it. In an interview for *The Paris Review,* Philip Larkin grumbled:

> A well-known publisher asked me how one punctuated poetry, and looked flabbergasted when I said, The same as prose. By which I mean that I write, or wrote, as everyone did till the mad lads started, using words and syntax in the normal way to describe recognizable experiences as memorably as possible. That doesn't seem to me a tradition. The other stuff, the mad stuff, is more an aberration.[4]

It's true that some poems seem to taunt us with willful misuse. In "th wundrfulness uv th mountees our secret police," Bill Bissett not only ignores punctuation and capitalization but misspells words, creating a narrative that is also a sort of manipulative graffiti:

> they opn our mail   petulantly
> they burn down barns they cant
> bug   they listn to our politikul
> ledrs phone conversashuns   what
> cud b less inspiring to ovrheer[5]

Sonia Sanchez takes a different tack in her "Song No. 3." Though she, too, ignores capitalization, she does make use of traditional punctuation. Nonetheless, she doesn't end every sentence with a period, only the last line of the stanza. Her choice affects how we imagine the speaker's voice and supports our absorption of the poem's blunt, childish, yet very clear pain.

> cain't nobody tell me any different
> i'm ugly and you know it too
> you just smiling to make me feel better
> but i see how you stare when nobody's watching you.[6]

Even as many poets experiment with deleting punctuation, others put traditional marks to new uses. For instance, rather than linking images with grammar, Melissa Stein's "So deeply that it is not heard at all, but" links them with punctuation:

> sister: the violin is blue. it plays stars, there was a field—
> sister: that swelling in your belly will be a milkweed, a duty, a friend—
> sister: goldenrod blossom: stippled ancillary: nonplussed bird—[7]

Russell Edson, on the other hand, gives us long grammatically complex sentences filled with traditional punctuation that, instead of clarifying the situation, contribute to the poem's ambiguity, as in this dense line from "Out of Whack":

> Too late, too late, because I am wearing the king's crown: and, in that we are married, and, in that the wearer of the king's crown is automatically the king, you are now *my* queen, who broke her crown like a typically silly woman, who doesn't quite realize the value of things, screamed the queen.[8]

But even when a poet follows less raucous patterns of punctuation, she chooses each comma, each period, each dash, precisely and deliberately. Punctuation marks, as Wormser and Cappella have said, add clarity; but they also are important elements of sound, affecting a line's cadence and tonality. The silence implied by a dash is longer than the silence implied by a comma. A question mark indicates a lift in tonal pitch, whereas a period indicates a drop. Even a hyphen or its absence has a subtle influence: the pacing of *fire truck* is different from *fire-truck* is different from *firetruck*.

Punctuation marks can be stylistic tics, as the dash was for Dickinson. They can even be stylistic anathemas. Richard Hugo, for instance, hated semicolons. In his essay "Nuts and Bolts," he declared, "No semicolons. Semicolons indicate relationships that only idiots need defined by punctuation. Besides, they are ugly."[9] Derek Walcott, among many other poets, would disagree passionately with that pronouncement. He uses semicolons throughout his book-length poem *The Prodigal,* often inserting them at line endings to indicate a pause of recognition or comprehension:

> Then through the thinned trees I saw a wraith
> of smoke, which I believed came from the house,
> but every smoker carries his own wreath;
> then I saw that this moving wreath was yours.[10]

In short, punctuation is both a flexible tool for experimentation and a formal structural element with rules and predictable patterns. Gerard Manley Hopkins was well aware of this duality, and he took advantage of both tradition and strangeness in the way in which he handled punctuation in his poems. Although I have chosen only three of his choices to discuss in this chapter, Hopkins thought intently about each punctuation mark in "The Soldier." Every one of them is significant.

THE PERIOD AFTER "YES"

"The Soldier" opens with this line:

> Yes. Why do we all, seeing of a soldier, bless him? bless

The effect of that first small word followed by a period is remarkable: a door slammed, a hand clapped over a mouth. If the poet had chosen a comma, a dash, or even a colon, I would have felt some sense of continued movement in the line. But "Yes." is a screeching halt.

Why did Hopkins use a period here? When I reread the poem, I don't see anything that parallels this usage. Perhaps "Here it is:" in line 3 is most similar, but in the second case the colon alerts us to a forthcoming example or explanation. In contrast, "Yes." ends all discussion. Flatly, it announces a fact.

According to *The Careful Writer,* "the period is the red light that brings the reader to a halt—in fact, it is known [in British English] as a full stop." Taking this power into account, *The Elements of Style* makes allowances for treating certain brief phrases as full sentences: "Do not use periods for commas. . . . [But] it is permissible to make an emphatic word or expression serve the purpose of a sentence and punctuate it accordingly."[11]

Although these style books address prose rather than poetry, Robert Frost understood that such fundamental principles of grammar were transferable to poems. In a notebook, he wrote, "Poets have lamented the lack in poetry of any such notation as music has for suggesting sound. But it is there and has always been there. The sentence is the notation. The sentence is before all else just that: a notation for suggesting significant tones of voice."[12]

Punctuation, as Hopkins knew, is crucial to that notation. "The Soldier" is rife with "significant tones of voice." It hesitates, doubles back, prevaricates . . . but not with "Yes." The first word of the poem overflows with what I can only call courage. Yes. I will bring myself to speak. Yes. You need to listen to me figure out what I need to say. Yes.

THE COMMA AFTER "THAT"

In the middle of line 3, Hopkins opens a new sentence that snakes its way through lines 4 and 5 until stalling out at a semicolon:

> Here it is: the heart,
> Since, proud, it calls the calling manly, gives a guess
> That, hopes that, makesbelieve, the men must be no less;

Encountering the commas in this passage is downright painful. Every one of them is a contortion, a stumble, a choke, a mistake. They chop up the cadence of the lines; they muddy the syntax of the phrasing. And the most uncomfortable of them all, to my ear, is "That," which appears at the beginning of line 5.

"That," could be the mirror opposite of "Yes." Whereas "Yes." was solidly decisive, "That," is timid and changeable. Whereas "Yes." was a brave loner, "That," repeats itself two words later in the same line, right before the sentence launches into the hurried mouthful of "makesbelieve." The poem's shift in tone is both dramatic and awkward, as if the speaker is playing two parts simultaneously.

"The Soldier" is a sonnet; and as I mentioned in my discussion of Shakespeare's sonnet 81, the first words in the lines of a sonnet often seem to propel the poem. I wasn't thinking of that power when I reacted to the word-punctuation combinations "Yes." and "That," but I am beginning to see that Hopkins's choice of punctuation both emphasizes and undercuts this natural propulsion. Instead of driving me forward into the sonnet, both the period and the comma force me to stop, look back, look ahead, scratch my head, ask, "Wait a minute: what's going on here?"

In the words of teacher Carlene Gadapee, Hopkins's punctuation functions as both "convention and invention."[13] The comma in "That," does, on one level, exactly what we'd expect of a comma. It indicates a pause—a brief moment of silence in the line that also gives the reader time to make sense of the sentence's syntactical shift. At the same time, the comma's placement is clumsy, even ugly: it is both visually and sonically unsettling.

THE ABSENCE OF COMMAS

If there's one thing I've learned after reading and rereading "The Soldier," it's that the poet is not shy about using commas. The poem overflows with them, and almost all contribute to the strained, contorted cadence of the lines and sentences. Hopkins's own term for this cadence was *sprung rhythm,* which, in Robert Pinsky's simplified explanation, "refers generally to the jamming in of stressed syllables."[14] By inserting pauses among the jammed-in syllables, the commas reinforce these unexpected stresses while also slowing the poem's pace.

"No doubt," Hopkins said in a letter to his friend Robert Bridges, "my poetry errs on the side of oddness."[15] One supreme oddness of "The Soldier" is the poet's inconsistency. He follows traditional spelling rules and then suddenly tosses in "makesbelieve." He revels in commas and then suddenly avoids them. Notice how his comma use changes in lines 12 through 14:

> For love he leans forth, needs his neck must fall on, kiss,
> And cry "O Christ-done-deed! So God-made-flesh does too:
> Were I come o'er again" cries Christ "it should be this."

Typically commas set off dialogue, so we might expect to see them after "And cry" in line 13 as well as "again" and "cries Christ" in line 14. But no: Hopkins hurries us straight into the punctuation-heavy dialogue, leaving me entirely confused, at first, as to whether Christ is doing all the talking or whether the man whose neck he "must fall on" is speaking line 13. I had to reread the entire poem to be sure that the problem wasn't a missing quotation mark.

In his novel *The Wapshot Chronicle,* John Cheever makes reference to historical figure Lord Timothy Dexter, a Massachusetts eccentric, who, in the second edition of his 1802 book *A Pickle for the Knowing Ones or Plain Truth in a Homespun Dress,* "put all punctuation marks, prepositions, adverbs, articles, etc., at end of communication and urged reader to distribute same as he saw fit."[16] When reading a Hopkins poem, I sometimes wish the poet had given me that option. His punctuation is visceral yet inscrutable; heavy-handed even in absence; strangely distracting, like a marble in the mouth. It seems as determined to mislead me as it is to force me to watch and listen.

Writing of Hopkins's poem "The Windhover," Ange Mlinko has said, "If we hear through our eyes when we read any page of text, Hopkins taught me that in a great poem's soundscapes, we 'see' through our ears as well."[17] By tinkering with his poems' punctuation, Hopkins manipulated the subtleties of these soundscapes. He showed that a comma or its absence is more than a visual sign. It can be a sonic presence, an intellectual and emotional presence. "It fancies, feigns, deems, dears the artist after his art."

Ideas for Writing

Punctuation is an important element of revision, but its presence or absence can also significantly influence the trajectory of a first draft. For example, in her poem "Question," Andrea Hollander demonstrates how the enforced absence of punctuation can drive a poet into revelation.

Question
Andrea Hollander

FOR (AND AFTER) JOHN BREHM

I've been reading the poems in your first book
between tasks or at the end of the day in bed
in my nightshirt sometimes tired sometimes
too awake sometimes first thing in the morning
still in bed just now I read the one about clouds
and wind and the way your mind leaps out of
control like my mind like all our minds and I
admire the way you guide me through all the leaps
the poem takes without holding my hand trusting
my instincts if not my intelligence and you do it
in one sentence without punctuation until the end
I almost wrote *the very end* but thought how
superfluous *very* is since end is end no matter
what kind and no adjective makes any difference
not even for emphasis someone is dead not
very dead not very pregnant or very divorced
as I am right now and I might have used *very*
in my own head but not out loud or in a poem
the last word in your poem is *you* meaning not
you but a woman which is what the poem's focus
finally is though we don't reach that word for many
lines yet I'm never confused in your one-sentence
poem that I'm not imitating if only to see where
it will lead if I keep it up the way I kept up my part
of my marriage even after I learned that my ex
did not he pretended to but isn't that the way
these things go when you finally relax and think
how good this is how easy to be yourself without
fuss without complaint and then the clouds you
were so grateful for in the Arkansas glare and heat
turn out to be storm clouds crouching over
the Ozarks about to devour everything in their wake
like a starving lion stalking the weakest in the herd
and along with the clouds the train sound that roar

you were warned about without time to rush
to the storm cellar the train sound after such
silence and that wind that wind but no *real* train
lifts the forest away like so many toothpicks
or rips off the roof of the carport and with it
the new car my heart felt like that and may as well
have been torn out because when that happens
you don't need it you don't want it you want to be
somewhere where you can't feel anything not even
if it's true that if you let yourself feel you will get
to the other side the fact that there is another side
to get to is hard enough to believe the way at the end
of your poem the clouds do what they want with you
you have no control the way you have no control
of the woman you want in your poem to stay
and she does not leave at least not when you wrote
the poem although that was then and this is now
isn't it?

In chapter 3, I mentioned that fast writing often helps us circumvent our internal
censor, and writing without punctuation can do the same. You or your students might try
Hollander's approach in your own first drafts. Think about something you've recently
been reading (a book, an article, a poem, a mean letter to the editor) or listening to
(a baseball game, a song, a sermon) and write a poem that opens by talking back to it.
Force yourself to avoid all punctuation and to write at least twenty-five lines as quickly as
possible.

As you begin to revise, you will probably find yourself changing words, adding
and deleting text, creating stanza and line breaks, and so on. But experimenting with
punctuation can also influence your thoughts about words and structure. Here are some
possibilities to try:

1. Add two commas to every line of your draft.
2. Turn three of the commas into dashes.
3. Turn one of the dashes into a colon.
4. Add a period after the first word in a line.
5. Insert periods at every natural sentence break in the poem.
6. Replace five of those periods with semicolons.

As you experiment with different combinations of punctuation, you may find yourself
preferring your original loose Hollander-like format. But you may also discover a
yearning for what, in "With Mercy for the Greedy," Anne Sexton calls "the tongue's
wrangle."[18] Punctuation, that modest battery of spots and strokes, can be a powerful ally
in your quest.

Thinking about Punctuation: An Anthology

Teresa Carson: Fill in the [Blanks] for July 3–25, 1986
Robert Francis: The Base Stealer
Li-Young Lee: The Hammock
Meg Kearney: Living in the Volcano
Sir Philip Sidney: "My Muse may well grudge at my heav'nly joy"

About punctuation my mind is clear: I can give a rule for everything I write myself, and even for other people, though they might not agree with me perhaps.
                                            —Gerard Manley Hopkins

Fill in the [Blanks] for July 3–25, 1986
Teresa Carson

During his last appointment with
the psychiatrist who prescribed the five
antipsychotic drugs—which he took
on a [time interval] basis—Joe asks [words].
Dr. Castillo replies [words].

I don't attend my brother Tom's wedding,
because a feud over [reason] has split
my siblings into non-speaking factions,
but Joe does and he's in an [adjective] mood.

Forty-two-year-old, 6'1" & 140 pounds Joe,
who doesn't drive, manages to haul 91 pounds
of cinder blocks and steel chains eight miles from Jersey City
to [location] near the Passaic River by [details of process].

A pleasure boat captain spots something
floating in the river. He feels [adjective] when he realizes
what it is. Fire Boat #1 recovers an Unknown Male.
Possible [crime type] says Det. Nankivell.
That afternoon, while someone cuts one chain from
the subject's body, I'm at work, [present participle verb],
and Joe hasn't even crossed my mind in [time interval].

The Base Stealer
Robert Francis

Poised between going on and back, pulled
Both ways taut like a tightrope-walker,
Fingertips pointing the opposites,
Now bouncing tiptoe like a dropped ball
Or a kid skipping rope, come on, come on,
Running a scattering of steps sidewise,
How he teeters, skitters, tingles, teases,
Taunts them, hovers like an ecstatic bird,
He's only flirting, crowd him, crowd him,
Delicate, delicate, delicate, delicate—now!

The Hammock

Li-Young Lee

When I lay my head in my mother's lap
I think how the day hides the stars,
the way I lay hidden once, waiting
inside my mother's singing to herself. And I remember
how she carried me on her back
between home and the kindergarten,
once each morning and once each afternoon.

I don't know what my mother's thinking.

When my son lays his head in my lap, I wonder:
Do his father's kisses keep his father's worries
from becoming his? I think, *Dear God,* and remember
there are stars we haven't heard from yet:
They have so far to arrive. *Amen,*
I think, and I feel almost comforted.

I've no idea what my child is thinking.

Between two unknowns, I live my life.
Between my mother's hopes, older than I am
by coming before me, and my child's wishes, older than I am
by outliving me. And what's it like?
Is it a door, and good-bye on either side?
A window, and eternity on either side?
Yes, and a little singing between two great rests.

Living in the Volcano
Meg Kearney

All I want is a falafel, a macramé purse,
and First Piccolo in the marching band.

Hey, my sunless tan puts an orange slant
on everything I say. I mean I want to *be*

first, and hippie free . . . but my tongue
is a branding iron shaped in an "X"

(I kiss your eyes and you're dead), First
Trombone turns left at the 40, and

the rest of us wave bye-bye, too grumpy
to follow. We say, Let's practice more, earn

this pride of prima donnas a scholarship
to Party University. We say, Let's melt

down the horns, buy us some brewskies
and vitamin M. We need to forget, for a two-

day bender, how much we can't stand
ourselves. But this is high school. And now

Mother, our First Fan, has skipped town
with the bake sale money and Finnegan,

our only tuba. Who needs TV drama? This
is life in the volcano. This as cold as it gets.

"My Muse may well grudge at my heav'nly joy"
Sir Philip Sidney

My Muse may well grudge at my heav'nly joy,
If still I force her in sad rhymes to creep:
She oft hath drunk my tears, now hopes t'enjoy
Nectar of mirth, since I *Jove*'s cup do keep.

Sonnets be not bound 'prentice to annoy;
Trebles sing high, as well as bases deep;
Grief but Love's winter liv'ry is; the boy
Hath cheeks to smile, as well as eyes to weep.

Come then, my Muse, show thou height of delight
In well-raised notes; my pen the best it may
Shall paint out joy, though but in black and white.

Cease eager Muse, peace pen, for my sake stay,
I give you here my hand for truth of this,
Wise silence is best music unto bliss.

5

Amy Lowell
Thompson's Lunch Room—Grand Central Station

No one expects a man to make a chair without first learning how, but there is a popular impression that the poet is born, not made, and that his verses burst from his overflowing heart of themselves. As a matter of fact, the poet must learn his trade in the same manner, and with the same painstaking care, as the cabinet-maker. His heart may overflow with high thoughts and sparkling fancies, but if he cannot convey them to his reader by means of the written word he has no claim to be considered a poet.
—Amy Lowell

About the Poet and the Poem

Amy Lowell (1874–1925) was born into a distinguished Boston family that included not only high-ranking military officers, intellectuals, and judges but also the poets James Russell Lowell and later Robert Lowell. In *A History of Modern Poetry,* David Perkins writes:

> Her brother, Abbott Lawrence Lowell, who became President of Harvard, made no public comment on the avant-garde writings and other eccentricities of his sister. She was enormously overweight because of a glandular disturbance, smoked cigars, slept with sixteen pillows, and worked from midnight to dawn, sleeping by day. These and other oddities contributed to her reputation, but what contributed more were her energy, shrewdness, determination, and pluck. By these virtues she thrust herself into prominence among the poets of the time, but her position was precarious.[1]

T. S. Eliot called her a "demon saleswoman" for Imagism, the early twentieth-century literary movement that brought poets such as Ezra Pound to prominence.[2] Yet the poets whom she championed often derided her in return, and her reputation has suffered over the years, often thanks to male poets and critics who ridiculed both her enthusiasms and her weight.

"Thompson's Lunch Room—Grand Central Station" is the second poem in a five-poem cycle titled *Towns in Color.* It appeared in Lowell's 1916 collection, also titled *Towns in Color.*

Thompson's Lunch Room—Grand Central Station
Amy Lowell

STUDY IN WHITES

Wax-white—
Floor, ceiling, walls.
Ivory shadows
Over the pavement
Polished to cream surfaces
By constant sweeping.
The big room is coloured like the petals
Of a great magnolia.
And has a patina
Of flower bloom
Which makes it shine dimly
Under the electric lamps.
Chairs are ranged in rows
Like sepia seeds
Waiting fulfilment.
The chalk-white spot of a cook's cap
Moves unglossily against the vaguely bright wall—
Dull chalk-white striking the retina like a blow
Through the wavering uncertainty of steam.
Vitreous-white of glasses with green reflections,
Ice-green carboys, shifting—greener, bluer—with the jar of moving water.
Jagged green-white bowls of pressed glass
Rearing snow-peaks of chipped sugar
Above the lighthouse-shaped castors
Of grey pepper and grey-white salt.
Grey-white placards: "Oyster Stew, Cornbeef Hash, Frankfurters":
Marble slabs veined with words in meandering lines.
Dropping on the white counter like horn notes
Through a web of violins,
The flat yellow lights of oranges,
The cube-red splashes of apples,
In high plated *épergnes.*
The electric clock jerks every half-minute:
"Coming!—Past!"
"Three beef-steaks and a chicken-pie,"
Bawled through a slide while the clock jerks heavily.
A man carries a china mug of coffee to a distant chair.
Two rice puddings and a salmon salad
Are pushed over the counter;
The unfulfilled chairs open to receive them.

A spoon falls upon the floor with the impact of metal striking stone,
And the sound throws across the room
Sharp, invisible zigzags
Of silver.

What's the Most Important Detail?

"We know there must be consciousness in things," writes Mark Jarman in "Astragaloi":

> In bits of gravel pecked up by a hen
> To grind inside her crop, and spider silk
> Just as it hardens stickily in air.[3]

Many poets might just as easily say, "We know there must be consciousness in words." By fitting together individual bits and pieces of language, they work to create a facsimile of life, one that may even reach across centuries to touch the most unsuspecting of readers.

A few summers ago, as I sat reading George Eliot's *Middlemarch* on the front porch of the Robert Frost Museum in Franconia, New Hampshire, a teenage boy came around the corner of the house. He was about eighteen years old—tall, curly-haired, athletic. Plopping himself down on a table, he crossed his arms and looked me in the eye. "Are you a poet?" he asked.

After I admitted that I was, he leaned back. Still holding my gaze, he announced, "'The Charge of the Light Brigade' is the bomb."

I did what anyone would have done under the circumstances, which was to become slack-jawed and slightly dizzy. Undeterred, the boy remarked that Alfred Tennyson was his favorite poet, that he'd accidentally discovered Tennyson's poems in a book in his grandfather's house; also, that he hadn't quite gotten his brain around "In Memoriam" and that other long stuff but "The Eagle" and "The Kracken" were also the bomb.

We talked. What he liked about these poems, he explained, were the details—those particular combinations of words that pulled him directly into the poet's imaginative world. "I like that he makes me be there."

Think of details as a poem's information. The poet relays this information by choosing words and phrases that evoke specific characters, places, or situations while also advancing narrative action, lyrical intensity, and thematic unity. As Theodore Roethke explains, "The poet must have a sense not only of what words were and are, but also what they are going to be."[4]

In her memoir *The Gift,* H. D. wrote of her child self's growing awareness of the link between observation and the urge to repeat, reframe, reinvent what one has seen: "It was not that I thought of the picture; it was that something was remembered. . . . You saw what was there, you knew that something was reminded of something. That something came true in a perspective and a dimension (though those words, of course, had no part in my mind) that was final."[5]

Image is the customary poetic term for a mental picture translated into words. Images are constructed of details, and precise nouns are their foundation. For instance, in the opening stanza of her poem "The Burn," Terry Blackhawk chooses a handful of plain yet exact nouns to solidify the details of place:

> I saw it once in a sycamore
> at a fishing spot near the lagoon,
> one of the tree's three trunks combusting.[6]

"Sycamore" is the accurate name of the tree. The compound noun "fishing spot" adds a casual connotation to the more exotic "lagoon." In the last line the poet avoids repeating "sycamore," this time allowing herself to draw back to the more general "tree," which visually and sonically reinforces the repeated *t* sounds in the line. Blackhawk's only adjective is "three." Her only verb (until the shock of the participle "combusting) is "saw." The imagery of this stanza depends primarily on those solid, simple nouns.

In "Christmas Eve in France," Jessie Redmon Fauset also chooses a handful of basic nouns, but she reveals and varies her details by adding adjectives:

> Oh, little Christ, why do you sigh
>   As you look down tonight
> On breathless France, on bleeding France,
>   And all her dreadful plight?
> What bows your childish head so low?
>   What turns your cheek so white?[7]

Even though "On breathless France, on bleeding France" repeats the same noun twice, Fauset's shift from "breathless" to "bleeding" entirely reconfigures the imagery. Yet the adjectives are similar in sound, so the line retains its songlike quality even as it disrupts my mental picture of the situation.

Some poets, such as Ted Hughes in "Sketching a Thatcher," choose details of ornament that seem as weighty as the nouns they modify:

> Lizard-silk of his lizard-skinny,
> Hands never still, twist of body never still—
> Bounds in for a cup of tea.[8]

The extract's grammar, like its subject, is jumpy. In "Lizard-silk of his lizard-skinny hands," the hyphenated repetition shifts from compound noun to compound adjective. Hughes repeats the noun "hands," the adverb-adjective combination "never still." In the last line he tosses us the vivid verb "bounds," yet we're hardly aware that it's the first verb in the extract. Thanks to the precise arrangement of his nouns and modifiers, Hughes has created the sensation of action from the details of a physical description.

The details in a poem do more than create specific images. They may also advance narrative action, develop character, hint at a back story, intensify a mood, reinforce sounds, and so on and so on. As Baron Wormser and David Cappella explain in *Teaching the Art of Poetry,* "Details are the confluence of observant intelligence, apt feeling, and thematic sense."[9] For example, the details in the opening stanza of Siegfried Sassoon's "The rank stench of those bodies haunts me still" draw together a present-tense situation and layered memories of other times and places to construct a unified moment of consciousness.

> The rank stench of those bodies haunts me still,
> And I remember things I'd best forget.
> For now we've marched to a green, trenchless land

Twelve miles from battering guns: along the grass
Brown lines of tents are hives for snoring men;
Wide radiant water sways the floating sky
Below dark, shivering trees. And living-clean
Comes back with thoughts of home and hours of sleep.[10]

A poet chooses specific details to accomplish specific purposes. Because every poem is different, the poet must constantly rethink her strategies. What details should she include or leave out? How should she organize them? How can she make certain details stand out while allowing others to recede? In "Thompson's Lunch Room—Grand Central Station," Amy Lowell was juggling an enormous amount of information and had to solve many problems as she worked to unify her disparate bits and pieces. I've chosen three of her poem's many details to discuss here.

STUDY IN WHITES

Before the poem opens, Lowell inserts a controlling detail: an odd subtitle that both adds ambiguity and lays out certain parameters for the poem. While the title proper is a jaunty description of the poem's busy setting, the subtitle, "Study in Whites," is vague and generalized. Rather than conjuring up a specific scene, it seems to retreat into academic neutrality. What could be blander than a study in whites? Already, even before I begin reading the poem, I don't know whether to expect clutter or flatness, passion or remoteness.

The two titles feel contradictory. Yet that seems to be exactly Lowell's intent. With only the primary title to guide me, I might have expected a more traditional dramatic approach. In contrast, the detached, intellectualized "Study in Whites" prepares me for the poem's structural idiosyncrasy—stacked images, incomplete sentences, a ragged right-hand margin—as well as a certain chilly emotional ambience.

The subtitle also leads me to believe that this poem will include many details about white objects and places, which indeed it does. The first nineteen lines of the poem are packed with white-focused imagery: wax, ivory, cream, magnolias, sepia seeds, chalk. But then Lowell changes her approach. Instead of continuing to limit her details to white, she starts adding colors to the mix:

Vitreous-white of glasses with green reflections,
Ice-green carboys, shifting—greener, bluer—with the jar of moving water.
Jagged green-white bowls of pressed glass
Rearing snow-peaks of chipped sugar
Above the lighthouse-shaped castors
Of grey pepper and grey-white salt.
Grey-white placards: "Oyster Stew, Cornbeef Hash, Frankfurters":
Marble slabs veined with words in meandering lines.
Dropping on the white counter like horn notes
Through a web of violins,
The flat yellow lights of oranges,
The cube-red splashes of apples,

In high plated *épergnes.*

"Study in Whites" has now also become a study of colors, yet the subtitle persists. By the time I reach the end of the poem, I don't know if it is ironic, if it posits the idea of white as a blank canvas or a negative space, if it demonstrates how the details of poem can subsume a poet's preconceived ideas, or if it indicates something entirely different from what I have hazarded here. A poem can surprise its maker. A reader may see what the poet never saw. As Adrienne Rich said in "Ghazals: Homage to Ghalib," "When they read this poem of mine, they are translators. / Every existence speaks a language of its own."[11]

A MAN CARRIES A CHINA MUG OF COFFEE

How does a poet arrange details so that they unify into a poem rather than remain a list of observations? Lowell organized her details in ways that guide her reader's imaginative eye. First, I see the space—"floor, ceiling, walls." Then she allows me to zero in on the smaller details of the lunch room—"Ice-green carboys," "Rearing snow-peaks of chipped sugar." The movement of "a cook's cap" hints at a human presence, and toward the end of the poem I hear, "'Three beef-steaks and a chicken-pie,' / Bawled through a slide while the clock jerks heavily." But the lunch room itself remains empty of life, until finally "A man carries a china mug of coffee to a distant chair."

I see, now, how very different this poem might have been. For instance, Lowell could so easily have focused my attention on the man. He might have prefigured Mona Van Duyn's "The Talker," a character who "spurts / all over the room in facts and puns and jokes," who "climbs the decibels toward some glorious view," who "only loves himself out loud."[12] Instead, she details a single, silent journey across the room. And by introducing the human character so quietly and so late in the poem, she reinforces my imaginative engagement with this grand, overwhelming, cavernous room. Even though it teems with human possessions, the people themselves remain insignificant.

Writing about Elizabeth Bishop's poem "At the Fishhouses," Seamus Heaney said, "She . . . submitted herself to the discipline of observation."

> This writing still bears a recognizable resemblance to the simple propositions of the geography text-book. There is not sentence which does not possess a similar clarity and unchallengeability. Yet since these concluding lines are poetry, not geography, they have a dream truth as well as a daylight truth about them, they are as hallucinatory as they are accurate.
>   . . . In the rift between what is going to happen and whatever we would wish to happen, poetry holds attention for a space, functions not as a distraction but as pure concentration, a focus where our power to concentrate is concentrated back on ourselves.[13]

Amy Lowell believed passionately in "'externality' (by which she meant objectivity, the rendering of outward events rather than impressions and subjective states) and a refusal to draw moral generalizations."[14] In "Thompson's Lunch Room," she, like Bishop, "submitted herself to the discipline of observation." But to create "a dream truth as well as a daylight truth," poets must order and arrange those observed details in ways that allow the reader to experience "the rift between what is going to happen and whatever we would wish to happen."

"A man carries a china mug of coffee to a distant chair." If Lowell had arranged the details in another way, I might have assumed that this was a happy man waiting to meet a friend. But in the context of the actual poem, the line strikes me as immensely sad. Lowell may have intended to remain cool and objective, yet she still managed to design a moment of pure loneliness.

A SPOON FALLS UPON THE FLOOR

"Thompson's Lunch Room" is a remarkably quiet poem. Nearly all of the details are visual; not until the end do I hear anything at all. "Bawled through a slide" is a surprise, yet the bawler remains invisible. Is this a man or a woman? Old or young? Is he or she the same person who pushes "Two rice puddings and a salmon salad . . . over the counter"?

In that case, Lowell detaches sound from its maker. But in the final four lines, she allows sound to take control of the poem:

> A spoon falls upon the floor with the impact of metal striking stone,
> And the sound throws across the room
> Sharp, invisible zigzags
> Of silver.

Not only does Lowell reveal exactly what makes the sound ("A spoon"), but she lingers over the moment to emphasize its importance. She also places the incident at the tail end of the poem, purposely choosing these particular details as the poem's final imaginative echo.

Yet even though she is describing the impact of sound, the comparison is composed of visual details: "Sharp, invisible zigzags / Of silver." The image seems to reach back to "Study in Whites," yet now white becomes silver, just as sound becomes sight. Once again, the poet subverts my expectations.

In "Sojourns in the Parallel World," Denise Levertov writes:

> No one discovers
> just where we've been, when we're caught up again
> into our own sphere (where we must
> return, indeed, to evolve our destinies)
> —but we have changed, a little.[15]

Her lines could be a structural description of "Thompson's Lunch Room," a poem that is deliberately, even coldly, organized but nonetheless manages a subtle shift in its tonal and emotional registers. A poem takes on a life of its own. The poet controls that life but is also controlled by it. Placing detail 1 next to detail 2 pushes a poem down one path. Dropping detail 3 between them may suddenly skew its direction.

Writing about the shifts in poetic style that took place early in the twentieth century, John Berryman said, "Poetry [by 1935] became ominous, flat, and social; elliptical and indistinctly allusive; casual in tone and form, frightening in import."[16] Amy Lowell was a prime force behind this stylistic movement, and "Thompson's Lunch Room" exemplifies nearly every characteristic on Berryman's list. Yet the individual details in the poem are often stunning. They glow in my memory like Georgia O'Keeffe's painted flowers.

Ideas for Writing

A poet lures in readers with sensory details. They upstage every brilliant intellectual argument, every complex intangible idea. "Dungan is the deidly dragon Lucifer, / The cruewall serpent with the mortal stang," wrote William Dunbar in "Done is a battle" in about 1500. "Here is this horse from a bad family, hating his burden and snaffle, not patient," wrote Rodney Jones in "Mule" in 1989.[17] These two poets, writing four hundred years and a continent apart, both turned instinctively to physical details to pull their readers into the orbit of their imagination. Yet when we feel a burgeoning need to write, we are often drawn to intangibles. "What is loneliness?" we find ourselves asking. "What is grief?" How can a poet use sensory details to frame such generalized questions?

When creating a character, a writer pulls together details that give it substance, that make us feel that the character has a physical place in the world. (Rodney Jones does this very simply with the phrase "horse from a bad family.") So one way to press your students or yourself into using sensory details is to transform an idea word into an actual character.

If you're writing alone and you're wrestling with issues of death, love, or beauty, or even procrastination, stinginess, or boredom, you might choose one of those touchstone words for this exercise. If you're working with students, you might have them brainstorm a group list of idea words and then have them choose a word from the list. Alternatively, you might write idea words on individual slips of paper and hand them out to students or choose one randomly from the pile yourself.

Then ask yourself or your students to answer a few of these or similar questions. I'm going to use the word *grief,* but you can replace it with any other idea word.

1. What does grief smell like?
2. What does grief cook for dinner?
3. Which tree does grief hide behind?
4. What song does grief's mother sing?
5. Which animal does grief fear?

Press yourself or your students to answer the questions in complete sentences. Then have them revise each original sentence:

1. Add three nouns to sentence 1.
2. Add two prepositional phrases to sentence 2.
3. Add a phrase beginning with "because" to sentence 3.
4. Replace "sing" with a different verb in sentence 4.
5. Replace "fear" with "eat" and then rewrite sentence 5 accordingly.

Don't think so much about making a poem as about making word pictures. Once you get comfortable with creating such imaginative sketches, you can weave them into a poem. It's important to remember that not every word you write needs to end up in a poem. Like novelists, poets often need to spend time creating a back story: clusters of images, observations, recollections, word experiments that we can shed or accumulate as we work toward writing the poem we need to write.

Thinking about Details: An Anthology

Jonathan Swift: A Description Of The Morning
Kim Addonizio: Garbage
Evening Star: Joe-Anne McLaughlin
Edward Thomas: Gone, Gone Again
Walt Whitman: There Was a Child Went Forth

For you, it was write poems or crack safes!
　　　　　　　　—Joe-Anne McLaughlin

A Description of the Morning
Jonathan Swift

Now hardly here and there an hackney-coach,
Appearing, showed the ruddy morn's approach.
Now Betty from her master's bed had flown,
And softly stole to discompose her own.
The slipshod prentice from his master's door
Had pared the dirt, and sprinkled round the floor.
Now Moll had whirled her mop with dextrous airs,
Prepared to scrub the entry and the stairs.
The youth with broomy stumps began to trace
The kennel-edge, where wheels had worn the place.
The small-coal man was heard with cadence deep,
Till drowned in shriller notes of chimney-sweep,
Duns at his lordship's gate began to meet,
And Brickdust Moll had screamed through half the street.
The turnkey now his flock returning sees,
Duly let out a-nights to steal for fees;
The watchful bailiffs take their silent stands;
And schoolboys lag with satchels in their hands.

Garbage
Kim Addonizio

Don't think about where it goes
after you tie it up in its white bag and squash it down
into the can dragged out to the curb. Don't think
of the stink of the truck backing up, or the men in their filthy gloves
hanging off the sides, cursing in the near-dark of a new day
in which, somewhere, someone is about to be thrown into a cell
the way garbage is thrown into a deep pit for burning,
the way bodies are thrown in to be shoveled over.
Don't think about the dump, the scavenging rats,
the reeking piles they tunnel through—the flattened shoes,
the dolls with their eyes torn out, the pennies, the lost
wedding ring, whatever's found its way there and won't return
except as a stain, a bad smell on the air, a poison
seeding the clouds until it rains back down. But today
the weather's lovely; look at the sky, its purity,
its nullity, only gulls crossing it on their way
to the beaches. Don't let the gulls remind you
of how they dive beak-first into fish, of fish floating up with the sewage.
Especially don't think of dead things, or of vultures, how they wait so patiently
while something is bleeding into the dirt, and then jostle each other
as they hunch black-frocked around it, feeding the way everyone feeds;
oh, don't think now of all the food you've wasted,
scraped off plates or gone bad on the shelf, in the fridge,
you couldn't help it, you meant to save everyone, the children especially,
but it keeps filling up the house: the thick black print of newspapers,
the petitions for money with lists of their names, their actual faces,
they're still alive, they're out there with the guards
and the soldiers and the flies, so don't think of how clean
your house is, don't for a minute think you've gotten it all,
look at your hands, they're covered with it, you can try
to wash them or else plunge them in; even one finger, take it and scrape
up a little of the sludge and the muck and the stench
of the human, feel how the barest hope clings there.

Evening Star

Joe-Anne McLaughlin

Let his breath come
          hard
            let his shoulders

kill him
    these late afternoons
        after his long illness

still he climbs
    the long hill out back
          through snow
            to his absent son's trailer

where he will sit for awhile
        with the old cat who gets
           lonely up there.

(What else?—with his son on the road
    week-in
        week-out.)

To change her water,
to clean her box
if needed, humbly, on all fours,
to feed her treats—in substance
no different from thousands
of manuscripts edited,
hundreds of blurbs written, letters
answered, hungers appeased. . . .

He will remove his boots
        just inside the door
         taking care

as always
      not to make a mess
               then
    as always
      steady his nerves
with a cigarette.

"Envy of the placid beasts
is a very widespread affliction
in this type of sadness,"
William James wrote in *The Varieties
of Religious Experience.*

                    Poetry? The old
cat's pleasure will warm him
                    halfway like heat
                              cast by an open
fireplace in a drafty hall
                    which falls
short
      which cannot quite
                    reach around
no matter how
      radiant—even at home
            in bed with his wife.

                         Snow
will have melted through
      his jeans to his calves. He will
                    remember then before
he leaves he must water his son's plants.

            Or at the windbreak
halfway down
            how he will count five
                         no six

male cardinals lighting
      on a wild choke cherry
         (getting it right   exactly)
                    this image he will carry

home for his wife
      who will be watching
            for him down there

in the little red house
      with its huge bird feeder
                    and neatly

stacked half-cord
      at which he will be stopping first

to gather more wood
    while there's still light.

Gone, Gone Again
Edward Thomas

Gone, gone again,
May, June, July,
And August gone,
Again gone by,

Not memorable
Save that I saw them go,
As past the empty quays
The rivers flow.

And now again,
In the harvest rain,
The Blenheim oranges
Fall grubby from the trees

As when I was young,
And when the lost one was here—
And when the war began
To turn young men to dung.

Look at the old house,
Outmoded, dignified,
Dark and untenanted,
With grass growing instead

Of the footsteps of life,
The friendliness, the strife;
In its beds have lain
Youth, love, age, and pain:

I am something like that;
Only I am not dead,
Still breathing and interested
In the house that is not dark: —

I am something like that:
Not one pane to reflect the sun,
For the schoolboys to throw at—
They have broken every one.

There Was a Child Went Forth
Walt Whitman

There was a child went forth every day,
And the first object he look'd upon, that object he became,
And that object became part of him for the day or a certain part of the day,
Or for many years or stretching cycles of years.

The early lilacs became part of this child,
And grass and white and red morning-glories, and white and red clover, and the song of
                    the phoebe-bird,
And the Third-month lambs and the sow's pink-faint litter, and the mare's foal and
                    the cow's calf,
And the noisy brood of the barnyard or by the mire of the pond-side,
And the fish suspending themselves so curiously below there, and the beautiful curious
                    liquid,
And the water-plants with their graceful flat heads, all became part of him.

The field sprouts of Fourth-month and Fifth-month became part of him,
Winter-grain sprouts and those of the light-yellow corn, and the esculent roots
                    of the garden,
And the apple-trees cover'd with blossoms and fruit afterward, and wood-berries,
                    and the commonest weeds by the road,
And the old drunkard staggering home from the outhouse of the tavern
                    whence he had lately risen,
And the schoolmistress that pass'd on her way to the school,
And the friendly boys that pass'd, and the quarrelsome boys,
And the tidy and fresh-cheek'd girls, and the barefoot negro boy and girl,
And all the changes of city and country wherever he went.

His own parents, he that had father'd him and she that had conceiv'd him in her womb
                    and birth'd him,
They gave this child more of themselves than that,
They gave him afterward every day, they became part of him.

The mother at home quietly placing the dishes on the supper-table,
The mother with mild words, clean her cap and gown, a wholesome odor falling off
                    her person and clothes as she walks by,
The father, strong, self-sufficient, manly, mean, anger'd, unjust,
The blow, the quick loud word, the tight bargain, the crafty lure,
The family usages, the language, the company, the furniture, the yearning and swelling
                    heart,
Affection that will not be gainsay'd, the sense of what is real, the thought if after all
                    it should prove unreal,
The doubts of day-time and the doubts of night-time, the curious whether and how,

Whether that which appears so is so, or is it all flashes and specks?
Men and women crowding so fast in the streets, if they are not flashes and specks
                              what are they?
The streets themselves and the façades of houses, and goods in the windows,
Vehicles, teams, the heavy-plank'd wharves, the huge crossing at the ferries,
The village on the highland seen from afar at sunset, the river between,
Shadows, aureola and mist, the light falling on roofs and gables of white or brown
                              two miles off,
The schooner nearby sleepily dropping down the tide, the little boat slack-tow'd astern,
The hurrying tumbling waves, quick-broken crests, slapping,
The strata of color'd clouds, the long bar of maroon-tint away solitary by itself, the spread
                              of purity it lies motionless in,
The horizon's edge, the flying sea-crow, the fragrance of salt marsh and shore mud,
These became part of that child who went forth every day, and who now goes,
                              and will always go forth every day.

6

Robert Hayden
Aunt Jemima of the Ocean Waves

Hayden took to heart Auden's principle that a problem in poetry should be treated like a problem in algebra, being essentially a search for fresh ways of handling subject matter.
—Pontheolla T. Williams

About the Poet and the Poem

Robert Hayden (1913–80), whose original name was Asa Sheffey, was born in Detroit to parents who then abandoned him, leaving the child with neighbors who raised and renamed him. As a teenager, he was already committed to becoming a poet; and despite his poverty, he managed to attend college and become a professor. By the 1930s he was writing seriously, but he did not become well known until 1966, when *Selected Poems* was published.

According to anthologist Stuart Friebert, "Hayden's poems deal with many compelling historical struggles—the Baha'i faith, slavery, Malcolm X, Kennedy, and King—and . . . many readers will be attracted to the 'romantic realist' spirit that Hayden himself felt infused the poems. Ultimately, however, Hayden's stature and power as a poet flow mainly from his uncanny ways of telling stories, both real and imagined. . . . And how his characters talk!"[1]

Even though many of his poems have, in Friebert's words, a certain "rough-cut abandon," Hayden was a passionate researcher, artist, and craftsman. Poetry historian David Perkins notes, "All that learning, intelligence, taste, sensitivity, and care can do, Hayden accomplished. He rewrote constantly, and he handled several different forms and styles superlatively."[2]

"Aunt Jemima of the Ocean Waves" is an example of Hayden's tendency to rewrite published poems. The version reprinted here appeared in *Words in Mourning Time* (1970), but the book's acknowledgments explain that part 1 of the poem is a revision of a piece from a previously published collection.

Aunt Jemima of the Ocean Waves
Robert Hayden

I

Enacting someone's notion of themselves
(and me), The One And Only Aunt Jemima
and Kokimo The Dixie Dancing Fool
do a bally for the freak show.

I watch a moment, then move on,
pondering the logic that makes of them
(and me) confederates
of The Spider Girl, The Snake-skinned Man . . .

Poor devils have to live somehow.

I cross the boardwalk to the beach,
lie in the sand and gaze beyond
the clutter at the sea.

II

Trouble you for a light?
I turn as Aunt Jemima settles down
beside me, her blue-rinsed hair
without the red bandanna now.

I hold the lighter to her cigarette.
Much obliged. Unmindful (perhaps)
of my embarrassment, she looks
at me and smiles: You sure

do favor a friend I used to have.
Guess that's why I bothered you
for a light. So much like him that I—
She pauses, watching white horses rush

to the shore. Way them big old waves
come slamming whopping in,
sometimes it's like they mean to smash
this no-good world to hell.

Well, it could happen. A book I read—
Crossed that very ocean years ago.
London, Paris, Rome,
Constantinople too—I've seen them all.

Back when they billed me everywhere
as the Sepia High Stepper.
Crowned heads applauded me.
Years before your time. Years and years.

I wore me plenty diamonds then,
and counts or dukes or whatever they were
would fill my dressing room
with the costliest flowers. But of course

there was this one you resemble so.
Get me? The sweetest gentleman.
Dead before his time. Killed in the war
to save the world for another war.

High-stepping days for me
were over after that. Still I'm not one
to let grief idle me for long.
I went out with a mental act—

mind-reading—Mysteria From
The Mystic East—veils and beads
and telling suckers how to get
stolen rings and sweethearts back.

One night he was standing by my bed,
seen him plain as I see you,
and warned me without a single word:
Baby, quit playing with that spiritual stuff.

So here I am, so here I am,
fake mammy to God's mistakes.
And that's the beauty part,
I mean, ain't that the beauty part.

She laughs, but I do not, knowing what
her laughter shields. And mocks.
I light another cigarette for her.
She smokes, not saying any more.

Scream of children in the surf,
adagios of sun and flashing foam,
the sexual glitter, oppressive fun. . . .
An antique etching comes to mind:

"The Sable Venus" naked on
a baroque Cellini shell—voluptuous
imago floating in the wake
of slave-ships on fantastic seas.

Jemima sighs, Reckon I'd best
be getting back. I help her up.
Don't you take no wooden nickels, hear?
Tin dimes neither. So long, pal.

Who's the Most Important Character?

Today, most of us automatically equate narrative with prose: stories, novels, memoirs, plays, and biographies that depend on skillful narrative control. This is understandable because many successful poems ride on the strength of their word choice, imagery, or cadence rather than their superior character development or plot construction. Nonetheless, as a narrative form, poetry predates prose by thousands of years. Poetry and storytelling are synonymous in the works of Homer, Virgil, Dante, the *Beowulf* poet, Chaucer, and many, many others. Even by the nineteenth century, when the novel began to dominate European and American literature, narrative poets such as Coleridge, Tennyson, Longfellow, and Browning remained enormously popular with a reading public hungry for stories.

A few contemporary narrative poets, such as Anne Carson and Rick Mullin, carry on this ancient storytelling tradition. But more often poets seem to turn to anecdotes, or brief narrative vignettes, rather than long, complex, plot-driven tales. Character development—particularly the first-person *I* character—is the linchpin of many of these anecdotal poems, which, in the guise of memoir scraps, informal conversations, or journal entries, lure a reader's attention toward the *I*.

Sometimes everything in an anecdotal poem seems to circle that central focus. In "The Quest," for instance, Sharon Olds recounts the horror of briefly losing track of a child in the city. Yet even though the poem is filled with references to the daughter, the *I* character is its emotional core. The poem is constructed around how *I* feels, not how the daughter feels.

> This is my quest, to know where it is,
> the evil in the human heart. As I walk home I
> look in face after face for it, I
> see the dark beauty, the rage, the
> grown-up children of the city she walks as a
> child, a raw target.[3]

"The Quest" blurs the line between fiction and nonfiction. Is the *I* really Olds herself? Or has Olds invented an *I* who is disguised as herself? In "Self-Portrait as Van Gogh," Peter Cooley plays more explicitly with these questions of character identity:

> Before a mirror at midnight I compose myself,
> donning the gold straw hat I tilt at just his angle
> to assure the vision will stay caged.
> I squint, ruffle my beard, henna the tips.[4]

Cooley's poem serves as a good reminder: although poems have the unique ability to make us believe in them as truth, we should never assume that the *I* in a poem is anything other than the poet's invention. Even the intimate, eloquent, heartbreaking *I* in John Keats's "Bright Star" is a character framed within a work of art. He's not the poet but the poet's creation.

Thus, characters, like so many other elements of poetry, can seem solid and simple even as they lead a poet to explore strange territory and make unanticipated disclosures.

Like her relationships with real people, a poet's relationship with her characters can be confusing, resentful, admiring, even dangerous. Yet she is also their creator and manipulator and thus remains separate and, to a certain degree, ambivalent about their behaviors and motivations.

In an essay about Shakespeare, W. H. Auden wrote about this necessary detachment: "A dramatist's characters are, normally, men-of-action, but he himself is a maker, not a doer, concerned not with disclosing himself to others in the moment, but with making a work which, unlike himself, will endure, if possible forever. . . . What a man does is irrevocable for good or ill; what he makes, he can always modify or destroy."[5]

In other words, as my sons used to say with exasperation when they discovered that once again I'd borrowed bits and pieces from our shared lives to create characters and a situation, "Mom! You exaggerate everything!" For when she's creating characters, a poet ruthlessly borrows from all the material she has at hand: her own internal motivations, her family's actions, her neighbor's peccadilloes. Sometimes the characters that emerge closely resemble the borrowed material. Sometimes the borrowed material becomes imaginative fodder for an invented persona.

Yet in poetry, it's not the character per se who charms, amuses, or repels the reader. It's the way in which the poet uses words to construct that character. As D. H. Lawrence noted in "When I Read Shakespeare," without his "language so lovely," even Shakespeare's most famous creations would be intolerable company:

> And Hamlet, how boring, how boring to live with,
> so mean and self-conscious, blowing and snoring
> his wonderful speeches, full of other folk's whoring![6]

Robert Hayden's poem "Aunt Jemima of the Ocean Ways" illustrates a few of the paths a poet may follow when developing characters. Like many twentieth-century poems, this one is not a story in the way in which Henry Wadsworth Longfellow's "Paul Revere's Ride" and Virgil's *Aeneid* are stories. Rather, Hayden uses a single chance meeting as an opportunity to create characters with complex, ambiguous histories. I will discuss three of those characters here.

AUNT JEMIMA

In her poem "Against Cinderella," Julia Alvarez rails against the way in which certain characters, such as the fairy-tale heroine Cinderella, seem to force their readers into uneasy or even false positions: "Whoever made it up is pulling my foot / so it'll fit my shoe."[7] Simply by choosing the name "Aunt Jemima" for the title character of his poem, Robert Hayden pushes us into similar territory.

Best known to most of us as a brand of pancake syrup, the commercial character Aunt Jemima arrives in this poem already carrying a great deal of cultural baggage. We have visual images of her from advertising, and we probably have an acquaintance with the troubling mammy stereotypes associated with some of those images.

In his poem Hayden both thwarts and reinforces our preconceptions about Aunt Jemima. He does so, in part, by creating a character who has both visual solidity and a believable voice. We, like the *I* character, find ourselves drawn into her tales and her talk.

Hayden manipulates us into paying attention to what she has to say by building up a series of conversational mannerisms, such as "Trouble you for a light?" and "You sure do favor a friend of mine," that make her monologue believable, casual, and compelling.

Hayden also includes plenty of physical details, many of which manage to be simultaneously specific and ambiguous. For instance, although the character's "blue-rinsed hair / without the red bandanna now" seems to refer us back to the commercial stereotype, her references to diamonds, flowers, and an entourage of "counts or dukes or whatever they were" build a back story that doesn't automatically mesh with the blue rinse and the red bandanna. This disconnect pushes us to recognize that the character is a performer, a shape shifter, a woman "enacting someone's notion of themselves." She plays the part of Aunt Jemima, just as she once played the role of the "Sepia High Stepper" and "Mysteria From the Mystic East."

In "For Primo Levy," poet Robert Cording asks, "What word / does not perjure itself?"[8] This is a question for all writers to ponder, not least when we are working to invent a character. Talk may conceal as much as it reveals, and a poet must choose words that bear this double burden, as Jemima's conversation demonstrates:

> So here I am, so here I am,
> fake mammy to God's mistakes.
> And that's the beauty part,
> I mean, ain't that the beauty part.
>
> She laughs, but I do not, knowing what
> her laughter hides. And mocks.
> I light another cigarette for her.
> She smokes, not saying any more.

Throughout this carefully controlled exchange, Hayden never allows Jemima to overdramatize, making sure that she maintains her privacy even as she speaks candidly. Yet the shift in her style of vocal repetition—from "So here I am, so here I am" to "And that's the beauty part, / I mean, ain't that the beauty part"—suggests an unspoken inner turbulence, one that she takes for granted, as the missing question mark seems to indicate. The subsequent stanza reiterates more directly what her speech only hints at, but here it does so by way of her listener's thoughts and her own silent actions. Thus, in the space of two stanzas, Hayden deepens our understanding of Aunt Jemima's character by giving her a solid, recognizable voice; subtly sketching her inner feelings; allowing her listener to draw inferences about the relationship between what she says and does not say; and showing her in physical action. An enormous amount of information is compressed into eight brief lines.

THE I CHARACTER
Aunt Jemima is clearly the central character, but is she the most important? Like Nick Carraway in F. Scott Fitzgerald's *The Great Gatsby,* the *I* character in Hayden's poem not only narrates the encounter but also observes, reacts, synthesizes, and forms opinions. He is not equivalent to the *I* character of Sharon Olds's "The Quest": his own emotions are

not the whirlpool of the poem. But neither is he a cipher, as Hayden makes clear in part 1 of the poem:

> Enacting someone's notion of themselves
> (and me), The One And Only Aunt Jemima
> and Kokimo The Dixie Dancing Fool
> do a bally for the freak show.

> I watch a moment, then move on,
> pondering the logic that makes of them
> (and me) confederates
> of The Spider Girl, The Snake-skinned Man . . .

> Poor devils have to live somehow.

> I cross the boardwalk to the beach,
> lie in the sand and gaze beyond
> the clutter at the sea.

In this brief opening section, the *I* character does a great deal of legwork for the reader. Not only does he introduce us to Aunt Jemima, the ostensible focus of the poem, but he also introduces us to himself. This character seems be an idle, solitary man, with plenty of leisure to watch "a bally for the freak show," to "cross the boardwalk to the beach" and "lie in the sand." He also seems to be an educated person, and his word choice is notably different from Jemima's in part 2. Whereas she uses words and phrases such as "slamming whopping" and "Don't you take no wooden nickels, hear?," he talks of "enacting someone's notion" and "pondering the logic." Yet these two very different voices have something in common, something unexplained and avoided but encapsulated in that small, repeated, parenthetical phrase "(and me)." From the moment he sees her, we realize, the *I* character recognizes a kinship with Aunt Jemima.

In part 2, she returns the favor, starting up a conversation with him because "there was this one you resemble so. / Get me? The sweetest gentleman." By such references, Hayden pulls the *I* into a relationship not only with the woman beside him on the sand but also with her history. The *I* is not himself "the sweetest gentleman," but he now stands in for him, serving as a beacon from the past, a messenger from the dead, as well as a courteous listener in the present.

In her collection *This Caravaggio,* Annie Boutelle considers the way in which the artist must "flood light / down on discrete body parts" so that the viewer "must work to piece it / together." Poets, too, must create these patches of light within a poem so that their readers have an opportunity to connect "hand to owner, or foot to leg. When / they contribute, then they admire."[9] Manipulation of time is an important element in this task. When a poet figures out how to move seamlessly among various levels of past and present, she is better able to deepen our acquaintance with a character. At the same time she can more easily control our focus and keep the poem compact.

Robert Hayden uses Aunt Jemima's storytelling urge as a way to juggle present and past and to reveal information about his characters. For instance, in the following stanza, Jemima seems to be focusing on her own story, yet she also shares significant information about the listening *I* character:

> Back when they billed me everywhere
> as the Sepia High Stepper.
> Crowned heads applauded me.
> Years before your time. Years and years.

We now know what we didn't know earlier in the poem: that the listener is much younger than the speaker. As a result, her previous remark, "You sure do favor a friend I used to have," which we might once have mistaken for flirtation, assumes a luster of sorrow and regret.

The Ocean Waves

Aunt Jemima isn't the only title character in the poem: the ocean waves also get marquee billing. Hayden makes the ocean an integral element throughout, shifting its role fluidly from simple setting to active participant. In the opening section, for instance, the sea is barely present. We don't realize where the characters are located until the last stanza:

> I cross the boardwalk to the beach,
> lie in the sand and gaze beyond
> the clutter at the sea.

Only in the final word—that plain, unadorned "sea"—does Hayden shift our vision away from the humans and their "clutter." Yet the ocean still remains more setting than character: it doesn't do anything, to this point, besides exist.

In part 2, however, the ocean waves take on more potency. Jemima pauses in her talk, "watching white horses rush / to the shore." Then she says,

> Way them big old waves
> come slamming whopping in,
> sometimes it's like they mean to smash
> this no-good world to hell.

Questions begin to arise in my mind. Are the waves still just the setting? Or are they something more dynamic and individual? Are they interacting with the other characters, exerting emotional pressure? Are they actively revealing and concealing? Their role here is ambiguous, both suggested and suggestive.

Jemima continues to talk, using the waves as a brief conversational vehicle for crossing space and time, back to her old days in as a performer in Europe. But late in the poem, the ocean rears again:

> Scream of children in the surf,
> adagios of sun and flashing foam,

the sexual glitter, oppressive fun. . . .
An antique etching comes to mind:

"The Sable Venus" naked on
a baroque Cellini shell—voluptuous
imago floating in the wake
of slave-ships on fantastic seas.

At first it seems as if Hayden has returned to using the sea as a simple setting. But
then "an antique etching comes to mind." What is the sea's role in bringing forth this
"voluptuous imago"? Without the trio of ocean, Aunt Jemima, and *I,* the vision would not
exist. The boundary between setting and character has become confused, interchangeable.

I hope that you are beginning to see that literary tropes such as setting and character
are not mutually exclusive but flexible, interdependent poetic elements. In "Fabrications,"
Richard Wilbur writes:

Each day men frame and weave
In their own way whatever looms in sight,
Though they must see with human scale and bias,
And though there is much unseen.[10]

Experimenting with shifts of time and voice, of actor and stage is how Robert Hayden
has worked to manage "in [his] own way whatever looms in sight." And if you go back and
look at poems we've already studied—say, Amy Lowell's "Thompson's Lunch Room" or
even Percy Shelley's "To a Skylark"—you may begin to suspect that many poets press their
settings to cross the line into becoming volatile elements of the situation.

Ideas for Writing
Charles Webb's "The Death of Santa Claus" opens with this stanza:

He's had the chest pains for weeks,
but doctors don't make house
calls to the North Pole.[11]

And this is the opening of Tim Seibles's "What Bugs Bunny Said to Red Riding Hood":

Say, good lookin, what brings you out thisaway
amongst the fanged and the fluffy?
Grandma, huh?
Some ol bag too lazy to pick up a pot, too feeble
to flip a flapjack—
and you all dolled up like a fire engine
to cruise these woods?[12]

Like Robert Hayden's "Aunt Jemima of the Ocean Waves," these two poems borrow preexisting characters and put them into new situations. This is a useful and interesting exercise for anyone who is learning how to manage characters in their poetry, and I've used it often in sessions with young writers, most of whom love inventing crazy connections between vastly different historical and cultural figures.

I've read student poems about Christopher Columbus and a Barbie doll struggling through cocktail-party small talk, about best friends Bambi the fawn and singer Justin Timberlake wandering the Hollywood streets at midnight. But as Hayden's poem makes clear, the exercise may lead to more than clever dialogue and comic scenarios. I suspect that when Hayden chose Aunt Jemima as a character, he was not entirely prepared for where she would lead him.

There are numbers of ways to begin a character-in-poetry exercise. For instance, you might choose two preexisting characters from different sorts of stories, as Seibles did when he matched up Bugs Bunny and Red Riding Hood. Invent a framing situation—an emergency room, a drivers' ed classroom, a wedding reception—and then force the characters to talk to one another in that context.

Another possibility is to concentrate on a single preexisting character, as Joe-Anne McLaughlin does in "Abishag's Brag." Abishag is a character with a double pedigree: she was an Old Testament beauty who reappears as an elderly woman in Robert Frost's poem "Provide, Provide." McLaughlin's poetic brag toys with both of those histories:

> Girl in my foxtails
> and fishnets, I was all
> city. Exotic as a Vatican
> bagel, accessible
> as Port Authority.[13]

McLaughlin chose to write a brag, but you could write a rant, a speech, an apology, or any other kind of monologue. As Hayden did in "Aunt Jemima of the Ocean Waves," push yourself to imagine the character's word choice and speech patterns. Include descriptive details. Think about the character's past, present, and future, and consider how you might introduce varying levels of time into the piece. Above all, find ways to *care* about the character. I don't mean that you have to love your creation . . . or even like her. But you must be willing to linger over her, to watch her and muse about her doings, to listen to what she presses you to say. "Accept this tribute from me, who was so different," wrote Czesław Miłosz in his poem "Allen Ginsberg."[14] Your characters, too, whether they are historical figures or complete inventions, are worth your scrutiny and your respect.

Thinking about Characters: An Anthology

Milly Jourdain: Watching the Meet
William Butler Yeats: Easter 1916
Gary Snyder: Why Log Truck Drivers Rise Earlier Than Students of Zen
Robert Browning: My Last Duchess
Ruth L. Schwartz: Highway Five Love Poem

I will frame you like this forever before and after
I abandon you
                              —Ruth L. Schwartz

Watching the Meet
Milly Jourdain

The air is still so new and fresh and cold,
It makes a warm excitement in our hearts
To drive beside the sad and lonely fields.
And now we see a wider space of road
Where groups of horsemen moving restlessly
Are waiting for the quiet-footed hounds.
The hounds come swiftly, covering the way
Like foaming water surging round our feet.
And then with cries and sound of cracking whips
All, all are gone: the distant beat of hoofs
Like trailing smoke of dreams, comes fitfully
To tell how near they were a moment past.
But we see only winter trees again,
And turning homewards meet a drifting rain.

Easter 1916
William Butler Yeats

I have met them at close of day
Coming with vivid faces
From counter or desk among grey
Eighteenth-century houses.
I have passed with a nod of the head
Or polite meaningless words,
Or have lingered awhile and said
Polite meaningless words,
And thought before I had done
Of a mocking tale of a gibe
To please a companion
Around the fire at the club,
Being certain that they and I
But lived where motley is worn:
All changed, changed utterly:
A terrible beauty is born.

The woman's days were spent
In ignorant good-will,
Her nights in argument
Until her voice grew shrill.
What voice more sweet than hers
When, young and beautiful,
She rode to harriers?
The man had kept a school
And rode our winged horse;
This other his helper and friend
Was coming into his force;
He might have won fame in the end,
So sensitive his nature seemed,
So daring and sweet his thought.
This other man I had dreamed
A drunken, vainglorious lout.
He had done most bitter wrong
To some who are near my heart,
Yet I number him in the song:
He, too, has resigned his part
In the casual comedy;
He, too, has been changed in his turn,
Transformed utterly:
A terrible beauty is born.

Hearts with one purpose alone
Through summer and winter seem
Enchanted to a stone
To trouble the living stream.
The horse that comes from the road,
The rider, the birds that range
From cloud to tumbling cloud,
Minute by minute they change;
A shadow of cloud on the stream
Changes minute by minute;
A horse-hoof slides on the brim,
And a horse plashes within it;
The long-legged moor-cocks call;
Minute by minute they live:
The stone's in the midst of all.

Too long a sacrifice
Can make a stone of the heart.
O when may it suffice?
That is Heaven's part, our part
To murmur name upon name,
As a mother names her child
When sleep has at last come
On limbs that had run wild.
What is it but nightfall?
No, no, not night but death;
Was it needless death after all?
For England may keep faith
For all that is done and said.
We know their dream; enough
To know they dreamed and are dead;
And what if excess of love
Bewildered them till they died?
I write it out in a verse—
MacDonagh and MacBride
And Connolly and Pearse
Now and in time to be,
Wherever green is worn,
Are changed, changed utterly:
A terrible beauty is born.

Why Log Truck Drivers Rise Earlier Than Students of Zen
Gary Snyder

In the high seat, before-dawn dark,
Polished hubs gleam
And the shiny diesel stack
Warms and flutters
Up the Tyler Road grade
To the logging on Poorman creek.
Thirty miles of dust.

There is no other life.

My Last Duchess
Robert Browning

Ferrara

That's my last Duchess painted on the wall,
Looking as if she were alive. I call
That piece a wonder, now: Frà Pandolf's hands
Worked busily a day, and there she stands.
Will't please you sit and look at her? I said
"Frà Pandolf" by design, for never read
Strangers like you that pictured countenance,
The depth and passion of its earnest glance,
But to myself they turned (since none puts by
The curtain I have drawn for you, but I)
And seemed as they would ask me, if they durst,
How such a glance came there; so, not the first
Are you to turn and ask thus. Sir, 't was not
Her husband's presence only, called that spot
Of joy into the Duchess' cheek: perhaps
Frà Pandolf chanced to say "Her mantle laps
Over my lady's wrist too much," or "Paint
Must never hope to reproduce the faint
Half-flush that dies along her throat:" such stuff
Was courtesy, she thought, and cause enough
For calling up that spot of joy. She had
A heart—how shall I say?—too soon made glad,
Too easily impressed; she liked whate'r
She looked on, and her looks went everywhere.
Sir, 't was all one! My favour at her breast,
The dropping of the daylight in the West,
The bough of cherries some officious fool
Broke in the orchard for her, the white mule
She rode with round the terrace—all and each
Would draw from her alike the approving speech,
Or blush, at least. She thanked men,—good! but thanked
Somehow—I know not how—as if she ranked
My gift of a nine-hundred-years-old name
With anybody's gift. Who'd stoop to blame
This sort of trifling? Even had you skill
In speech—(which I have not)—to make your will
Quite clear to such a one, and say, "Just this
Or that in you disgusts me; here you miss,
Or there exceed the mark"—and if she let
Herself be lessoned so, nor plainly set

Her wits to yours, forsooth, and made excuse,
—E'en then would be some stooping; and I choose
Never to stoop. Oh sir, she smiled, no doubt,
Whene'er I passed her; but who passed without
Much the same smile? This grew; I gave commands;
Then all smiles stopped together. There she stands
As if alive. Will 't please you rise? We'll meet
The company below, then. I repeat,
The Count your master's known munificence
Is ample warrant that no just pretence
Of mine for dowry will be disallowed;
Though his fair daughter's self, as I avowed
At starting, is my object. Nay, we'll go
Together down, sir. Notice Neptune, though,
Taming a sea-horse, thought a rarity,
Which Claus of Innsbruck cast in bronze for me!

Highway Five Love Poem
Ruth L. Schwartz

FOR ANNA

This is a love poem for all the tomatoes
spread out in the fields along Highway Five,
their gleaming green and ruddy faces like a thousand
moons prostrate in praise of sun.
And for every curd of cloud,
clotted cream of cloud spooned briskly
by an unseen hand into the great blue bowl,
then out again, into a greedy mouth.
Cotton baled up beside the road,
altars to the patron saint of dryer lint.
Moist fudge of freshly-planted dirt.
Shaggy neglected savage grasses
bent into the wind's designs.
Sheep scattered over the landscape like fuzzy confetti,
or herded into stubbled funnels, moving like rough water
toward its secret source.
Egrets praying in the fields like
white-cloaked priests.
A dozen wise and ponderous cows
suddenly spurred to run, to gallop, even,
down a flank of hill.
Horses for sale, goats for sale, nopales for sale, orange groves for sale,
topless trailers carrying horses,
manes as loose and lovely as tomorrow in our mouths,
and now a giant pig, jostling majestic in the open
bed of a red pickup.

7

Joe Bolton
In Memory of the Boys of Dexter, Kentucky

To say that Bolton is an American Keats is to overstate the case but it is to make the reader aware of the very rare value of Bolton's poetry—something remarkable occurred, something that will never be duplicated and something that can put the reader under a spell.
—Baron Wormser

About the Poet and the Poem

Joe Bolton (1961–90) grew up in western Kentucky and studied poetry in creative writing programs in Texas, Florida, and Arizona. These regional attachments, simultaneously transient and penetrating, became central themes of his poetry, as his teacher Donald Justice noted:

> A number of his poems deal with that side of the South which a generation of Southern storytellers has virtually made iconographic—the lower-middle-class life of rental apartments and loud neighbors, of motel rooms, of bars and highways, small towns and rundown urban neighborhoods. But Bolton's style of looking and noticing is not the same as that of the storytellers. He had a kind of helpless love for the subjects of his poems; and that, I think, cannot fairly be said of the writers whose fiction shares the locales of these poems.

Bolton committed suicide at the age of twenty-nine, and in many ways the poems in his posthumous collection are an elegy to the pervasive melancholia that eventually drove him to take his life. Yet as Justice said, "confession just does not seem the point of these poems. Effortlessly they transcend the merely anecdotal; they are always edging toward something emblematic. And they can be immensely moving in their modesty."[1]

The day before he killed himself, Bolton submitted a collection of his poems to his degree committee at the University of Arizona. That thesis manuscript included the poem in this chapter, "In Memory of the Boys of Dexter, Kentucky," which appeared among a group of poems labeled "The New Cities of the Tropics." Donald Justice edited the manuscript, which retained Bolton's own preferred title, *The Last Nostalgia.*

In Memory of the Boys of Dexter, Kentucky
Joe Bolton

West of Murray, just off 641,
It is forever summer in my mind.
I see land darken under a red sun
And hear lost music drift back on the wind.
Blind fingers read the initials *D.P.*
Carved in the oak from which he was found hung;
In the creek, *J.* holds his breath endlessly.
Did they think they were late, leaving so young?—
Chain-smoking only to bypass cancer,
Washing down pills with whiskey, wrapping cars
Round poles like a girl's love-ring. . . . In answer,
The sky fades like a chord behind first stars.
Their dying, it seems now, started at birth—
Dying to find out what their lives were worth.

What's the Most Important Sound?

Sound may be our deepest and most instinctive connection to poetry, for we respond to sound as not only individuals but also members of the human community and inheritors of its ancient traditions. "The hearing knowledge we bring to a line of poetry," writes Robert Pinsky, "is a knowledge of patterns of speech we have known to hear since we were infants."[2] That childhood comfort stretches beyond the confines of our private selves, back through the history of language and our species.

In "The Hymn to Earth," a Greek poem dating from about 650 B.C., the speaker reaches out to his listeners, coaxing them to recognize their agency in his creations:

> farewell:
> but if you liked what I sang here
> give me this life too
> 　　　then,
> 　　　in my other poems
> 　　　　　I will remember you[3]

No page lay between this poet and his first listeners. Sound was the primary element of communication, and poet and listeners shared a direct physical experience.

Today poetry has become as much a visual as a sonic art. Yet the sound of a poem still transmits an intensely emotional message, even in those moments before a reader begins to engage with the poem's narrative or thematic threads.

Take the opening couplet of Donald Justice's "Psalm and Lament":

> The clocks are sorry, the clocks are very sad.
> One stops, one goes on striking the wrong hours.[4]

The poem doesn't rhyme, nor does it scan as blank verse. Except for its couplet format, it looks rather like a version of spoken English. Yet if you study these two modest lines, you will see that Justice makes extravagant use of sound: he repeats individual *k* and *s* sounds; he repeats entire words and phrases; he uses commas as silent beats within the cadence. Try reading the couplet aloud, and you will feel, too, how his syntax and word choice force you to modify your pacing. It would be almost impossible to read this couplet quickly.

For contrast, look at the opening of Edna St. Vincent Millay's famous "Recuerdo."

> We were very tired, we were very merry—
> We had gone back and forth all night on the ferry.[5]

In certain ways the lines look very similar to Justice's. The two poems share a simple subject/predicate nominative construction: "The clocks are very sad." "We were very tired." Both use comma splices as musical devices. But while Justice's poem moves slowly and heavily, almost to the point of exhaustion, Millay's speeds across the page. Her rhymes sparkle; her commas denote breathlessness rather than weighty moments of silence. Like the ferry, her lines go "back and forth," hustling between the rhymes, riding the alliterative vowels: short *e*'s, long *i*'s, the repetition of *We*.

In other words, a poet's sound devices are intimate elements of a poem's essential being. From the very first moments of creation, a poet begins to hear her poem take shape. In my own case, I usually feel the pressure of a metrical stress or a letter sound before I begin to consider what words I might try out next in a line. This is true whether I am writing formal or free verse. The sounds in my ear lead me to pursue the sense of what I am trying to articulate.

I chose to feature Joe Bolton in this chapter on sound because, to me, he exemplifies a poet who uses sound as a vehicle to discovery. His well-tuned ear drives the sinuous arc of his poems, yet his narrative is never obscure, and his rhythms and rhymes rarely command my instant attention. As a way to gather the myriad subtle ways in which Bolton uses sound, I grouped my thoughts about his poem into three umbrella categories: rhyme, repetition, and cadence.

RHYME

"In Memory of the Boys of Dexter, Kentucky" is a sonnet; and as I mentioned in an earlier chapter, sonnets are a notoriously difficult and deceptive form to write. Much of that difficulty lies in the allure of the rhyme scheme. The task can seem so simple: just find a few rhyming words and then fill in the rest of the poem around them. But rhyme is both powerful and manipulative, and it may destroy a poem as often as it strengthens it. A controlling rhyme scheme can make the rest of the poem seem frail and unimportant, and this is fatal in an art that depends on the precision of every single word.

So, for a sonnet writer, the rhyme scheme must be a means to several ends. First, the rhymes must be integral to the progression of the poem—moving the poet through the end of each line, through the end of each quatrain and couplet, and into the end of the poem. In other words, the rhymes are essential elements of the movement of the poem, just as the sound of a crashing wave is woven into a perception of the physical movement of the water.

Second, the rhymes must work simultaneously in the realms of sound and sense. This is another way of saying that they must feel *inevitable*—as if no other word could replace them in this context. Sometimes this inevitability means that the end rhyme is modest, almost invisible, among the other words of the poem. Sometimes it means that the end rhyme vibrates with sonic, emotional, or connotative intensity. Learning to hover between these extremes is a complicated and necessary task.

In terms of its basic rhyme structure, "In Memory of the Boys of Dexter, Kentucky" is a predictable example of the sonnet form. Bolton has chosen to follow a Shakespearean, or English, pattern composed of three quatrains and a final couplet. The rhyme scheme can be notated as *a b a b, c d c d, e f e f, g g,* and here are the poet's word choices:

641

mind

a red sun

wind

D.P.
hung
endlessly
young

cancer
cars
answer
stars

birth
worth

Yet now that I've transcribed Bolton's rhyming words, I begin to notice that he's made a number of subtle decisions. He starts off with an unusual combination, rhyming the numeral "641" with the phrase "a red sun." While the sound of the rhyme is reasonably smooth, the numeral itself is a visual oddity. Then, in the second rhyme of the quatrain, he completely inverts his approach: he chooses two words, "mind" and "wind," that are visually soothing but sonically grating. In other words, Bolton immediately tinkers with my expectations of rhyme, and this puts me on my guard. What strange choice will come next?

His second quatrain continues to push at my expectations. The opening rhyme, "D.P." and "endlessly," makes me feel both visually and sonically uneasy. The sound is crooked (two syllables versus three syllables), and it doesn't help that the initials are my own. I mention this point because I think these sorts of personal identifications may be just as important to a reader as more general links are. A reader meets a poem as an individual— as a person with particular experiences, particular hauntings. When "blind fingers read the initials *D.P.*," I shiver. Now I know the poet is talking to *me*.

Yet the closing rhyme of the second quatrain is more restrained, a pattern that Bolton continues into the third quatrain and the couplet. Now he doesn't need to depend on visual or sonic surprise because he has taken his rhymes to a different place. The word sounds themselves are steady and staid: "hung" and "young," "cancer" and "answer," "cars" and "stars." But the connotations are cosmic.

As I glance back into the lines and re-immerse myself in the tale they tell, I have the strong sense that the rhymes were an essential outburst of both the narrative arc and Bolton's emotional state. In the first two quatrains, he concentrates on the specificity of the details—"West of Murray," "*J.* holds his breath"—but by the second half of the sonnet he has broadened into similes: "like a girl's love ring," "like a chord behind first stars." When this metaphorical language takes hold of the poem, the rhymes become more stately and their emotional import becomes more universal.

REPETITION

Repetition—of individual letter sounds, syllables, words, phrases, sentences, and even stanzas—is a powerful tool for both musicians and poets. In many ways, music has the advantage here because each repeated sound in a song can carry vastly different

WATCHING A POET MAKE A POEM

dynamic and emotional weight. Written English can't convey the subtleties of musical performance—which is to say, "Baby, *baby, BABY!*" may be a convincing song chorus but it's an awkward line of poetry.

Because poetry on the page can't depend on interpretive performance in the air, poets tend to use repetition in ways that link sound, sight, and sense. This not only draws the reader into a finished poem but also pulls the poet further into a poem under construction. For instance, in line 2 of his sonnet, Bolton writes, "It is forever summer in my mind." Although the opening *it is* may seem like a throwaway phrase, the short *i* sounds both look and sound like quick skips. Moreover, they push poet and reader to fill in the blank. "*It is* what?" we wonder. Bolton chooses *forever summer* to fill in the blank. And how does he continue to press himself into the poem? He chooses another quick-skipping short-*i* word: *in*. Like all prepositions, *in* demands details and Bolton fills them in with *my mind*, a pronoun-noun phrase that suddenly launches us into the sound world of long *i*. Thus, sound, sight, and sense forge connections and break down barriers as the poet imagines himself into the budding world of a poem.

Bolton's internal repetitions also work in harness with his end rhymes. As I mentioned in the previous section, the rhyme scheme of "In Memory of the Boys of Dexter, Kentucky" becomes more stable as the poem becomes more metaphoric. At the same time the poet begins to heighten the musicality within the lines. Now, instead of depending on *it is* and *in* to drive himself into the sonnet, he sweeps into watery, rushing *w* sounds ("Washing down pills with whiskey, wrapping cars"), the curl of *l* and the breath of *r* ("Round poles like a girl's love ring"), the hiss of *s* and the thud of *d* ("The sky fades like a chord behind first stars"). The consonants are dramatic, weighty, insistent; they enforce my engagement with both the situation and the language. At the same time, unnervingly, they beautify an ugly incident. In other words, Bolton uses them as a tool of emotional manipulation . . . certainly for me, possibly for himself.

CADENCE

Cadence is a musical term, which the Imagist movement borrowed in the early years of the twentieth century as way to describe the rhythmic movement of free verse. In the March 1913 issue of *Poetry*, Ezra Pound announced the Imagist goal "as regarding rhythm: to compose in sequence of the musical phrase, not in sequence of the metronome." In his preface to the 1915 Imagist anthology, Richard Aldington expanded upon Pound's pronouncement:

> To create new rhythms—as the expression of new moods—and not to copy old rhythms, which merely echo old moods. We do not insist upon "free-verse" as the only method of writing poetry. We fight for it as a principle of liberty. We believe that the individuality of a poet may often be better expressed in free-verse than in conventional forms. In poetry, a new cadence means a new idea.[6]

There's a certain contemptuous inaccuracy to these Imagist manifestos. Of course Shakespeare, Milton, Barrett Browning, and Millay never wrote their sonnets to "the sequence of the metronome." Meter, like rhyme, is a framework that poets have always polished and bent. Nonetheless, the Imagist declarations did give many young poets the courage to begin using their own everyday rhythms as creative sources—and for poets such as Plath, Carruth, Rich, and many others who continued to respect, emulate, and argue with the great formalists, this new freedom was tonic. Poets found themselves experimenting with meter and rhythm as a composer or an improviser might experiment with time signature. "A new cadence means a new idea."

By the 1980s, when Joe Bolton was writing his sonnets, the Imagist prescriptions were old hat. Most young poets were writing in free verse, and Bolton's attachment to the sonnet form (he wrote many of them) may have seemed old-fashioned. Yet when I look at his lines, I see that he is not writing in iambic pentameter. Instead, he shifts his stress and syllable patterns, varying the rhythm of each line while working to keep his rhyme scheme intact.

Did Bolton choose rhythmic variety because writing in iambic pentameter was too difficult? Given his subtle control of rhyme and repetition, I find that assumption hard to believe. So let's consider Aldington's statement: "a new cadence means a new idea." If I think of cadence as the language analogue of what composers define as "a progression of two or more chords . . . used to convey a feeling of permanent or temporary repose," can I track the way in which Bolton has grouped the cadences within his lines to lead his reader and himself into new discoveries?[7]

For the sake of space, I'll limit myself here to studying a single pair of lines chosen at random from the poem. In my transcription, I've italicized and boldfaced the heavy stresses, italicized the lighter stresses, and left the unstressed syllables in roman type.

> *I see land dar-*ken *un-*der a *red sun*
> And *hear lost mu-*sic *drift back* on the *wind.*

As you can see and hear, Bolton begins line 1 with the lightly stressed "I" and then moves into three weighty stressed syllables. To my ear the cadence ends with the falling second syllable of "darken." He starts again with a new group of sounds: the lightly stressed-unstressed-unstressed "under a" and then two more weighty stressed syllables. Although I've now reached the end of the line, I don't feel as if this rhythmic phrase has finished. It seems to push into line 2, through the unstressed "and," the heavily stressed "hear lost mu," until ending on the unstressed syllable "sic." The third cadence begins with two strongly stressed syllables, flows through the unstressed "on the," and ends with a stressed "wind."

Like those of any interpreter, my reactions are subjective. You might hear the cadences differently. Yet I think both of us are likely to notice Bolton's predilection for sets of stressed one-syllable words: "see land," "red sun," "hear lost," "drift back." I find it interesting that even though these pairings cross grammatical boundaries (verb-noun, adjective-noun, verb-adjective, verb-adverb), the cadences themselves tend to stay within their grammatical clusters. That is, they end after subjects, before prepositional phrases, and at points of punctuation; they incorporate modifiers and compound predicates. In other words, I can easily work out a grammatical reasoning behind the movement of the cadence.

For instance, you might argue that "drift back" and "on the wind" are two separate cadences. After all, I've already heard a cadence break before the prepositional phrase in line 1, between "I see land darken" and "under a red sun." But in line 2, the words in "drift back on the wind" feel sonically interdependent, partly, I think, because the short *a* sound in "back" pushes me to linger on that word rather than pause and collect myself before moving into the prepositional phrase. Moreover, the adverb "back" functions grammatically as a connector, linking the verb "drift" and to the prepositional phrase "on the wind." No such connector exists in line 1.

So let's return to Aldington's statement: "a new cadence means a new idea." If a new grammatical move means a new idea, then, yes, Bolton's poem is built on such sounds. This may seem like a boring discovery; but if I also consider that language is constantly shifting and evolving, then I begin to recognize that sentence structure is itself a means of arranging sound. Recall Frost's statement: "Poets have lamented the lack in poetry of any such notation as music has for suggesting sound. But it is there and has always been there. The sentence is the notation. The sentence is before all else just that: a notation for suggesting significant tones of voice."[8] Once again, the intersections of sound and sense lead poet and reader into mysterious territory.

Ideas for Writing

Vowel sounds have remarkable power. In *Western Wind,* John Frederick Nims discusses how "the upness and downness of vowel sounds affect us physically in different ways." For instance, comparing *ee* to *oo,* he explains that "the high-frequency *ee* is busier, gives the ear more to process. Its greater [wave] activity suggests greater vitality, speed, excitement than the slower moving, more sluggish waves of the *oo.*"[9]

Try reading the following poem aloud, listening for Emily Pauline Johnson's shifts among up and down vowel sounds and noting how her choices influence the upness or downness of both your physical manner of reading aloud and your emotional reaction to the words you read.

Marshlands
Emily Pauline Johnson

A thin wet sky, that yellows at the rim,
And meets with sun-lost lip the marsh's brim.

The pools low lying, dank with moss and mould,
Glint through their mildews like large cups of gold.

Among the wild rice in the still lagoon,
In monotone the lizard shrills his tune.

The wild goose, homing, seeks a sheltering,
Where rushes grow, and oozing lichens cling.

Late cranes with heavy wing, and lazy flight,
Sail up the silence with the nearing night.

And like a spirit, swathed in some soft veil,
Steals twilight and its shadows o'er the swale.

Hushed lie the sedges, and the vapours creep,
Thick, grey and humid, while the marshes sleep.

Now choose one of the writing exercises you did in a previous chapter and revise it, keeping your main focus on your vowel sounds.

1. In your first revision, add more long-*i* sounds.
2. In your second revision, add more short-*a* sounds.
3. In your third revision, add more short-*i* sounds.
4. In your fourth revision, add more long-*a* sounds.

You can choose to keep elements of each revision intact in the subsequent draft, or you can replace one entire group of revision words with another. The results will be quite different, but in both cases you should begin to hear how powerful sound repetitions can be in setting tone and pacing, highlighting themes, and adjusting your preconceptions about the poem you thought you might be writing.

Thinking about Sounds: An Anthology

Christopher Marlowe: The Passionate Shepherd to His Love
A. E. Stallings: An Ancient Dog Grave, Unearthed During Construction
    of the Athens Metro
Alfred Tennyson: The Charge of the Light Brigade
William Carlos Williams: Paterson: The Falls
Anonymous: The Demon Lover

Lyrics are arias.

                    —*A. E. Stallings*

The Passionate Shepherd to His Love
Christopher Marlowe

Come live with me, and be my love,
And we will all the pleasures prove
That hills and valleys, dales and fields,
And all the craggy mountains yields.

And we will sit upon the rocks,
Seeing the shepherds feed their flocks
By shallow rivers, to whose falls
Melodious birds sing madrigals.

And I will make thee beds of roses,
And a thousand fragrant posies,
A cap of flowers and a kirtle
Embroider'd all with leaves of myrtle.

A gown made of the finest wool
Which from our pretty lambs we pull,
Fair linèd slippers for the cold,
With buckles of the purest gold;

A belt of straw and ivy-buds,
With coral clasps and amber studs,
And if these pleasures may thee move,
Come live with me, and be my love.

Thy silver dishes for thy meat,
As precious as the gods do eat,
Shall on an ivory table be
Prepar'd each day for thee and me.

The shepherd swains shall dance and sing
For thy delight each May-morning;
If these delights thy mind may move,
Then live with me, and be my love.

An Ancient Dog Grave, Unearthed During Construction of the Athens Metro
A. E. Stallings

It is not the curled up bones, nor even the grave
That stops me, but the blue beads on the collar
(Whose leather has long gone the way of hides)—
The ones to ward off evil. A careful master
Even now protects a favorite, just so.
But what evil could she suffer after death?
I picture the loyal companion, bereaved of her master,
Trotting the long, dark way that slopes to the river,
Nearly trampled by all the nations marching down,
One war after another, flood or famine,
Her paws sucked by the thick, caliginous mud,
Deep as her dewclaws, near the riverbank.
In the press for the ferry, who will lift her into the boat?
Will she cower under the pier and be forgotten,
Forever howling and whimpering, tail tucked under?
What stranger pays her passage? Perhaps she swims,
Dog-paddling the current of oblivion.
A shake as she scrambles ashore sets the beads jingling.
And then, that last, tense moment—touching noses
Once, twice, three times, with unleashed Cerberus.

The Charge of the Light Brigade

Alfred Tennyson

I

Half a league, half a league,
Half a league onward,
All in the valley of Death
   Rode the six hundred.
"Forward the Light Brigade!
Charge for the guns!" he said.
Into the valley of Death
   Rode the six hundred.

II

"Forward the Light Brigade!"
Was there a man dismay'd?
Not tho' the soldier knew
   Some one had blunder'd.
Theirs not to make reply,
Theirs not to reason why,
Theirs but to do and die.
Into the valley of Death
   Rode the six hundred.

III

Cannon to right of them,
Cannon to left of them,
Cannon in front of them
   Volley'd and thunder'd:
Storm'd at with shot and shell,
Boldly they rode and well,
Into the jaws of Death,
Into the mouth of hell
   Rode the six hundred.

IV

Flash'd all their sabres bare,
Flash'd as they turn'd in air
Sabring the gunners there,
Charging an army, while
   All the world wonder'd.
Plung'd in the battery-smoke
Right thro' the line they broke;
Cossack and Russian

Reel'd from the sabre-stroke
   Shatter'd and sunder'd.
Then they rode back, but not,
   Not the six hundred.

      V
Cannon to right of them,
Cannon to left of them,
Cannon behind them
   Volley'd and thunder'd;
Storm'd at with shot and shell,
While horse and hero fell,
They that had fought so well,
Came thro' the jaws of Death,
Back from the mouth of hell,
All that was left of them,
   Left of six hundred.

      VI
When can their glory fade?
O the wild charge they made!
   All the world wonder'd.
Honor the charge they made!
Honor the Light Brigade,
   Noble six hundred.

Paterson: The Falls
William Carlos Williams

What common language to unravel?
The Falls, combed into straight lines
from that rafter of a rock's
lip. Strike in! the middle of

some trenchant phrase, some
well packed clause. Then . . .
This is my plan. 4 sections. First,
the archaic persons of the drama.

An eternity of bird and bush,
resolved. An unraveling:
the confused streams aligned, side
by side, speaking! Sound

married to strength, a strength
of falling—from a height! The wild
voice of the shirt-sleeved
Evangelist rivaling, Hear

me! I am the Resurrection
and the Life! echoing
among the bass and pickerel, slim
eels from Barbados, Sargasso

Sea, working up the coast to that
bounty, ponds and wild streams—
Third, the old town: Alexander Hamilton
working up from St. Croix,

from that sea! and a deeper, whence
he came! stopped cold
by that unmoving roar, fastened
there: the rocks silent

but the water, married to the stone,
voluble, though frozen; the water
even when and though frozen
still whispers and moans—

And in the brittle air
a factory bell clangs, at dawn, and
snow whines under their feet. Fourth,
the modern town, a

disembodied roar! the cataract and
its clamor broken apart—and from
all learning, the empty
ear struck from within, roaring . . .

The Demon Lover

Anonymous

"O where have you been, my long, long love,
    This long seven years and more?"
"O I'm come to seek my former vows
    Ye granted me before."

"O hold your tongue of your former vows,
    For they will breed sad strife;
O hold your tongue of your former vows
    For I am become a wife."

He turn'd him right and round about,
    And the tear blinded his ee;
"I wad never hae trodden on Irish ground,
    If it had not been for thee.

"I might have had a king's daughter,
    Far, far beyond the sea;
I might have had a king's daughter,
    Had it not been for love o' thee."

"If ye might have had a king's daughter,
    Yersell ye had to blame;
Ye might have taken the king's daughter,
    For ye kend that I was nane.

"If I was to leave my husband dear,
    And my two babes also,
O what have you to take me to,
    If with you I should go?"

"I hae seven ships upon the sea,
    The eighth brought me to land;
With four-and-twenty bold mariners,
    And music on every hand."

She has taken up her two little babes,
    Kiss'd them baith cheek and chin;
"O fair ye weel, my ain two babes,
    For I'll never see you again."

She set her foot upon the ship,
   No mariners could she behold;
But the sails were o' the taffetie,
   And the masts o' the beaten gold.

She had not sail'd a league, a league,
   A league but barely three,
When dismal grew his countenance,
   And drumlie grew his ee.

They had not sail'd a league, a league,
   A league but barely three,
Until she espied his cloven foot,
   And she wept right bitterlie.

"O hold your tongue of your weeping," says he,
   "Of your weeping now let me be;
I will show you how the lilies grow
   On the banks of Italy."

"O what hills are yon, yon pleasant hills,
   That the sun shines sweetly on?"
"O yon are the hills of heaven," he said,
   "Where you will never win."

"O whaten a mountain is yon," she said,
   "All so dreary with frost and snow?"
"O yon is the mountain of hell," he cried,
   "Where you and I will go."

He struck the tapmast wi' his hand,
   The foremast wi' his knee;
And he brak that gallant ship in twain,
   And sank her in the sea.

8

John Donne
The Triple Foole

Donne felt his thought as immediately as the odour of a rose.
—A. S. Byatt

About the Poet and the Poem

Over the course of his life John Donne (1572–1631) was a Catholic, a Protestant, a soldier, a member of Parliament, an eloping lover, a jailbird, a royal chaplain, and the dean of Saint Paul's Cathedral, but today he is most often remembered as one of the greatest poets in the English language. His fame has been variable, however. During Donne's lifetime a set of staunch admirers circulated his manuscripts among themselves. Yet later generations disliked his metaphysical style (a loose term that might be roughly defined as "thought-based"), preferring instead the musical metrics and more idealized visions of love that became fashionable during the latter half of the seventeenth century. Although poets such as Coleridge and Browning continued to champion Donne, his work did not become popular until after World War I, when scholar H.J.C. Grierson published the first large critical edition of his poetry. With this new source available, writers began discovering Donne's work, and the excitement of readers such as T. S. Eliot and Virginia Woolf helped revive the poet's reputation.

According to M. H. Abrams, "Donne wrote in a diction and meter modeled on the rough give-and-take of actual speech, and usually organized his poems in the dramatic and rhetorical form of an urgent or heated argument. . . . He employed a subtle and often deliberately outrageous logic."[1] He was a committed poet and consciously wrote for a readership. But as was usual in his day, he was not interested in publishing his poems, and "The Triple Foole" did not appear in print until after his death. Charles M. Coffin explains the editorial complications: "The establishment of a good text . . . has been difficult, not only because Donne is not an easy poet, but because of the considerable variation among the numerous manuscript copies and among the early printed editions."[2] In other words, the details of language we see on the page may or may not have been the details that Donne actually meant his readers to see.

The Triple Foole
John Donne

I am two fooles, I know,
For loving, and for saying so
   In whining Poëtry;
But where's that wiseman, that would not be I,
   If she would not deny?
Then as th'earths inward narrow crooked lanes
Do purge sea waters fretfull salt away,
   I thought, if I could draw my paines,
Through Rimes vexation, I should them allay.
Griefe brought to numbers cannot be so fierce,
For, he tames it, that fetters it in verse.

But when I have done so,
Some man, his art and voice to show,
   Doth Set and sing my paine,
And, by delighting many frees againe
   Griefe, which verse did restraine.
To Love, and Griefe tribute of Verse belongs,
But not of such as pleases when 'tis read,
   Both are increased by such songs:
For both their triumphs so are published,
And I, which was two fooles, do so grow three;
Who are a little wise, the best fooles bee.

What's the Most Important Sentence?

In many ways, "what's the most important sentence?" is the linchpin question of this book. Individual words, punctuation, and sounds cohere into the grammatical unity of a sentence. Details accumulate among these words and sounds. Lines and stanzas fracture or link burgeoning sentences. The sentences collectively construct characters and images.

Theodore Roethke wrote that "the poem . . . means an entity, a unity has been achieved that transcends by far the organization of the lecture, the essay, even the great speech."[3] The sentence is key to reaching such poetic unity. It's a blueprint for working out what and how the poet thinks and feels. It's a conduit for curiosity, a path into mystery.

But sentences in poetry are not simply blocks of meaning. As I discussed in the previous chapter, they also exist as patterns of sound. A sentence is supple and musical and physical; and more than one poet can recall a childhood moment in which she experienced that viscerality. In her essay "The Province of Radical Solitude," Carolyn Forché writes:

> The world hummed, and my own speech rose above the humming and was measured by it. I didn't know what metered verse was, but I remember knowing that language rose and fell, and that it occurred most pleasurably in utterances of similar length. One could recite for hours the flow of language in patterns. My early musical and rhythmic training derived from the Latin liturgy, most especially from litany recitations and Gregorian plainsong. Rhythm, however, is of the body, and it was during walks in childhood that I first sensed the relation between breath, phrase, and heart. I spoke to the pounding.[4]

How does a poet write the kinds of sentences that create a response like Forché's? The answer is more flexible than you might imagine. Because grammar books tend to treat sentences as recipes requiring precise ingredients, many students think of a sentence as correct or incorrect, not as a personal exploration. In contrast, *The Oxford English Dictionary*'s definition focuses on the individuality of articulation rather than the rules of the game: "[a sentence is] a series of words complete in itself as the expression of a thought, containing or implying a subject and predicate, and conveying a statement, question, exclamation, or command."[5]

In other words, sentences comprise a large variety of language patterns, many of which don't follow official grammar-book prescriptions. So when I talk about sentences in poetry, I'm not celebrating tidy subject-predicate combos and snarling about fragments and comma splices. Rather, I'm thinking about the way in which a poet arranges words to express a thought. In an effective sentence, the arrangement of words is "complete in itself." That is, the articulation has a beginning, a middle, and an end. In addition, an effective sentence displays a particular pattern of language: "a statement, question, exclamation, or command."

The variations are as individual as the poets who invent them. For instance, sentences may be identical to lines of poetry, as they are in Jeanne Marie Beaumont's "Afraid So":

Is it starting to rain?
Did the check bounce?
Are we out of coffee?
Is this going to hurt?[6]

A sentence can fill up an entire stanza, as it does in Maxine Kumin's "Rehearsing for the Final Reckoning in Boston":

During the Berlioz *Requiem* in Symphony Hall
which takes even longer than extra innings
in big league baseball, this restless Jewish agnostic
waits to be pounced on, jarred by the massive fanfare
of trombones and trumpets assembling now in the second
balcony, left side, right side, and at the rear.[7]

A sentence may cross stanzas, as it does in Alexander Pope's "Ode on Solitude":

Blest, who can unconcern'dly find
    Hours, days, and years slide soft away,
In health of body, peace of mind,
        Quiet by day,

Sound sleep by night; study and ease,
    Together mixt; sweet recreation;
And Innocence, which most does please
        With meditation.[8]

Sentence boundaries may be ambiguous, as they are in Lynn Emmanuel's "Dressing the Parts":

So, here we are,
I am a kind of diction[9]

Despite their many differences, all of these examples maintain allegiance to what Forché has called "the flow of language in patterns." Robert Frost named this flow the "sentence-sound," defining a sentence as "a sound in itself on which other sounds called words may be strung." By this, he didn't mean any random clump of words. "You may string words together without a sentence-sound to string them on just as you may tie clothes together by the sleeves and stretch them without a clothes-line between two trees but—it is bad for the clothes." Thus, *dog buttermilk the in* is not a sentence-sound. But rearrange the words as *dog in the buttermilk* and suddenly "the sound of sense" is "apprehended by the ear."[10]

John Donne's "The Triple Foole" is an intricate maze of sentences, all of which are important to the poem. Nonetheless, I've chosen three different constructions to consider more closely.

I AM TWO FOOLES. . . .

Lucille Clifton's poem "sorrows" opens with "who would believe them winged," an unpunctuated, uncapitalized line that is a clear, straightforward question.[11] Her sentence doesn't require punctuation or capitalization to convey what Frost called "the sound of sense." In contrast, John Donne relies on ornate, heavy-handed punctuation to demarcate the sentences in "The Triple Foole." Nevertheless, at first reading I'm not always convinced that what Donne has marked out as a sentence is, in the *OED*'s terms, "complete in itself as the expression of a thought."

But what is "the expression of a thought"? My own thoughts are frequently clotted, unclear, and ambiguous; and it seems that Donne may have felt the same about his, for not much in "The Triple Foole" can be called straightforward. Let's look at the opening sentence and track how the speaker moves grammatically through his own perplexity.

> I am two fooles, I know,
> For loving, and for saying so
> In whining Poëtry;
> But where's that wiseman, that would not be I,
> If she would not deny?

The sentence breaks neatly into halves. The first section, which ends at the semicolon, lays out a claim ("I am two fooles, I know") and follows with supporting reasons. Foole 1 is foolish "For loving," and Foole 2 is foolish "for saying so / In whining Poëtry." Thus far, the sentence seems to express a coherent thought "complete in itself."

But after the semicolon, things get stranger. As the sentence shifts from a statement to a question, the speaker lays out a series of linked but incongruous phrases. "But where's that wiseman," he asks. Immediately he undercuts the question with the self-deprecating "that would not be I." Or should I read this as an excuse rather than as modesty? Suddenly I find myself not entirely trusting this speaker. What is he trying to evade? The sentence continues, deepening my confusion. "If she would not deny?" Deny what? Are words missing here? The sentence feels as if it's been chopped off mid-phrase. Typically, "deny" would be followed by a noun phrase or a dependent clause: for instance, *deny my love, deny that I am a foole.* As it is, the question leaves me hanging. I don't understand what's going on. All I know is that I am confused, suspicious of the speaker, and curious about this enigmatic "she," this mysterious "deny."

"The Triple Foole" is an early seventeenth-century poem. No doubt there's a scholarly edition that would translate its archaic sentences into contemporary English, lifting my spirits and erasing my puzzlement. But even though I honor such scholarship, I want to argue for the value of coming to a poem as it exists, unadorned, on the page. I think it's important to meet a difficult poem on your own ground, to rely on your own wits and reactions as you wrestle with it.

Are my reactions to this sentence "correct"? If I were faced with a multiple-choice question about "The Triple Foole," I'd probably get the answer wrong. But when I ask myself what I've learned, I see that I've made an important discovery. Pushing myself to look closely at the structure of the sentence has also pushed me look closely at the structure of a thought. And what I've learned is that, for some poets, sentences really do seem to mirror thoughts. Clear or confused, simple or complex, Donne's thoughts unwind as his sentences unwind. When I read his lines, I feel as if I am wandering along the pathways of his brain, at one moment basking in his rational neatness, at another drowning in his tortuous evasions. "Donne felt his thought as immediately as the odour of a rose," writes A. S. Byatt. Now I know what she means.

GRIEFE BROUGHT TO NUMBERS. . . .

"The Triple Foole" is composed of five sentences. Four of those sentences are constructed as intricate stacks of clauses that fill between four and six lines. But the fifth sentence is notably different:

> Griefe brought to numbers cannot be so fierce,
> For, he tames it, that fetters it in verse.

At only two lines long, it is much shorter than every other sentence in the poem. This brevity might not have surprised me if it had shown up in some other place. For instance, if the poem had begun with a short sentence and then gradually accrued into denser and denser sentences, I might have speculated about the way in which the sentence structure was mirroring the speaker's increasing emotional turmoil. If the poem had ended with a short sentence, I might have seen it as an epigrammatic conclusion, a succinct comment analogous to the moral at the end of a fable.

But Donne's short sentence appears in the middle of the poem. Two long sentences precede it; two more follow it. So I begin to mull over visual and structural associations: *fulcrum, keystone, waist, hourglass, heart.* Does anything within this sentence support these associations?

Most of you have done enough close reading in college English courses to follow up on that question yourself. My point here isn't to give you answers about meaning but to show you that a sentence's style and its position in a poem can trigger a curiosity that leads toward literary analysis. Sometimes scholarship and craft can feel like two different roads into reading a difficult poem. If you teach, you might find yourself focusing on analysis skills rather than creative writing skills, or vice versa, as if the two are entirely unrelated. By bringing them together, you allow both yourself and your students to think of complex canonical literature, such as Donne's poetry, as work that a real person actually constructed from movable materials.

TO LOVE AND GRIEFE. . . .

At six lines long, the final sentence of "The Triple Foole" accounts for nearly a quarter of the poem.

> To Love, and Griefe tribute of Verse belongs,
> But not of such as pleases when 'tis read,
> > Both are increased by such songs:
> For both their triumphs so are published,
> And I, which was two fooles, do so grow three;
> Who are a little wise, the best fooles bee.

Despite its length, the sentence seems to visually comply with traditional sentence expectations. It begins with a capital letter and ends with a period. It is composed of linked clauses, several of which begin with coordinating conjunctions such as *but, and,* and *for.* These kinds of conjunctions tend to make a reader feel rhetorically safe. They hint at a balanced argument, a weighing of options. They imply logical progress from one idea to the next. But is logical progress really what's happening in this sentence? When I look more closely at the punctuation, I begin to feel uneasy.

Lines 1 and 2 open smoothly enough. In fact, "To Love, and Griefe tribute of Verse belongs, / But not of such as pleases when 'tis read," reads like a sentence unto itself. Though the order is archaic and convoluted, the lines have a subject ("tribute of Verse") and an accompanying verb ("belongs") with an attached prepositional phrase ("To Love, and Griefe"). The second line is a dependent clause that explains the qualities of this particular "tribute of Verse" (it's not pleasant when read). So far, so clear.

But line 2 ends with a comma, indicating that the sentence isn't over yet. So why, when I read line 3, do I feel as if I am now in a completely different sentence? The simplest response is because Donne has relied on a comma splice. That is, instead of inserting a period or a semicolon after line 2, he has used a comma to link an independent clause ("Both are increased by such songs:") to what was already a complete sentence.

You may be a person with a hot, hot hate for so-called bad grammar. You may revile *its* versus *it's* errors and snarl about dangling modifiers and split infinitives. But for now I want you to stop spitting and snarling. I want you forget the fact that seventeenth-century punctuation styles don't follow the rules of twenty-first-century grammar manuals. I also want you to ignore the manuscript issues I mentioned in "About the Poet and the Poem." Simply I want you to reread these three lines and ask yourself, "Why is there a comma here?"

In my earlier chapter about punctuation, I thought about some of the ways in which Hopkins chose to punctuate his poem "The Soldier." To me, many of those choices seemed to relate to sound. In this case, however, I am less sure about the influence of sound. Does the sound of "The Triple Foole" change radically if I insert a strong end-stopped pause rather than a lighter comma pause? Yes, each reading does create a different effect in my voice and on my ear. But more than the echo of music I hear the echo of thought.

In lines 1 and 2, Donne states that verse can be a tribute to either love or grief, and he tells us that such tributes aren't necessarily a pleasure to read about. Then in line 3 he rushes into his next idea: such tributes aren't pleasant because verse intensifies both love and grief. Is he making logical sense? Not necessarily. I might argue that an increase in love can be pleasurable, even that an increase in grief can have its self-absorbed allurements. But I think it's important to remember that thought isn't logic. Thought is exploration. To my mind, Donne's comma splice is somewhat analogous to the light bulb that appears over a cartoon character's head. "Idea!" it shouts.

Let's keep pushing into the sentence. Line 3 ends with a colon. Here again, we have a situation that might be called a sentence break. Why did Donne choose to break his thought with a long exhale rather than an actual stop?

Read further down into line 5, which ends with a semicolon. In modern English grammar, a semicolon links two independent clauses. In other words, it functions as a

kind of hybrid period/comma. But this isn't a case of two independent clauses. Line 6 is
a straightforward dependent clause—a place I might have expected to see a comma. Why
didn't Donne choose to use one here?

How do these punctuation choices—a colon, then a semicolon—affect your sense
that the poet is working, in the *OED*'s terms, with "a series of words complete in itself as
the expression of a thought"? I'm not going to answer such questions for you, although I
hope you take the time to puzzle over them yourself. As I've already said, my goal in this
chapter is to show you how to open doors into the poem, not to explicate it for you. By
paying attention to sentence structure, sentence punctuation, and sentence position, you
will be using the solid elements of language as touchstones for your own curiosity. You can
analyze for meaning; you can focus on dramatic movement; you can bask in the cadence
of the language. There are many ways to read a poem, and there are moments in your life
when one type of reading will be more vital than another. But the poet's language choices
always remain at the root of those readings.

Ideas for Writing
When we think about sentences, most of us tend to think about prose. What's the
difference between a sentence in prose and a sentence in poetry? As a way to begin
thinking about this question, let's look at some samples from Walt Whitman's writing.
First, here's a prose extract from his preface to the 1855 edition of *Leaves of Grass:*

> Who knows the curious mystery of the eyesight? The other senses corroborate
> themselves, but this is removed from any proof but its own and foreruns the
> identities of the spiritual world. A single glance of it mocks all the investigations
> of man and all the instruments and books of the earth and all reasoning. What is
> marvelous? what is unlikely? what is impossible or baseless or vague? after you
> have once just opened the space of a peachpit and given audience to far and near
> and to the sunset and had all things enter with electric swiftness softly and duly
> without confusion or jostling or jam.[12]

On the surface, the language in this excerpt is almost stereotypically poetic. Whitman's
word choice is varied and memorable; the sentences float smoothly off the tongue; he
uses rhetorical devices such as the repetition of questions to intensify the musicality of the
passage. So let's try breaking the sentences into the long, dense lines typical of a Whitman
poem. What has changed in your reaction to this passage now that I've transformed it
from a block of prose into a series of sentences in lines?

> Who knows the curious mystery of the eyesight?
> The other senses corroborate themselves, but this is removed from any proof
>   but its own and foreruns the identities of the spiritual world.
> A single glance of it mocks all the investigations of man and all the instruments
>   and books of the earth and all reasoning.
> What is marvelous? what is unlikely? what is impossible or baseless or vague?
>   after you have once just opened the space of a peachpit and given audience
>   to far and near

and to the sunset and had all things enter with electric swiftness softly and
duly
without confusion or jostling or jam.

While you're still thinking about the previous sentence experiment, let's look at a passage from an actual Whitman poem and start drawing some comparisons. Here's the opening of "Crossing Brooklyn Ferry":

> Flood-tide below me! I see you face to face!
> Clouds of the west—sun there half an hour high—I see you also face to face.
>
> Crowds of men and women attired in the usual costumes, how curious you are
>   to me!
> On the ferry-boats the hundreds and hundreds that cross, returning home, are
>   more curious to me than you suppose,
> And you that shall cross from shore to shore years hence are more to me,
>   and more in my meditations, than you might suppose.[13]

One difference that I'm noticing is the place in which the repetitions tend to appear in the sentences. In the prose excerpt, Whitman repeats "what is?" to begin a series of internal mini-sentences: "What is marvelous? what is unlikely? what is impossible or baseless or vague?" In the poetry excerpt, his repetitions appear at the ends of sentences. "I see you face to face!" is followed by "I see you also face to face." "How curious you are to me!" is followed by "are more curious to me than you suppose," which is followed by "more in meditations, than you might suppose." Notably, those sentence endings are not exact matches but variations on a phrase. The initial phrase is always the most concise, whereas the repetitions add or replace words and substitute new punctuation marks.

There are other differences as well. The sentences in "Crossing Brooklyn Ferry" are shorter and airier than most of the sentences in the prose extract. I never think of Whitman as a poet who writes in compact sentences, but his prose seems to be much denser than his poetry. Yet the opening question of that prose extract is so evocative!

What would have happened if he had used that sentence to open a poem? Why not try it out for yourself? Write a draft that takes Whitman's sentence as your opening cue:

> Who knows the curious mystery of the eyesight?

Using that sentence as a trigger, think your way into at least four more sentences. Write out the sentences as lines, not as prose, but feel free to break those lines however you'd like. Create long sentence-lines (as Whitman does), break your lines at the punctuation (as Donne does), or borrow from the styles of any of the poets that I've anthologized at the end of this chapter.

However you choose to experiment, don't allow yourself to forget that thought is freedom . . . most importantly, the freedom to change. Work to make your sentences vehicles of this freedom. As Virginia Woolf wrote in "Romance and the Heart," "the heart is not, as we should like it to be, a stationary body, but a body which moves perpetually, and is thus always standing in a new relation to the emotions which are its sun. Chaucer, Donne, Dickens—each, if you read him, shows this change of the heart."[14]

Thinking about Sentences: An Anthology

George Herbert: Sinne
Howard Levy: Polish Prism
Lady Mary Wortley Montagu: Epistle from Mrs. Yonge to Her Husband
John Clare: Badger
Lucille Clifton: sleeping beauty

Whatever I write will be the real thought of that hour, and I know you will no more expect it of me to persevere till death in every sentiment or notion I now set down, than you would imagine a man's face should never change after his picture was once drawn.
                              —Alexander Pope to Lady Mary Wortley Montagu

Sinne
George Herbert

Lord, with what care hast thou begirt us round!
   Parents first season us: then schoolmasters
   Deliver us to laws; they send us bound
To rules of reason, holy messengers,
Pulpits and Sundayes, sorrow dogging sinne,
   Afflictions sorted, anguish of all sizes,
   Fine nets and stratagems to catch us in.
Bibles laid open, millions of surprises,
Blessings beforehand, tyes of gratefulnesse,
   The sound of glorie ringing in our eares:
   Without, our shame; within, our consciences;
Angels and grace, eternall hopes and fears.
   Yet all these fences and their whole aray
   One cunning bosome-sinne blows quite away.

Polish Prism
Howard Levy

In the scuttlebutt of Warsaw
someone is always running into a wall
while the night throws powerful stencils of the crash,
and the trees, lounging, leap to attention at the noise.
This is their contribution
to the need for seriousness.

Meanwhile, an army officer
outflanks the reticence of a maid.
He unbuttons her blouse, she imagines doves.
He cups her breasts, she imagines
the long bus ride back to her distant province.
A merchant in the building net door tallies
his books. They are an atlas
of bankruptcy, the numbers attack him
like swarms of red bees.

What can be said of ruin,
whether fanciful or factual?
Toward what dark churches do the poets go
to attend that litany,
to learn how many candles they need light
when the mind can sufficiently plot
the decaying orbitals of history
and yet the eye, relishing independence,
wanders into restaurants
and signals for sausage, for the strongest
vodka.

IN MEMORY OF ZBIGNIEW HERBERT

Epistle from Mrs. Yonge to Her Husband
Lady Mary Wortley Montagu

Think not this paper comes with vain pretense
To move your pity, or to mourn th' offense.
Too well I know that hard obdurate heart;
No softening mercy there will take my part,
Nor can a woman's arguments prevail,
When even your patron's wise example fails.
But this last privilege I still retain;
Th' oppressed and injured always may complain.
   Too, too severely laws of honor bind
The weak submissive sex of womankind.
If sighs have gained or force compelled our hand,
Deceived by art, or urged by stern command,
Whatever motive binds the fatal tie,
The judging world expects our constancy.
   Just heaven! (for sure in heaven does justice reign,
Though tricks below that sacred name profane)
To you appealing I submit my cause.
Nor fear a judgment from impartial laws.
All bargains but conditional are made;
The purchase void, the creditor unpaid;
Defrauded servants are from service free;
A wounded slave regains his liberty.
For wives ill used no remedy remains,
To daily racks condemned, and to eternal chains.
   From whence is this unjust distinction grown?
Are we not formed with passions like your own?
Nature with equal fire our souls endued,
Our minds as haughty, and as warm our blood;
O'er the wide world your pleasures you pursue,
The change is justified by something new;
But we must sigh in silence—and be true.
Our sex's weakness you expose and blame
(Of every prattling fop the common theme),
Yet from this weakness you suppose is due
Sublimer virtue than your Cato knew.
Had heaven designed us trials so severe,
It would have formed our tempers then to bear.
   And I have borne (oh what have I not borne!)
The pang of jealousy, the insults of scorn.
Wearied at length, I from your sight remove,
And place my future hopes in secret love.
In the gay bloom of glowing youth retired,

I quit the woman's joy to be admired,
With that small pension your hard heart allows,
Renounce your fortune, and release your vows.
To custom (though unjust) so much is due;
I hide my frailty from the public view.
My conscience clear, yet sensible of shame,
My life I hazard, to preserve my fame.
And I prefer this low inglorious state
To vile dependence on the thing I hate—
But you pursue me to this last retreat.
Dragged into light, my tender crime is shown
And every circumstance of fondness known.
Beneath the shelter of the law you stand,
And urge my ruin with a cruel hand,
While to my fault thus rigidly severe,
Tamely submissive to the man you fear.

   This wretched outcast, this abandoned wife,
Has yet this joy to sweeten shameful life:
By your mean conduct, infamously loose,
You are at once my accuser and excuse.
Let me be damned by the censorious prude
(Stupidly dull, or spiritually lewd),
My hapless case will surely pity find
From every just and reasonable mind.
When to the final sentence I submit,
The lips condemn me, but their souls aquit.

   No more my husband, to your pleasures go,
The sweets of your recovered freedom know.
Go: court the brittle friendship of the great,
Smile at his board, or at his levee wait;
And when dismissed, to madam's toilet fly,
More than her chambermaids, or glasses, lie,
Tell her how young she looks, how heavenly fair,
Admire the lilies and the roses there.
Your high ambition may be gratified,
Some cousin of her own be made your bride,
And you the father of a glorious race
Endowed with Ch——l's strength and Low——r's face.

Badger
John Clare

When midnight comes a host of dogs and men
Go out and track the badger to his den,
And put a sack within the hole, and lie
Till the old grunting badger passes by.
He comes and hears—they let the strongest loose.
The old fox hears the noise and drops the goose.
The poacher shoots and hurries from the cry,
And the old hare half wounded buzzes by.
They get a forkèd stick to bear him down
And clap the dogs and take him to the town,
And bait him all the day with many dogs,
And laugh and shout and fright the scampering hogs.
He runs along and bites at all he meets:
They shout and hollo down the noisy streets.

He turns about to face the loud uproar
And drives the rebels to their very door.
The frequent stone is hurled where'er they go;
When badgers fight, then everyone's a foe.
The dogs are clapt and urged to join the fray.
The badger turns and drives them all away.
Though scarcely half as big, demure and small,
He fights with dogs for hours and beats them all.
The heavy mastiff, savage in the fray,
Lies down and licks his feet and turns away.
The bulldog knows his match and waxes cold,
The badger grins and never leaves his hold.
He drives the crowd and follows at their heels
And bites them through—the drunkard swears and reels.

The frightened women take the boys away,
The blackguard laughs and hurries on the fray.
He tries to reach the woods, an awkward race,
But sticks and cudgels quickly stop the chase.
He turns agen and drives the noisy crowd
And beats the dogs in noises loud.
He drives away and beats them every one,
And then they loose them all and set them on.
He falls as dead and kicked by boys and men,
Then starts and grins and drives the crowd agen;
Till kicked and torn and beaten out he lies
And leaves his hold and cackles, groans, and dies.

sleeping beauty
Lucille Clifton

when she woke up
she was terrible.
under his mouth her mouth
turned red and warm
then almost crimson as the coals
smothered and forgotten
in the grate.
she had been gone so long.
there was much to unlearn.
she opened her eyes.
he was the first thing she saw
and she blamed him.

Writing about Poets and Poetry

William Blake
America: A Prophecy

If I should dream before I wake,
may I dream of William Blake.

—*Nancy Willard*

About the Poet and the Poem

Today William Blake (1757–1827) is seen as a central figure of English Romanticism, but during his lifetime few people were familiar with either his poetry or his artwork. His talents and oddities appeared early. Biographer Peter Ackroyd writes, "Keats was [later] to remark, 'That which is creative must create itself,' but the process was not an easy one for Blake. He might have been some star-child, or changeling, who withdrew into himself and into his own myth because he could not deal directly or painlessly even with the human beings closest to him."[1] Even as a child, he claimed to see visions, and his drawings were striking and precocious. At age fourteen, he was apprenticed to an engraver; and although throughout his life he made various attempts to move into more prominent artistic circles, his livelihood always depended on his engraving skills. In addition to illustrating his own poetry, he created paintings, prints, and drawings for (among other works) Dante's *Inferno,* the Bible's Book of Job, and Chaucer's *The Canterbury Tales.*

Blake's long poem "America: A Prophecy" is dated 1793, a volatile year. In their introduction to the poem, editors Mary Lynn Johnson and John E. Grant summarize the climate of the times:

> In 1793 Louis XVI was executed. Britain went to war against the French revolutionary government, Parliament passed harsh laws against seditious publications, and the French Revolution was becoming so violent that English sympathizers like Blake found revolutionary activity increasingly difficult to justify. . . . For Blake, a prophet is a seer rather than a forecaster; he perceives the outlines of contemporary events and understands the implications of public issues; above all, he speaks out fearlessly to awaken his contemporaries. 1793 was a time to reflect on the imaginative origins of the contemporary revolution: why was it going wrong? Was the American Revolution more successful?[2]

America: A Prophecy
William Blake

Preludium

The shadowy daughter of Urthona stood before red Orc
When fourteen suns had faintly journey'd o'er his dark abode;
His food she brought in iron baskets, his drink in cups of iron;
Crown'd with a helmet & dark hair the nameless female stood.
A quiver with its burning stores, a bow like that of night
When pestilence is shot from heaven—no other arms she need:
Invulnerable tho' naked, save where the clouds roll round her loins
Their awful folds in the dark air. Silent she stood as night:
For never from her iron tongue could voice or sound arise,
But dumb till that dread day, when Orc assay'd his fierce embrace.

"Dark virgin," said the hairy youth, "thy father stern abhorr'd
Rivets my tenfold chains while still on high my spirit soars:
Sometimes an eagle screaming in the sky, sometimes a lion
Stalking upon the mountains, & sometimes a whale I lash
The raging fathomless abyss; anon a serpent folding
Around the pillars of Urthona, and round thy dark limbs.
On the Canadian wilds I fold, feeble my spirit folds,
For chained beneath I rend these caverns. When thou bringest food
I howl my joy: and my red eyes seek to behold thy face—
In vain! these clouds roll to & fro, & hide thee from my sight.

Silent as despairing love, and strong as jealousy,
The hairy shoulders rend the links. Free are the wrists of fire;
Round the terrific loins he siez'd the panting struggling womb;
It joy'd: she put aside her clouds & smiled her first-born smile:
As when a black cloud shews its light'nings to the silent deep.

Soon as she saw the terrible boy, then burst the virgin cry:

"I know thee, I have found thee, & I will not let thee go:
Thou art the image of God who dwells in the darkness of Africa.
And thou art fall'n to give me life in regions of dark death.
On my American plains I feel the struggling afflictions
Endur'd by roots that writhe their arms into the nether deep:
I see a serpent in Canada, who courts me to his love;
In Mexico an Eagle, and a Lion in Peru;
I see a Whale in the South-sea, drinking my soul away.
O what limb rending pains I feel. Thy fire & my frost
Mingle in howling pains, in furrows by thy lightnings rent.
This is eternal death; and this the torment long foretold.

* * *

The stern Bard ceas'd, asham'd of his own song; enrag'd he swung
His harp aloft sounding, then dash'd its shining frame against
A ruin'd pillar in glittring fragments; silent he turn'd away,
And wander'd down the vales of Kent in sick & drear lamentings.

    A Prophecy
The Guardian Prince of Albion burns in his nightly tent.
Sullen fires across the Atlantic glow to America's shore:
Piercing the souls of warlike men, who rise in silent night.
Washington, Franklin, Paine & Warren, Gates, Hancock & Green
Meet on the coast, glowing with blood from Albion's fiery Prince.

Washington spoke: "Friends of America, look over the Atlantic sea;
A bended bow is lifted in heaven, & a heavy iron chain
Descends link by link from Albion's cliffs across the sea to bind
Brothers & sons of America, till our faces pale and yellow,
Heads deprest, voices weak, eyes downcast, hands work-bruis'd,
Feet bleeding on the sultry sands, and the furrows of the whip
Descend to generations that in future times forget.—"

The strong voice ceas'd; for a terrible blast swept over the heaving sea.
The eastern cloud rent· on his cliffs stood Albion's wrathful Prince.
A dragon form clashing his scales at midnight, he arose
And flam'd red meteors round the land of Albion beneath.
His voice, his locks, his awful shoulders, and his glowing eyes

Appear to the Americans upon the cloudy night.

Solemn heave the Atlantic waves between the gloomy nations,
Swelling, belching from its deeps red clouds & raging Fires.
Albion is sick. America faints! enrag'd the Zenith grew,
As human blood shooting its veins all round the orbed heaven,
Red rose the clouds from the Atlantic in vast wheels of blood,
And in the red clouds rose a Wonder o'er the Atlantic sea.
Intense! naked! a Human fire fierce glowing, as the wedge
Of iron heated in the furnace: his terrible limbs were fire,
With myriads of cloudy terrors, banners dark, & towers
Surrounded; heat but not light went thro' the murky atmosphere.

The King of England looking westward trembles at the vision.

Albion's Angel stood beside the Stone of night, and saw
The terror like a comet, or more like the planet red

That once inclos'd the terrible wandering comets in its sphere.
Then, Mars, thou wast our center, & the planets three flew round
Thy crimson disk; so e'er the Sun was rent from thy red sphere.
The Spectre glowed his horrid length, staining the temple long
With beams of blood, & thus a voice came forth and shook the temple:

"The morning comes, the night decays, the watchmen leave their stations;
The grave is burst, the spices shed, the linen wrapped up;
The bones of death, the cov'ring clay, the sinews shrunk & dry'd,
Reviving shake, inspiring move, breathing! awakening!
Spring like redeemed captives when their bonds & bars are burst.
Let the slave grinding at the mill run out into the field:
Let him look up into the heavens & laugh in the bright air;
Let the inchained soul shut up in darkness and in sighing,
Whose face has never seen a smile in thirty weary years,
Rise and look out; his chains are loose, his dungeon doors are open.
And let his wife and children return from the oppressor's scourge.
They look behind at every step & believe it is a dream,
Singing, 'The Sun has left his blackness, & has found a fresher morning
And the fair Moon rejoices in the clear & cloudless night;
For Empire is no more, and now the Lion & Wolf shall cease.'"

In thunders ends the voice. Then Albion's Angel wrathful burnt
Beside the Stone of Night; and like the Eternal Lion's howl
In famine & war, reply'd, "Art thou not Orc; who serpent-form'd
Stands at the gate of Enitharmon to devour her children?
Blasphemous Demon, Antichrist, hater of Dignities;
Lover of wild rebellion, and transgressor of God's Law,
Why dost thou come to Angels' eyes in this terrific form?"

The terror answered: "I am Orc, wreath'd round the accursed tree:
The times are ended; shadows pass, the morning 'gins to break;
The fiery joy, that Urizen perverted to ten commands,
What night he led the starry hosts thro' the wide wilderness:
That stony law I stamp to dust: and scatter religion abroad
To the four winds as a torn book, & none shall gather the leaves;
But they shall rot on desert sands, & consume in bottomless deeps,
To make the deserts blossom, & the deeps shrink to their fountains,
And to renew the fiery joy, and burst the stony roof,
That pale religious letchery, seeking Virginity,
May find it in a harlot, and in coarse-clad honesty
The undefil'd, tho' ravish'd in her cradle night and morn:
For every thing that lives is holy, life delights in life;
Because the soul of sweet delight can never be defil'd.
Fires inwrap the earthly globe, yet man is not consumed;

Amidst the lustful fires he walks: his feet become like brass,
His knees and thighs like silver, & his breast and head like gold."

"Sound! sound ! my large war-trumpets & alarm my Thirteen Angels!
Loud howls the eternal Wolf! the eternal Lion lashes his tail!
America is darkened; and my punishing Demons terrified
Crouch howling before their caverns deep, like skins dry'd in the wind.
They cannot smite the wheat, nor quench the fatness of the earth.
They cannot smite with sorrows, nor subdue the plow and spade.
The cannot wall the city, nor moat round the castle of princes.
They cannot bring the stubbed oak to overgrow the hills.
For terrible men stand on the shores, & in their robes I see
Children take shelter from the lightnings. There stands Washington
And Paine and Warren with their foreheads reared toward the east.
But clouds obscure my aged sight. A vision from afar!
Sound! sound! my loud war-trumpets & alarm my thirteen Angels!
Ah vision from afar! Ah rebel form that rent the ancient
Heavens, Eternal Viper self-renew'd, rolling in clouds:
I see thee in thick clouds and darkness on America's shore.
Writhing in pangs of abhorred birth. Red flames the crest rebellious
And eyes of death; the harlot womb oft opened in vain
Heaves in enormous circles. Now the times are return'd upon thee,
Devourer of thy parent, now thy unutterable torment renews.
Sound! sound! my loud war trumpets & alarm my thirteen Angels!
Ah terrible birth! a young one bursting! where is the weeping mouth?
And where the mother's milk? Instead those ever-hissing jaws
And parched lips drop with fresh gore; now roll thou in the clouds.
Thy mother lays her length outstretch'd upon the shore beneath.
Sound! sound! my loud war-trumpets & alarm my thirteen Angels!
Loud howls the eternal Wolf! the eternal Lion lashes his tail!"

Thus wept the Angel voice & as he wept the terrible blasts
Of trumpets blew a loud alarm across the Atlantic deep.
No trumpets answer; no reply of clarions or of fifes;
Silent the Colonies remain and refuse the loud alarm.

On those vast shady hills between America & Albion's shore,
Now barr'd out by the Atlantic sea, call'd Atlantean hills
Because from their bright summits you may pass to the Golden world,
An ancient palace, archetype of mighty Emperies,
Rears its immortal pinnacles, built in the forest of God
By Ariston the king of beauty for his stolen bride.

Here on their magic seats the thirteen Angels sat perturb'd
For clouds from the Atlantic over o'er the solemn roof.

Fiery the Angels rose, & and as they rose deep thunder roll'd
Around their shores: indignant burning with the fires of Orc;
And Boston's Angel cried aloud, as they flew thro' the dark night:

He cried: "Why trembles honesty and, like a murderer,
Why seeks he refuge from the frowns of his immortal station?
Must the generous tremble & leave his joy, to the idle: to the pestilence!
That mock him? Who commanded this? what God? what Angel!
To keep the gen'rous from experience till the ungenerous
Are unrestrained performers of the energies of nature,
Till pity is become a trade, and generosity a science
That men get rich by, & the sandy desart is giv'n to the strong!
What God is he writes laws of peace, & clothes him in a tempest?
What pitying Angel lusts for tears, and fans himself with sighs?
What crawling villain preaches abstinence & wraps himself
In fat of lambs? No more I follow, no more obedience pay!"

So cried he, rending off his robe & throwing down his scepter
In sight of Albion's Guardian. And all the thirteen Angels
Rent off their robes to the hungry wind, & threw their golden scepters
Down on the land of America. Indignant they descended
Headlong from out their heav'nly heights, descending swift as fires
Over the land; naked & flaming are their lineaments seen
In the deep gloom. By Washington & Paine & Warren they stood,
And the flame folded, roaring fierce within the pitchy night
Before the Demon red, who burnt towards America
In black smoke, thunders, and loud winds, rejoicing in its terror,
Breaking in smoky wreaths from the wild deep, & gath'ring thick
In flames as of a furnace on the land from North to South.

What time the thirteen Governors that England sent convene
In Bernard's house, the flames covered the land. They rouze, they cry,
Shaking their mental chains; they rush in fury to the sea
To quench their anguish; at the feet of Washington down fall'n
They grovel on the sand and writhing lie, while all
The British soldiers thro' the thirteen states sent up a howl
From their encampments and dark castles seeking where to hide
From the grim flames; and from the vision of Orc; in sight
Of Albion's Angel, who, enrag'd, his secret clouds open'd
From north to south, and burnt outstretched wings of wrath, cov'ring
The eastern sky, spreading his awful wings across the heavens.
Beneath him roll'd his num'rous hosts, all Albion's Angels camp'd,
Darkend the Atlantic mountains, & their trumpets shook the valleys,
Arm'd with diseases of the earth to cast upon the Abyss
Their numbers forty millions, must'ring in the eastern sky.

In the flames stood & view'd the armies drawn out in the sky
Washington, Franklin, Paine & Warren, Allen, Gates & Lee;
And heard the voice of Albion's Angel give the thunderous command;
His plagues obedient to his voice flew forth out of their clouds,
Falling upon America, as a storm to cut them off
As a blight cuts the tender corn when it begins to appear.
Dark is the heaven above, & cold & hard the earth beneath;
And as a plague wind fill'd with insects cuts off man & beast;
And as a sea o'erwhelms a land in the day of an earthquake;

Fury! rage! madness! in a wind swept through America,
And the red flames of Orc that folded roaring fierce around
The angry shores, and the fierce rushing of th' inhabitants together:
The citizens of New York close their books & lock their chests;
The mariners of Boston drop their anchors and unlade;
The scribe of Pennsylvania casts his pen upon the earth;
The builder of Virginia throws his hammer down in fear.
Then had America been lost, o'erwhelm'd by the Atlantic,
And Earth had lost another portion of the infinite,
But all rush together in the night in wrath and raging fire.
The red fires rag'd! the plagues recoil'd! then rolld they back with fury.

On Albion's Angels; then the Pestilence began in streaks of red
Across the limbs of Albion's Guardian, the spotted plague smote Bristol's
And the Leprosy London's Spirit, sickening all their bands.
The millions sent up a howl of anguish and threw off their hammerd mail,
And cast their swords & spears to earth, & stood a naked multitude.
Albion's Guardian writhed in torment on the eastern sky.
Pale, quivring toward the brain his glimmering eyes, teeth chattering,
Howling & shuddering, his legs quivering, convuls'd each muscle & sinew,
Sick'ning, lay London's Guardian, and the ancient miter'd York:
Their heads on snowy hills, their ensigns sick'ning in the sky.

The plagues creep on the burning winds, driven by the flames of Orc,
And by the fierce Americans rushing together in the night;
Driven o'er the Guardians of Ireland and Scotland and Wales,
They, spotted with plagues, forsook the frontiers; & their banners seard
With fires of hell, deform their ancient heavens with shame & woe.
Hid in his caves, the Bard of Albion felt the enormous plagues.
And a cowl of flesh grew o'er his head & scales on his back & ribs;
And rough with black scales all his Angels fright their ancient heavens.

The doors of marriage are open, and the Priests in rustling scales
Rush into reptile coverts, hiding from the fires of Orc
That play around the golden roofs in wreaths of fierce desire,
Leaving the females naked and glowing with the lusts of youth.

For the female spirits of the dead, pining in bonds of religion,
Run from their fetters, reddening, & in long drawn arches sitting;
They feel the nerves of youth renew, and desires of ancient times
Over their pale limbs as a vine when the tender grape appears.

Over the hill, the vales, the cities, rage the red flames fierce;
The Heavens melted from north to south; and Urizen who sat
Above all heavens in thunders wrap'd, emerg'd his leprous head
From out his holy shrine, his tears in deluge piteous
Falling into the deep sublime! Flag'd with grey-brow'd snows
And thunderous visages, his jealous wings wav'd over the deep;
Weeping in dismal howling woe he dark descended, howling
Around the smitten bands, clothed in tears & trembling, shudd'ring cold.
His stored snows he poured forth, and his icy magazines
He open'd on the deep, and on the Atlantic sea white shiv'ring.
Leprous his limbs, all over white, and hoary was his visage.
Weeping in dismal howlings before the stern Americans,
Hiding the Demon red with clouds & cold mists from the earth;
Till Angels & weak men twelve years should govern o'er the strong,
And then their end should come, when France reciev'd the Demon's light.

Stiff shudderings shook the heav'nly thrones! France, Spain & Italy,
In terror view'd the bands of Albion, and the ancient Guardians
Fainting upon the elements smitten with their own plagues
They slow advance to shut the five gates of their law-built heaven,
Fill'd with blasting fancies and with mildews of despair,
With fierce disease and lust, unable to stem the fires of Orc:
But the five gates were consum'd, & their bolts and hinges melted,
And the fierce flames burnt round the heavens, & round the abodes of men.

Two Essays about Blake

It took me a long time to learn how to write prose about poetry. In large part this was because, like many of you, I had grown up in an education system that encouraged me to think of literature as something separate from myself rather than something that I could engage with personally and idiosyncratically. I knew as a reader that poetry could change me as a human being, but the English papers I wrote in high school and college ignored that inner knowledge. Instead, I worked to convince myself that cool objectivity and critical analysis were my true nature and that my passion for literature was sober and precise rather than mutable and intoxicating.

I have come to understand that writing essays about poetry is a way to articulate links among reading, reaction, inspiration, and daily life. Essays don't need to be analytical pieces written to impress a teacher with the breadth of my knowledge. Rather, they can help me clarify and expand my personal relationship to the art.

In the two essays anthologized in this chapter, I write about a single poet, William Blake, yet the pieces cover different ground. In the first, "For the Eye altering alters all," I imagine how Blake might have responded to one of my own poems. This was a nerve-wracking assignment: it is always difficult to give myself permission to speak to a great poet as a colleague. But it also pushed me to look closely at the similarities and differences between our styles, to consider what I trusted and did not trust in the work we were doing as poets. Unlike my discussions in the first section of this book, which focused on elements of language, the essay takes up broader questions of morality and responsibility, referring specifically to the central Blake poem in this chapter, "America: A Prophecy."

The second essay, "Blake the Terrible," considers the two best-known Blake poems in the canon, "The Lamb" and "The Tyger," in the context of my own life history. For me it's been important to articulate the power of personal reactions to literature. Like scholarly analysis, this is a form of critical thinking: a route to discovery, a forum for asking questions and drawing conclusions. Likewise, I think it's important to engage with literary stereotypes. I know both of these Blake poems so well that I found it challenging to look at them with new wonder. But when I pressed myself to do so, I also found that I was reexamining my own perceptions and motivations.

"For the Eye altering alters all"

When a Blake scholar asked me to speculate on how William Blake might have responded to one of my own poems, I knew immediately that I had stumbled into an assignment that would be both a nightmare and a joy. More to the point, however, no matter how I felt, be it burdened or excited, I knew this essay would be hard to write. Even the simple step of allowing myself to visualize crazy, ardent, single-minded Blake leaning a shoulder against the casement of his small window, the better to cast a scorching eye over my work, is an arduous one. The image seems both absurdly arrogant and deeply humiliating; and whenever I picture that scene, my strongest impulse is to run away. Yet as I write these words, I'm angry at my craven reaction. "Turn around!" I want to shout. "Sit down! Keep still and listen to the man!" For I recognize that my fears—these public revelations of my weakness and my vanity, of the gaps in my art and my goodness—are exactly what Blake demands from me. He is a terrifying, unrelenting master. And yet: he is a master.[3]

So I chose a poem for Blake to read.

The Fate of Captain Fetterman's Command

December 21, 1866

At first light we saw our enemies
on the bluff
silver flashing in their hair

a glory of sun as they rode away laden
with tunics saddles boots arrows
still piercing the cracked boots

piercing our silent comrades
and just visible in the dawn
we saw wolves and coyotes

skulking along the verge
crows buzzards eagles circling
the sun-spattered meadow

but not one white body was disturbed
for we hear that salt permeates
the whole system of our race

which protects us from the wild
to some degree but it was strange
that nothing had eaten the horses either

except for flies which swarmed in thick
like the stench
all day we waited

till the doctor finished his report then
they told us to pack our friends
into the ammunition wagons

this was our job they said to retch
to stumble into the field to grasp
at wrists at ankles dissolving to pulp

under our grip to vomit to weep
to stare at masks pounded bloody with stones
bloated crawling with flies who were they

this was our job but we could not sort
cavalry from infantry all stripped
naked slashed skulls crushed

with war clubs ears noses legs
hacked off and some had
crosses cut on their breasts

faces to the sky
we walked on their hearts
but did not know it in the high grass

As I steel myself to picture Blake at his window, scowling over this poem, my first
thought is to wonder what he would think of its mechanics: punctuation, for instance.
I am, in general, priggish about punctuation . . . not like William, who appreciates
ampersands but otherwise could care less. In this poem, however, I've dropped my usual
sentence tidiers—my commas and periods, my predictable capitalization—a choice that
has forced the lines and stanza breaks to shoulder the poem's metric and syntactic load.
That technical decision feels brave to me, but it's a bravery that Blake would probably
never notice. Nonetheless, he would certainly notice that the poem doesn't rhyme or
thrust itself into the rhythms of blank verse; and my guess is that he wouldn't much
like the quavering sonic result. But to tell the truth, I don't much like the sounds of his
lines either, neither his pedantic little melodies nor his prosy ranting. We would quarrel.
Possibly he would find something cutting to say about literary women, and I would throw
up my hands and spill his ink bottle. I wouldn't mean to spill his ink, but I wouldn't be
altogether sorry I'd done it either.

Yet if I can manage to mop up the ink and he can manage to laugh (he does claim to
"love laughing"), we may find our way into a common space. For I do think that, as poets

and as human beings, Blake and I share at least two traits. We both have energy, and we both believe that "Severity of judgment is a great virtue."[4]

These qualities were crucial to my invention of "The Fate of Captain Fetterman's Command," which is, by the way, unquestionably the most violent poem I have ever written. Its impetus was my immersion in *Son of the Morning Star,* Evan S. Connell's account of the bloody war between the U.S. Army and the plains tribes in the years after the American Civil War. While General George Custer is the book's central focus, Connell also relies on innumerable primary-source accounts from soldiers, officers, tribal warriors, merchants, and bureaucrats, not to mention their wives, children, and servants. By combining these many one-sided accounts, Connell was able to create both a panorama and a general thesis about the cruelty and wrongheadedness of the U.S. government. But my poem doesn't do that work. It remains a one-sided account—fictional yet arising in both spirit and dramatic arc from the journal entries of soldiers involved in a specific incident: the 1866 slaughter known as the Fetterman Massacre, when the captain and seventy-nine of his men were ambushed and killed by Sioux warriors.[5]

To Blake, this narrowed vision might well be the most unattractive characteristic of my poem. His gift was his ability—his urgent need—to take every side and to castigate every side. Even the small poems are massive in scope and complication. "The Little Vagabond," for instance, has always struck me as one of the most subversive poems I have ever read.

> But if at the Church they would give us some Ale,
> And a pleasant fire, our souls to regale:
> We'd sing and we'd pray, all the live-long day,
> Nor ever once wish from the Church to stray.

Who but Blake would ever suggest that churches should be more like bars? Who but Blake would then slam on an ending like this one?

> And God like a father rejoicing to see
> His children as pleasant and happy as he;
> Would have no more quarrel with the Devil or the Barrel,
> But kiss him & give him both drink and apparel.[6]

At once cynical and idealistic, scornful and hopeful, rigid and chaotic, humane and poisonous, the poem is a pipe bomb wrapped up in a blanket of prim singsong.

Blake never seemed to fear the possibility of supporting the wrong political or moral or religious issue. This isn't to say that he never erred. Rather, I think he believed that speaking was more important than not speaking. Moreover, speaking vehemently was more important than speaking timidly. "Active Evil is better than passive Good," he scrawled recklessly in the margin of Johann Caspar Lavater's 1788 *Aphorisms on Man.*[7] If questioned, I doubt he would have stood up for that statement. What really mattered, I think, was the word *active*—the reckless resolve to declare to any listener, "What a contemptible Fool is This [Francis] Bacon"; to paint an image of the evening sky so dense and green and tumultuous that the inks soak through the paper and stain the table beneath.[8]

But as Blake also knew, vehemence doesn't necessarily draw in readers. And in my own case, I'm fairly sure that it explains, at least in part, why the poem has been so difficult to publish. The issue has been, I believe, more a problem of politics than of quality of work. For by calling the Sioux "the enemies," by limiting itself to the viewpoint of the soldiers, the poem seems to be taking the Wrong Side.

Somehow we are no longer allowed to admit publicly that native Americans have ever behaved badly. Yes, the government took away their land, their culture, and in too many cases their future. But I'm not talking about the big story here: I'm talking about the smaller, messier stories of brutality. And neither side is exempt from that brutality. As Blake writes in "America: A Prophecy," when honesty "trembles . . . and like a murder . . . seeks refuge from the frowns of his immortal station," then the pestilence of violence and dissent can spread to all involved. It no longer matters who is right and who is wrong. Using the American Revolution as his metaphor, he writes,

> The plagues creep on the burning winds, driven by the flames of Orc,
> And by the fierce Americans rushing together in the night;
> Driven o'er the Guardians of Ireland and Scotland and Wales,
> They spotted with plagues, forsook the frontiers; & their banners seard
> With fires of hell, deform their ancient heavens with shame & woe.

In other words, everyone, on every side, is tainted by injustice.

Simultaneously, however, everyone, on every side, clings to the shreds of his humanity. Blake, by way of "Boston's Angel," may seem to support the colonial revolutionaries, but he doesn't exult over the defeat of "the thirteen Governors that England sent":

> They rouze, they cry,
> Shaking their mental chains; they rush in fury to the sea
> To quench their anguish; at the feet of Washington down fall'n
> They grovel on the sand and writhing lie, while all
> The British soldiers thro' the thirteen states set up a howl
> Of anguish: threw their swords & muskets to the earth & ran
> From their encampments & dark castles seeking where to hide
> From the grim flames.

This is the pity that I felt for those men under Captain Fetterman's command. They may have been agents of government evil, but they were also men. No, really they were mostly boys: graceful, curious, impetuous, clumsy, pimple-faced, shock-haired, laughing, screaming. The same could be said for the Sioux warriors. I just didn't happen to find myself writing that poem.

To a certain degree, we are trapped by our own history. Those slaughtered white men were my ancestors. The Sioux who were slaughtered in other battles were not. I don't see the white soldiers as better than the Sioux, but I know them better; I recognize the details of their cowardice and their bravery. The situation is analogous to, say, the question among American animal-rights activists of reintroducing wolves into domesticated territory. Yes, the wolves have the right of primogeniture. Yes, farmers stole the wolves' homeland

and murdered them in great numbers simply because the animals were following their predatory instincts. I know this history, and I share the guilt of my species. But when a predator invades my henhouse and kills my fat chicks, I still cry, and I'm still angry.

In the eyes of Blake's "Bard of Albion," the plagues that revolution unleashes "deform [the Angels'] ancient heavens with shame & woe." *Woe* is what drew me to the story of the Fetterman Massacre, a woe that I, for whatever reason, was able not only to share but to imagine—its violence and ineptitude, its scavenging beasts, its tall grass. Meanwhile, the Sioux "on their magic seats . . . sat perturb'd." They remained distant, mythological. It is my flaw that, in this moment of the poem, I could not imagine them otherwise. Yet perhaps Blake would forgive me my limits, so long as I refuse to forgive myself. Like Milton before him, his mission was to reveal the minute and infinite coilings of human immorality; but neither poet ever exempted himself from sin. "The grandest Poetry is Immoral," claimed Blake; "the Poet is Independent & Wicked[;] the Philosopher is Dependent & Good."[9] And God knows I am no philosopher.

"Severity of judgment is a great virtue." And yet "Some cannot tell what they can write tho they dare."[10] It seems to me that, as a writer, as a living being, I negotiate day and night between these instructions—now bowing to the impossible demands of clarity and culpability, now recklessly chronicling my ignorance. I think that Blake, standing at his window, frowning over my lines, would give that desperation its due, even as he pounces on my timidity of vision. At least I hope he would. "We walked on their hearts / but did not know it in the high grass" are the words I chose to circle this painful beauty, this hideous despair. His words, as usual, are starker:

> And none can touch that frowning form,
> Except it be a Woman Old;
> She nails him down upon the Rock,
> And all is done as I have told.[11]

Blake the Terrible

This morning, very early, as Monday light insinuated itself among the reddening maples and our pines that imprison my yard, I took down my frayed Norton edition of William Blake's poetry and opened it at random. For the past several days, I had been toying with writing about Blake, which was strange because I had not lately been reading his poems or even consciously thinking about them. Merely the idea of Blake had begun to rise in my imagination, rather as recalcitrant bread dough rises in a chilly room: irresistibly yet with a laborious pessimism.

When I opened my Blake anthology this morning, the words I happened upon did not ease my ambivalence about the undertaking, for I immediately tumbled into a section of *The Marriage of Heaven and Hell* innocuously titled, as many of the sections are, "A Memorable Fancy." Memorable indeed. Blake writes: "As I was walking among the fires of hell, delighted with the enjoyments of Genius, which to Angels look like torment and insanity, I collected some of their Proverbs: thinking that as the sayings used in a nation mark its character, so the Proverbs of Hell shew the nature of Infernal wisdom better than any description of buildings or garments."[12] Following in short order are the "Proverbs of Hell," two pages of aphorisms that fill me with dread. I understand, when I read these proverbs, that Blake is messing with me, but I don't always know why, and I don't always know how.

For instance, here is the first proverb: "In seed time learn, in harvest teach, in winter enjoy." What makes this proverb hellish? Though didactic, it otherwise seems harmless enough, and I feel my sons may once have owned a picture book on the subject, perhaps one of those tales that feature friendly mice industriously collecting kernels in the autumn and tuning their fiddles by the fireside in the winter.

But Blake doesn't allow me to waste time pondering the harvest proverb; he instantly undercuts it with a second one: "Drive your cart and your plow over the bones of the dead."[13] At this point I stop reading and put my head down on the desk.

I think I never knew what a poem was until my father read Blake to me. I was very young, barely a reader myself. My literary mother, of course, read aloud very often, so I knew a good deal about nursery rhymes. But no one dignified them with the word *poem*. A poem, I now began to gather, was different. It was far graver, far more formal. It should not be read cozily in a lap but was rather like the Bible, requiring a deep voice and special, hushed family attention. The implication was "Sit up straight. You are learning something here."

My father chose first to read "The Lamb" from *Songs of Innocence*.

> Little Lamb who made thee?
> Dost thou know who made thee?
> Gave thee life & bid thee feed
> By the stream and o'er the mead;
> Gave thee clothing of delight,
> Softest clothing wooly bright;
> Gave thee such a tender voice,

> Making all the vales rejoice:
>   Little Lamb who made thee?
>   Dost thou know who made thee?
>
>   Little Lamb I'll tell thee,
>   Little Lamb I'll tell thee:
> He is called by thy name,
> For he calls himself a Lamb:
> He is meek & he is mild,
> He became a little child:
> I a child & thou a lamb,
> We are called by his name.
>   Little Lamb God bless thee.
>   Little Lamb God bless thee.[14]

At the time, of course, I had no idea that this is one of the two Blake poems that most readers ever know. But I did instantly discover that, for a well-loved child, it is a very embarrassing one. My father's seriousness of presentation interacted almost chemically with the verse's sugary diction. It was all too obvious that my father was peering at Blake's lyric through his own caretaker eyeglass and that the tender-voiced, "wooly bright" lamb was a stand-in for my little sister and myself. I may not have been clear about what exactly God-as-lamb was up to in the final stanza, but unquestionably "meek and mild" equaled "little child" equaled "blessed lamb" equaled me.

Like most children, I was perfectly aware that I was not at all meek but a bastion of wickedness. I picked my nose and bit my nails and told lies. I hated cooked carrots and washing my hair. I didn't put away the doll town that was taking over the living room until my father threatened to throw it out, and I told my sister she was fat even though she wasn't. Clearly "The Lamb" had nothing to do with me. What's more, being the granddaughter of farmers, I knew "The Lamb" had nothing to with real lambs, which as a class were loud, muddy, and dimwitted. My father, the farmer's son, also knew about real lambs and presumably about real children too since on most days he found himself yelling at me about something or other.

In short, there was nothing I could call truth in "The Lamb," except for the way in which it revealed my father's vast and painfully abiding love for his daughters. But this was truth in the way a boil in the armpit is truth—a throbbing rawness that no one should be allowed to see. I certainly didn't want any part of this weighted, embarrassing knowledge. I wanted my father to "act regular," by which I meant serene and briskly self-confident. I wanted to walk down the street chattering and swinging from his hand. I did not want to know that he needed me desperately, that he was using his daughters to fill a hole in his heart.

But I begin to think now that the boil's exposure was more Blake's fault than my father's. Even the collection's title, *Songs of Innocence,* is a setup, as if Blake had chosen it for the sole purpose of pasting wool over my father's innocent spectacles. For though he had unaccountably grown up to be a college professor, my father remained, in his clothes, his eating habits, and his comprehension of art, nearly as unsophisticated as the

Presbyterian farm boy he once was. How could he know he wasn't supposed to take "The Lamb" at face value? It appears to be a tender, sentimental, spiritual lyric, childlike in execution and intent. It paints a Sunday-school picture, using Sunday-school language. My father therefore took it to be a Sunday-school poem.

Whether or not he believed that his love for his daughters was equivalently childlike, I cannot say. The poem took the words out of his mouth.

As I sat at my desk this autumn morning trying to figure out "The Lamb," I found myself writing, "I would not call it a lie, but it is, and very deliberately, I think, a manipulation." Yet as soon as I hemmed and hawed my way into that tenuous assertion, I wondered if I might be misreading the situation. Blake, like Robert Frost, chooses to assume an innocuous demeanor, and often enough readers enjoy falling for it. Maybe there's some truth in that persona. Why shouldn't a masked man occasionally be reliable?

Floundering, I turned for advice to Peter Ackroyd's *Blake: A Biography*. And I discovered that, as regards *Songs of Innocence,* Ackroyd and I share a similar suspicion. The poems are not to be trusted.

> These are often poems with an argumentative or satirical intent, and they are emphatically not expressions of lyrical feeling or the spontaneous overflowing of emotion in the conventional "romantic" mode. That is why the *Songs* aspire to be as formal and as impersonal as the folk ballads and nursery rhymes from which Blake borrowed; he could thereby dramatise the spiritual significance, as well as the possible deficiencies, of "Innocence" itself.[15]

Ackroyd is right: there is precious little spontaneous overflow in "The Lamb." It sits primly on its page, as tidily awkward as a paint-by-number. Exhibit 1: fake sheep. Exhibit 2: fake child. Do they naturally lead to Exhibit 3: fake savior? I'm not so sure. For when I reread the second verse, the sentences throw me into confusion. Who is Blake talking about? Who is the child? The infant Jesus? Humankind as the collective child of God? Who is the lamb versus the Lamb? Does the final repeated line, "Little Lamb God bless thee," imply that God is blessing himself? Faced with my questions, the smug little verse coils up around itself, defeating syntactic logic. Somehow, despite the poem's lack of spontaneous overflow, ambiguity manages to rise like floodwater.

Yet I'm surprised, when I recall my docility to instruction, that I didn't resign myself to accepting "The Lamb" as truth. I was a young female accustomed to assuming that her father's opinions were universal: in that regard, I could have stepped out of a Victorian bandbox. My distaste for the poem might have centered on the mealy-mouthed falsity of the characters, but I was also a devotee of fairy tales, which overflow with falsity. It was the emotional fraudulence of the poem that distressed me, but how did I know enough at age six or seven to recognize its presence?

I think I knew because "The Lamb" wasn't the only Blake poem that my father read aloud that evening. He chose also to read that other standby, "The Tyger."

Tyger, Tyger, burning bright,
In the forests of the night:
What immortal hand or eye,
Could frame thy fearful symmetry?

In what distant deeps or skies
Burnt the fire of thine eyes?
On what wings dare he aspire?
What the hand dare seize the fire?

And what shoulder, & what art,
Could twist the sinews of thy heart?
And when thy heart began to beat,
What dread hand? & what dread feet?

What the hammer? What the chain?
In what furnace was thy brain?
What the anvil? what dread grasp,
Dare its deadly terrors clasp?

When the stars threw down their spears
And water'd heaven with their tears:
Did he smile his work to see?
Did he who made the Lamb make thee?

Tyger, Tyger, burning bright,
In the forests of the night:
What immortal hand or eye,
Dare frame thy fearful symmetry?[16]

Since the moment in which I first heard this poem, on that faraway winter evening
under the lamplight, the tyger has glittered behind my eyes, always changing but never
eroding. The poet's tyger is no more a real tiger than the lamb is a real lamb, but my
thoughts never carp at this as they do at the priggish lamb. For the tyger is sensation; he
is seducing and dangerous; he has dragged me into his lair and I will not try to escape . .
. though, in truth, there is no escape. And Blake did not escape either. "Did he who made
the Lamb make thee?" Who can doubt that "The Tyger" is a *Song of Experience* because the
poet capitulated to his own invention?

But why would the tyger's inventor choose to write a poem as cloying as "The Lamb"?

Innocence connotes a milk-white purity; yet it is also inexperience, also naïveté, also
ignorance. If experience tarnishes us, it enriches us as well, not least because it forces us
to confront the fact of our immorality. It may prove that a tyger will indeed tear apart
a lamb, but it also presses us to admit that perhaps we don't care overmuch about the
lamb's bloody fate.

According to Peter Ackroyd, poems such as "The Lamb" allowed Blake "to dramatise
. . . the possible deficiencies" of innocence. And in this particular case, I begin to see
that the poet created his drama by way of a speaking persona who is both parson and
sugar-tongued serpent. Try reading the poem with that voice in your head, and the
malevolence becomes breathtaking. Because now it seems clear that the poem really
doesn't make any sense. One sentence doesn't lead to the next, to the next, to the
next. Merely "The Lamb" is a stack of well-worn phrases and images, a homily designed
to stupefy, not illuminate.

"For he calls himself a Lamb." How easily a poet can employ words as bait; how sleekly
he borrows from his own experience to prey upon a reader's innocence. Such revelation
chills both reader-victim and poet-predator, for what lover of art cares to acknowledge
that she's been gulled? Worse, what bard wants to admit the pleasures of inflicting
damage? And there may be a third party in unwitting collusion: the listener. I was that
listener, unsophisticated in the ways of poets but with a child's alarmed antennae attuned
to any shift in her father's mood. In a voice thick with love, he read aloud "The Lamb,"
but "The Lamb" did not return his love. It stood apart from him, it mocked him, and I
winced. Nearly forty years later, I undergo that identical twinge of guilt, that prick of
serpent knowledge, each time I reread the poem.

Poetry can be a cruel art, and Blake is its most pitiless practitioner. In the "Proverbs of
Hell," he tells me:

> Prisons are built with stones of Law, Brothels with bricks of Religion.
> The pride of the peacock is the glory of God.
> The wrath of the lion is the wisdom of God.
> The nakedness of woman is the work of God.
> Excess of sorrow laughs. Excess of joy weeps.
> The roaring of lions, the howling of wolves, the raging of the stormy sea
> and the destructive sword, are portions of eternity
> too great for the eye of man.
> The fox condemns the trap, not himself.
> Joys impregnate. Sorrows bring forth.[17]

I sit at my desk reading a sheaf of printed words, but all the while Blake the terrible
puppet master jerks the strings. This time he does not allow me the predatory pleasures
of the tyger. I cannot leap into the heavens alongside him, seizing the fire, twisting the
sinews. Again, and yet again, he requires me to document my unveiled ignorance. For
I cannot dredge up anything coherent to say about these proverbs—except that they
frighten me. They seem to exist in order prove that I am a trapped animal, a doomed
beast, a burden of dust, who knows nothing, nothing at all, of death or life, good or evil,
hell or paradise.

"Where man is not nature is barren," Blake declares. Outside my window, a small
wind clatters among the dry leaves and raps against the pane. Tomorrow is my forty-fifth
birthday, and all have I learned about myself is to keep reading. I look down at my book,
and Blake says, "He who has suffered you to impose on him knows you."[18] For a moment

the wind quiets, and now a single car sifts past, tires sighing on the damp tarmac. I don't know what the poet wants from me. But if nothing else, I can be sure he intends no comfort.

Ideas for Writing

In later chapters I will focus more intently on suggestions for writing and revising essays about poetry. For now, I will simply ask: how does Blake's "America: A Prophecy" intersect with your daily life, your confusions, your curiosities, your puzzlements, your angers?

Write a page and see what you discover.

10

John Milton
Paradise Lost, Book 7

I confess that her taste is very uncertain and rather promiscuous. For instance, she likes Whitman and at the same time loves Milton.

—*A. R. Orage*

About the Poet and the Poem

Although John Milton (1608–74) is best known for his epic poem *Paradise Lost,* he was a prolific writer in many different forms and styles. Not only did he compose a great deal of other poetry, including sonnets, Latin epistles, and the masque *Comus,* but he was dangerously active in politics, turning out tracts, satires, and attacks, most of them lambasting the Royalist party and the Church of England. Milton was a staunch Puritan at a time when conservative Protestantism attracted and promoted intellectual rigor. He was enormously well read, and *Paradise Lost* is filled with references to Greek and Roman literature, geography, and the natural and physical sciences.

Milton conceived of *Paradise Lost* as a didactic poem with a specific theological intent: to "justify the ways of God to men."[1] Yet he was equally ambitious as a poet, convinced that his masterpiece would stand alongside the epics of Homer, Virgil, and Dante. Such arrogance is breathtaking, yet in the end he was right. *Paradise Lost* does stand in that inner circle. Enormous, difficult, tiresome, complicated, and relentless, it remains a miracle of thought and risk, of diction and image, of moral complexity and frailty. As Milton's friend Andrew Marvell wrote in "On Mr. Milton's 'Paradise Lost,'"

> Thou sing'st with so much gravity and ease;
> And above human flight dost soar aloft,
> With plume so strong, so equal, and so soft.
> The bird named from that paradise you sing
> So never flags, but always keeps on wing.[2]

This chapter features book 7 of *Paradise Lost,* much of which focuses on the biblical story of creation. Milton's foundation text is Genesis, but he embroiders on the Bible's concise version of the tale, not only manipulating time and narrative but also painting a compelling imaginative portrait of the natural world.

Paradise Lost, Book 7
John Milton

Descend from Heav'n *Urania,* by that name
If rightly thou art call'd, whose Voice divine
Following, above th' *Olympian* Hill I soar,
Above the flight of *Pegasean* wing.
The meaning, not the Name I call: for thou
Nor of the Muses nine, nor on the top
Of old *Olympus* dwell'st, but Heav'nly born,
Before the Hills appear'd, or Fountain flow'd,
Thou with Eternal Wisdom didst converse,
Wisdom thy Sister, and with her didst play
In presence of th' Almighty Father, pleas'd
With thy Celestial Song. Up led by thee
Into the Heav'n of Heav'ns I have presum'd,
An Earthly Guest, and drawn Empyreal Air,
Thy temp'ring; with like safety guided down
Return me to my Native Element:
Lest from this flying Steed unrein'd, (as once
Bellerephon, though from a lower Clime)
Dismounted, on th' *Aleian* Field I fall
Erroneous there to wander and forlorn.
Half yet remains unsung, but narrower bound
Within the visible Diurnal Sphere;
Standing on Earth, not rapt above the Pole,
More safe I Sing with mortal voice, unchang'd
To hoarse or mute, though fall'n on evil days,
On evil days though fall'n, and evil tongues;
In darkness, and with dangers compast round,
And solitude; yet not alone, while thou
Visit'st my slumbers Nightly, or when Morn
Purples the East: still govern thou my Song,
Urania, and fit audience find, though few.
But drive far off the barbarous dissonance
Of *Bacchus* and his Revellers, the Race
Of that wild Rout that tore the *Thracian* Bard
In *Rhodope,* where Woods and Rocks had Ears
To rapture, till the savage clamor drown'd
Both Harp and Voice; nor could the Muse defend
Her Son. So fail not thou, who thee implores:
For thou art Heavn'ly, shee an empty dream.
Say Goddess, what ensu'd when *Raphaël,*
The affable Arch-angel, had forewarn'd
Adam by dire example to beware

Apostasy, by what befell in Heaven
To those Apostates, lest the like befall
In Paradise to *Adam* or his Race,
Charg'd not to touch the interdicted Tree,
If they transgress, and slight that sole command,
So easily obey'd amid the choice
Of all tastes else to please thir appetite,
Though wand'ring. He with his consort *Eve*
The story heard attentive, and was fill'd
With admiration, and deep muse to hear
Of things so high and strange, things to thir thought
So unimaginable as hate in Heav'n,
And War so near the Peace of God in bliss
With such confusion: but the evil soon
Driv'n back redounded as a flood on those
From whom it sprung, impossible to mix
With Blessedness. Whence *Adam* soon repeal'd
The doubts that in his heart arose: and now
Led on, yet sinless, with desire to know
What nearer might concern him, how this World
Of Heav'n and Earth conspicuous first began,
When, and whereof created, for what cause,
What within *Eden* or without was done
Before his memory, as one whose drouth
Yet scarce allay'd still eyes the current stream,
Whose liquid murmur heard new thirst excites,
Proceeded thus to ask his Heav'nly Guest.
    Great things, and full of wonder in our ears,
Far differing from this World, thou hast reveal'd
Divine Interpreter, by favor sent
Down from the Empyrean to forewarn
Us timely of what might else have been our loss,
Unknown, which human knowledge could not reach:
For which to th' infinitely Good we owe
Immortal thanks, and his admonishment
Receive with solemn purpose to observe
Immutably his sovran will, the end
Of what we are. But since thou hast voutsaf't
Gently for our instruction to impart
Things above Earthly thought, which yet concern'd
Our knowing, as to highest wisdom seem'd,
Deign to descend now lower, and relate
What may no less perhaps avail us known,
How first began this Heav'n which we behold
Innumerable, and this which yields or fills

All space, the ambient Air wide interfus'd
Imbracing round this florid Earth, what cause
Mov'd the Creator in his holy Rest
Through all Eternity so late to build
In *Chaos,* and the work begun, how soon
Absolv'd, if unforbid thou mayst unfold
What wee, not to explore the secrets ask
Of his Eternal Empire, but the more
To magnify his works, the more we know.
And the great Light of Day yet wants to run
Much of his Race though steep, suspense in Heav'n
Held by thy voice, thy potent voice he hears,
And longer will delay to hear thee tell
His Generation, and the rising Birth
Of Nature from the unapparent Deep:
Or if the Star of Ev'ning and the Moon
Haste to thy audience, Night with her will bring
Silence, and Sleep list'ning to thee will watch,
Or we can bid his absence, till thy Song
End, and dismiss thee ere the Morning shine.
    Thus *Adam* his illustrious Guest besought:
    And thus the Godlike Angel answer'd mild.
This also thy request with caution askt
Obtain: though to recount Almighty works
What words or tongue of Seraph can suffice,
Or heart of man suffice to comprehend?
Yet what thou canst attain, which best may serve
To glorify the Maker, and infer
Thee also happier, shall not be withheld
Thy hearing, such Commission from above
I have receiv'd, to answer thy desire
Of knowledge within bounds; beyond abstain
To ask, nor let thine own inventions hope
Things not reveal'd, which th' invisible King,
Only Omniscient, hath supprest in Night,
To none communicable in Earth or Heaven:
Anough is left besides to search and know.
But Knowledge is a food, and needs no less
Her Temperance over Appetite, to know
In measure what the mind may well contain,
Oppresses else with Surfeit, and soon turns
Wisdom to Folly, as Nourishment to Wind.
    Know then, that after *Lucifer* from Heav'n
(So call him, brighter once amidst the Host
Of Angels, than that Star the Stars among)

Fell with his flaming Legions through the Deep
Into his place, and the great Son return'd
Victorious with his Saints, th' Omnipotent
Eternal Father from his Throne beheld
Thir multitude, and to his Son thus spake.
　　At least our envious Foe hath fail'd, who thought
All like himself rebellious, by whose aid
This inaccessible high strength, the seat
Of Deity supreme, us dispossest,
He trusted to have seiz'd, and into fraud
Drew many, whom thir place here knows no more;
Yet the far greater part have kept, I see,
Thir station, Heav'n yet populous retains
Number sufficient to possess her Realms
Though wide, and this high Temple to frequent
With Ministeries due and solemn Rites:
But lest his heart exalt him in the harm
Already done, to have dispeopl'd Heav'n,
My damage fondly deem'd, I can repair
That detriment, if such it be to lose
Self-lost, and in a moment will create
Another World, out of one man a Race
Of men innumerable, there to dwell,
Not here, till by degrees of merit rais'd
They open to themselves at length the way
Up hither, under long obedience tri'd,
And Earth be chang'd to Heav'n, and Heav'n to Earth,
One Kingdom, Joy and Union without end.
Meanwhile inhabit lax, ye Powers of Heav'n;
And thou my Word, begotten Son, by thee
This I perform, speak thou, and be it done:
My overshadowing Spirit and might with thee
I send along, ride forth, and bid the Deep
Within appointed bounds be Heav'n and Earth,
Boundless the Deep, because I am who fill
Infinitude, nor vacuous the space
Though I uncircumscrib'd myself retire,
And put not forth my goodness, which is free
To act or not, Necessity and Chance
Approach not mee, and what I will is Fate.
　　So spake th' Almighty, and to what he spake
His Word, the Filial Godhead, gave effect.
Immediate are the Acts of God, more swift
Than time or motion, but to human ears
Cannot without process of speech be told,

So told as earthly notion can receive.
Great triumph and rejoicing was in Heav'n
When such was heard declar'd the Almighty's will;
Glory they sung to the most High, good will
To future men, and in thir dwellings peace:
Glory to him whose just avenging ire
Had driven out th' ungodly from his sight
And th' habitations of the just; to him
Glory and praise, whose wisdom had ordain'd
Good out of evil to create, instead
Of Spirits malign a better Race to bring
Into thir vacant room, and thence diffuse
His good to Worlds and Ages infinite.
So sang the Hierarchies: Meanwhile the Son
On his great Expedition now appear'd
Girt with Omnipotence, with Radiance crown'd
Of Majesty Divine, Sapience and Love
Immense, and all his Father in him shone.
About his Chariot numberless were pour'd
Cherub and Seraph, Potentates and Thrones,
And Virtues, winged Spirits, and Chariots wing'd,
From the Armory of God, where stand of old
Myriads between two brazen Mountains lodg'd
Against a solemn day, harness't at hand,
Celestial Equipage; and now came forth
Spontaneous, for within them Spirit liv'd,
Attendant on thir Lord: Heav'n op'n'd wide
Her ever-during Gates, Harmonious sound
On golden Hinges moving, to let forth
The King of Glory in his powerful Word
And Spirit coming to create new Worlds.
On heav'nly ground they stood, and from the shore
They view'd the vast immeasurable Abyss
Outrageous as a Sea, dark, wasteful, wild,
Up from the bottom turn'd by furious winds
And surging waves, as Mountains to assault
Heav'n's highth, and with the Centre mix the Pole.
    Silence, ye troubl'd waves, and thou Deep, peace,
Said then th' Omnific Word, your discord end:
    Nor stay'd, but on the Wings of Cherubim
Uplifted, in Paternal Glory rode
Far in *Chaos,* and the World unborn;
For *Chaos* heard his voice: him all his Train
Follow'd in bright procession to behold
Creation, and the wonders of his might.

Then stay'd the fervid Wheels, and in his hand
He took the golden Compasses, prepar'd
In God's Eternal store, to circumscribe
This Universe, and all created things:
One foot he centred, and the other turn'd
Round through the vast profundity obscure,
And said, Thus far extend, thus far thy bounds,
This be thy just Circumference, O World.
Thus God the Heav'n created, thus the Earth,
Matter unform'd and void: Darkness profound
Cover'd th' Abyss: but on the wat'ry calm
His brooding wings the Spirit of God outspread,
And vital virtue infus'd, and vital warmth
Throughout the fluid Mass, but downward purg'd
The black tartareous cold Infernal dregs
Adverse to life; then founded, then conglob'd
Like things to like, the rest to several place
Disparted, and between spun out the Air,
And Earth self-balanc't on her Centre hung.
    Let there be Light, said God, and forthwith Light
Ethereal, first of things, quintessence pure
Sprung from the Deep, and from her Native East
To journey through the airy gloom began,
Spher'd in a radiant Cloud, for yet the Sun
Was not; shee in a cloudy Tabernacle
Sojourn'd the while. God saw the Light was good;
And light from darkness by the Hemisphere
Divided: Light the Day, and Darkness night
He nam'd. Thus was the first Day Ev'n and Morn:
Nor pass uncelebrated, nor unsung
By the Celestial Choirs, when Orient Light
Exhaling first from Darkness they beheld;
Birth-day of Heav'n and Earth; with joy and shout
The hollow Universal Orb they fill'd,
And touch'd thir Golden Harps, and hymning prais'd
Both when first Ev'ning was, and when first Morn.
    Again, God said, let there be Firmament
Amid the Waters, and let it divide
The Waters from the Waters: and God made
The Firmament, expanse of liquid, pure,
Transparent, Elemental Air, diffus'd
In circuit to the uttermost convex
Of this great Round: partition firm and sure,
The Waters underneath from those above
Dividing: for as Earth, so hee the World

Built on circumfluous Waters calm, in wide
Crystalline Ocean, and the loud misrule
Of *Chaos* far remov'd, lest fierce extremes
Contiguous might distemper the whole frame:
And Heav'n he nam'd the Firmament: So Ev'n
And Morning *Chorus* sung the second Day.
    The Earth was form'd, but in the Womb as yet
Of Waters, Embryon immature involv'd,
Appear'd not: over all the face of Earth
Main Ocean flow'd, not idle, but with warm
Prolific humor soft'ning all her Globe,
Fermented the great Mother to conceive,
Satiate with genial moisture, when God said,
Be gather'd now ye Waters under Heav'n
Into one place, and let dry Land appear
Emergent, and thir broad bare backs upheave
So high as heav'd the tumid Hills, so low
Down sunk a hollow bottom broad and deep,
Capacious bed of Waters: thither they
Hasted with glad precipitance, uproll'd
As drops on dust conglobing from the dry;
Part rise in crystal Wall, or ridge direct,
For haste; such flight as the great command impress'd
On the swift floods: as Armies at the call
Of Trumpet (for of Armies thou hast heard)
Troop to thir Standard, so the wat'ry throng,
Wave rolling after Wave, where way they found,
If steep, with torrent rapture, if through Plain,
Soft-ebbing; nor withstood them Rock or Hill,
But they, or under ground, or circuit wide
With Serpent error wand'ring, found thir way,
And on the washy Ooze deep Channels wore;
Easy, ere God had bid the ground be dry,
All but within those banks, where Rivers now
Stream, and perpetual draw thir humid train.
The dry Land, Earth, and the great receptacle
Of congregated Waters he call'd Seas:
And saw that it was good, and said, Let th' Earth
Put forth the verdant Grass, Herb yielding Seed,
And Fruit Tree yielding Fruit after her kind;
Whose Seed is in herself upon the Earth.
He scarce had said, when the bare Earth, till then
Desert and bare, unsightly, unadorn'd,
Brought forth the tender Grass, whose verdure clad
Her Universal Face with pleasant green,

Then Herbs of every leaf, that sudden flow'r'd
Op'ning thir various colors, and made gay
Her bosom smelling sweet: and these scarce blown,
Forth flourish'd thick the clust'ring Vine, forth crept
The smelling Gourd, up stood the corny Reed
Embattl'd in her field: and th' humble Shrub,
And Bush with frizzl'd hair implicit: last
Rose as in Dance the stately Trees, and spread
Thir branches hung with copious Fruit: or gemm'd
Thir Blossoms: with high Woods the Hills were crown'd,
With tufts the valleys and each fountain side,
With borders long the Rivers. That Earth now
Seem'd like Heav'n, a seat where Gods might dwell,
Or wander with delight, and love to haunt
Her sacred shades: though God had yet not rain'd
Upon the Earth, and man to till the ground
None was, but from the Earth a dewy Mist
Went up and water'd all the ground, and each
Plant of the field, which ere it was in the Earth
God made, and every Herb, before it grew
On the green stem; God saw that it was good:
So Ev'n and Morn recorded the Third Day.
    Again th' Almighty spake: Let there be Lights
High in th' expanse of Heaven to divide
The Day from Night; and let them be for Signs,
For Seasons, and for Days, and circling Years,
And let them be for Lights as I ordain
Thir Office in the Firmament of Heav'n
To give Light on the Earth; and it was so.
And God maded two great Lights, great for thir use
To Man, the greater to have rule by Day,
The less by Night altern: and made the Stars
And set them in the Firmament of Heav'n
To illuminate the Earth, and rule the Day
In thir vicissitude, and rule the Night,
And Light from Darkness to divide. God saw,
Surveying his great Work, that it was good:
For of Celestial Bodies first the Sun
A mighty Sphere he fram'd, unlightsome first,
Though of Ethereal Mould: then form'd the Moon
Globose, and every magnitude of Stars,
And sow'd with Stars the Heav'n thick as a field:
Of Light by far the greater part he took,
Transplanted from her cloudy Shrine, and plac'd
In the Sun's Orb, made porous to receive

And drink the liquid Light, firm to retain
Her gather'd beams, great Palace now of Light.
Hither as to thir Fountain other Stars
Repairing, in thir gold'n Urns draw Light,
And hence the Morning Planet gilds her horns;
By tincture or reflection they augment
Thir small peculiar, though from human sight
So far remote, with diminution seen.
First in his East the glorious Lamp was seen,
Regent of Day, and all th' Horizon round
Invested with bright Rays, jocund to run
His Longitude through Heav'n's high road: the gray
Dawn, and the *Pleiades* before him danc'd
Shedding sweet influence: less bright the Moon,
But opposite in levell'd West was set
His mirror, with full face borrowing her Light
From him, for other light she needed none
In that aspect, and still that distance keeps
Till night, then in the East her turn she shines,
Revolv'd on Heav'n's great Axle, and her Reign
With thousand lesser Lights dividual holds,
With thousand thousand Stars, that then appear'd
Spangling the Hemisphere: then first adorn'd
With thir bright Luminaries that Set and Rose,
Glad Ev'ning and glad Morn crown'd the fourth day.
    And God said, let the Waters generate
Reptile with Spawn abundant, living Soul:
And let Fowl fly above the Earth, with wings
Display'd on the op'n Firmament of Heav'n.
And God created the great Whales, and each
Soul living, each that crept, which plenteously
The waters generated by thir kinds,
And every Bird of wing after his kind;
And saw that it was good, and bless'd them, saying,
Be fruitful, multiply, and in the Seas
And Lakes and running Streams the waters fill;
And let the Fowl be multipli'd on the Earth.
Forthwith the Sounds and Seas, each Creek and Bay
With Fry innumerable swarm, and Shoals
Of Fish that with thir Fins and shining Scales
Glide under the green Wave, in Sculls that oft
Bank the mid Sea: part single or with mate
Graze the Seaweed thir pasture, and through Groves
Of Coral stray, or sporting with quick glance
Show to the Sun thir wav'd coats dropt with Gold,

Or in thir Pearly shells at ease, attend
Moist nutriment, or under Rocks thir food
In jointed Armor watch: on smooth the Seal,
And bended Dolphins play: part huge of bulk
Wallowing unwieldy, enormous in thir Gait
Tempest the Ocean: there Leviathan
Hugest of living Creatures, on the Deep
Stretcht like a Promontory sleeps or swims,
And seems a moving Land, and at his Gills
Draws in, and at his Trunk spouts out a Sea.
Meanwhile the tepid Caves, and Fens and shores
Thir Brood as numerous hatch, from th' Egg that soon
Bursting with kindly rupture forth disclos'd
Thir callow young, but feather'd soon and fledge
They summ'd thir Pens, and soaring th' air sublime
With clang despis'd the ground, under a cloud
In prospect; there the Eagle and the Stork
On Cliffs and Cedar tops their Eyries build:
Part loosely wing the Region, part more wise
In common, rang'd in figure wedge thir way,
Intelligent of seasons, and set forth
Thir Aery Caravan high over Seas
Flying, and over Lands with mutual wing
Easing thir flight; so steers the prudent Crane
Her annual Voyage, born on Winds; the Air
Floats, as they pass, fann'd with unnumber'd plumes:
From Branch to Branch the smaller Birds with song
Solac'd the Woods, and spread thir painted wings
Till Ev'n, nor then the solemn Nightingale
Ceas'd warbling, but all night tun'd her soft lays:
Others on Silver Lakes and Rivers Bath'd
Thir downy Breast; the Swan with Arched neck
Between her white wings mantling proudly, Rows
Her state with Oary feet: yet oft they quit
The Dank, and rising on stiff Pennons, tow'r
The mid Aereal Sky: Others on ground
Walk'd firm; the crested Cock whose clarion sounds
The silent hours, and th' other whose gay Train
Adorns him, color'd with the Florid hue
Of Rainbows and Starry Eyes. The Waters thus
With Fish replenisht, and the Air with Fowl,
Ev'ning and Morn solemniz'd the Fift day.
    The Sixt, and of Creation last arose
With Ev'ning Harps and Matin, when God said,
Let th' Earth bring forth Soul living in her kind,

Cattle and Creeping things, and Beast of the Earth,
Each in their kind. The Earth obey'd, and straight
Op'ning her fertile Womb teem'd at a Birth
Innumerous living Creatures, perfet forms,
Limb'd and full grown: out of the ground up rose
As from his Lair the wild Beast where he wons
In Forest wild, in Thicket, Brake, or Den;
Among the Trees in Pairs they rose, they walk'd:
The Cattle in the Fields and Meadows green:
Those rare and solitary, these in flocks
Pasturing at once, and in broad Herds upsprung.
The grassy Clods now Calv'd, now half appear'd
The Tawny Lion, pawing to get free
His hinder parts, then springs as broke from Bonds,
And Rampant shakes his Brinded mane; the Ounce,
The Libbard, and the Tiger, as the Mole
Rising, the crumbl'd Earth above them threw
In Hillocks; the swift Stag from under ground
Bore up his branching head: scarce from his mould
Behemoth biggest born of Earth upheav'd
His vastness: Fleec't the Flocks and bleating rose,
As Plants: ambiguous between Sea and Land
The River Horse and scaly Crocodile.
At once came forth whatever creeps the ground,
Insect or Worm; those wav'd thir limber fans
For wings, and smallest Lineaments exact
In all the Liveries deckt of Summer's pride
With spots of Gold and Purple, azure and green:
These as a line thir long dimension drew,
Streaking the ground with sinuous trace; not all
Minims of Nature; some of Serpent kind
Wondrous in length and corpulence involv'd
Thir Snaky folds, and added wings. First crept
The Parsimonious Emmet, provident
Of future, in small room large heart enclos'd,
Pattern of just equality perhaps
Hereafter, join'd in her popular Tribes
Of Commonalty: swarming next appear'd
The Female Bee that feeds her Husband's Drone
Deliciously, and builds her waxen Cells
With Honey stor'd: the rest are numberless,
And thou thir Natures know'st, and gav'st them Names,
Needless to thee repeated; nor unknown
The Serpent, subtl'st Beast of all the field,
Of huge extent sometimes, with brazen Eyes

And hairy Mane terrific, though to thee
Not noxious, but obedient at thy call.
Now Heav'n in all her Glory shone, and roll'd
Her motions, as the great first-Mover's hand
First wheel'd thir course; Earth in her rich attire
Consummate lovely smil'd; Air, Water, Earth,
By Fowl, Fish, Beast, was flown, was swum, was walkt
Frequent; and of the Sixt day yet remain'd;
There wanted yet the Master work, the end
Of all yet done; a Creature who not prone
And Brute as other Creatures, but endu'd
With Sanctity of Reason, might erect
His Stature, and upright with Front serene
Govern the rest, self-knowing, and from thence
Magnanimous to correspond with Heav'n,
But grateful to acknowledge whence his good
Descends, thither with heart and voice and eyes
Directed in Devotion, to adore
And worship God Supreme who made him chief
Of all his works: therefore th' Omnipotent
Eternal Father (For where is not hee
Present) thus to his Son audibly spake.
   Let us make now Man in our image, Man
In our similitude, and let them rule
Over the Fish and Fowl or Sea and Air,
Beast of the Field, and over all the Earth,
And every creeping thing that creeps the ground.
This said, he form'd thee, *Adam,* thee O Man
Dust of the ground, and in thy own Image hee
Created thee, in the Image of God
Express, and thou becam'st a living Soul.
Male he created thee, but thy consort
Female for Race; then bless'd Mankind, and said,
Be fruitful, multiply, and fill the Earth,
Subdue it, and throughout Dominion hold
Over Fish of the Sea, and Fowl of the Air,
And every living thing that moves on the Earth.
Wherever thus created, for no place
Is yet distinct by name, thence, as thou know'st
He brought thee into this delicious Grove,
This Garden, planted with the Trees of God,
Delectable both to behold and taste;
And freely all thir pleasant fruit for food
Gave thee, all sorts are here that all th' Earth yields,
Variety without end; but of the Tree

Which taste works knowledge of Good and Evil,
Thou may'st not; in the day thou eat'st, thou di'st;
Death is the penalty impos'd, beware,
And govern well thy appetite, lest sin
Surprise thee, and her black attendant Death.
Here finish'd hee, and all that he had made
View'd, and behold all was entirely good;
So Ev'n and Morn accomplish'd the Sixt day:
Yet not till the Creator from his work,
Desisting, though unwearied, up return'd
Up to the Heav'n of Heav'ns his high abode,
Thence to behold this new Empire, how it show'd
In prospect from his Throne, how good, how fair,
Answering his great Idea. Up he rode
Follow'd with acclamation and the sound
Symphonious of ten thousand Harps that tun'd
Angelic harmonies: the Earth, the Air
Resounded, (thou remember'st, for thou heard'st)
The Heav'ns and all the Constellations rung,
The Planets in thir station list'ning stood,
While the bright Pomp ascended jubilant.
Open, ye everlasting Gates, they sung,
Open, ye Heav'ns, your living doors; let in
The great Creator from his work return'd
Magnificent, his Six days' work, a World;
Open, and henceforth oft; for God will deign
To visit oft the dwellings of just Men
Delighted, and with frequent intercourse
Thither will send his winged Messengers
On errands of supernal Grace. So sung
The glorious Train ascending: He through Heav'n,
That open'd wide her blazing Portals, led
To God's Eternal house direct the way,
A broad and ample road, whose dust is Gold
And pavement Stars, as Stars to thee appear,
Seen in the Galaxy, that Milky way
Which nightly as a circling Zone thou seest
Powder'd with Stars. And now on Earth the Seventh
Ev'ning arose in *Eden,* for the Sun
Was set, and twilight from the East came on,
Forerunning Night; when at the holy mount
Of Heav'n's high-seated top, th' Imperial Throne
Of Godhead, fixt for ever firm and sure,
The Filial Power arriv'd, and sat him down
With his great Father, for he also went

Invisible, yet stay'd (such privilege
Hath Omnipresence) and the work ordain'd,
Author and end of all things, and from work
Now resting, bless'd and hallow'd the Sev'nth day,
As resting on that day from all his work,
But not in silence holy kept; the Harp
Had work and rested not, the solemn Pipe,
And Dulcimer, all Organs of sweet stop,
All sounds on Fret by String or Golden Wire
Temper'd soft Tunings, intermixt with Voice
Choral or Unison; of incense Clouds
Fuming from Golden Censers hid the Mount.
Creation and the Six days' acts they sung:
Great are thy works, *Jehovah,* infinite
Thy power; what thought can measure thee or tongue
Relate thee; greater now in thy return
Than from the Giant Angels; thee that day
Thy Thunders magnifi'd; but to create
Is greater than created to destroy.
Who can impair thee, mighty King, or bound
Thy Empire? easily the proud attempt
Of Spirits apostate and thir Counsels vain
Thou hast repell'd, while impiously they thought
Thee to diminish, and from thee withdraw
The number of thy worshippers. Who seeks
To lessen thee, against his purpose serves
To manifest the more thy might: his evil
Thou usest, and from thence creat'st more good.
Witness this new-made World, another Heav'n
From Heaven Gate not far, founded in view
On the clear *Hyaline,* the Glassy Sea;
Of amplitude almost immense, with Stars
Numerous, and every Star perhaps a World
Of destin'd habitation; but thou know'st
Thir seasons: among these the seat of men,
Earth with her nether Ocean circumfus'd,
Thir pleasant dwelling-place. Thrice happy men,
And sons of men, whom God hath thus advanc't,
Created in his Image, there to dwell
And worship him, and in reward to rule
Over his Works, on Earth, in Sea, or Air,
And multiply a Race of Worshippers
Holy and just: thrice happy if they know
Thir happiness, and persevere upright.
  So sung they, and the Empyrean rung,

With *Halleluiahs:* Thus was Sabbath kept.
And thy request think now fulfill'd, that ask'd
How first this World and face of things began,
And what before thy memory was done
From the beginning, that posterity
Inform'd by thee might know; if else thou seek'st
Aught, not surpassing human measure, say.

Two Chapters from *Tracing Paradise: Two Years in Harmony with John Milton*

"Every poem can be considered in two ways—as what the poet has to say, and as a *thing* which he *makes*. From the one point of view it is an expression of opinions and emotions; from the other, it is an organization of words which exist to produce a particular kind of patterned experience in the readers."[3]

   C. S. Lewis was the author of those sentences, and he happened to include them in a book he wrote about John Milton's epic poem *Paradise Lost*. I like his remark and am pleased to have discovered it. But even though I, too, have published a book about *Paradise Lost*, I didn't come across Lewis's book until last week. In fact, I had no idea he'd ever written about the poem.

   Many, many people have written about *Paradise Lost,* and I am probably the most ignorant of the bunch. I have read almost no Milton scholarship. You might wonder how I had the gall to write a book about *Paradise Lost* without paying any attention to what the experts had to say about it. But my purposeful avoidance wasn't an offshoot of either laziness or arrogance. Rather, it was a way to circumvent my tongue-tied humility.

   How does a not very religious American woman who lives in the woods and writes poems talk to a seventeenth-century urban Puritan firebrand and canonized epic poet? My initial reaction was to avoid talking to him at all. I had never really liked *Paradise Lost,* and I had no confidence in my ability to interact with it. Yet at the same time I was in need of a challenge. I wanted to expand myself as a poet. I wanted to learn from difficult work, from poems that made me uncomfortable, even angry.

   Timidly I decided to copy out a few pages of the poem. As I discuss in the introduction to this book, copying out poems is the best way I know to get inside the head of another poet, to undergo word for word, comma by comma, what the poet experienced as he worked on the poem. But in this case my little copying experiment snowballed, and I ended up transcribing every single word of *Paradise Lost*. In the afterword of my memoir of that project, I talk about the strange, absorbing, unexpected task:

> In early December 2007 I finished copying out the final lines of *Paradise Lost*. Accomplishing the job had occupied me for more than two years. Some weeks I copied out page after page. Some weeks I managed only a few lines. Some hours my fingers chased each other fluidly over the keyboard like Rogers and Astaire sparkling in easy tandem across a spotlit stage. Some hours I mangled every word, stuttering through typos and flawed punctuation, misunderstood verbs and unanticipated line breaks—an epic chore narrowed to "backspace and try again, backspace and try again."
>
>   Copying was a hard job, and not just because typing is dull and Milton is a mountain. Living with myself as copyist was equivalently hard. When I undertook the task, I thought of myself as a poet, not a memoirist. But I was anxious about my worth as a poet: I needed to do something important, something improving. Transcribing Milton's masterpiece seemed to be a quick solution and a weighty preoccupation, yet I couldn't define why it might be improving or important. Even though I saw the job as special, even glamorous, I couldn't take myself seriously. That I may have been the only person on the

planet who imagined copying out all of *Paradise Lost* to be glamorous increased both my absurdity and my conceit. And once I began to write about the project, my sense of inadequacy grew. As hard as I pressed myself intellectually, I could not, in the end, truly understand *Paradise Lost*. The poem was too large for me.[+]

Although I say "the poem was too large for me," I don't mean that I gained nothing from the experience. The most important lesson was how vital it can be to build an unmediated relationship with a work of art. My discoveries about *Paradise Lost* may have been pedestrian, but they were *my* discoveries. I had only myself to depend on as I made my way through this immense and thorny poem. The undertaking was vast and daunting, but I learned to think, to question, to argue, to weigh my opinions, to change my mind.

There are times when research and scholarly analysis are necessary ingredients of art and the study of art. But there are also times when the exercise of one's own mind is the stimulant. In each chapter of my memoir, I wrote about *Paradise Lost* as it intersected with my life on that particular day, at that particular moment. Thus, the chapters are very different.

I've chosen two of them to include in this book. The first, "Celestial Song," deals specifically with the language of the poem's book 7, which you have just read. The second, "Killing Ruthie," applies *Paradise Lost* to a fraught moment in my non-reading life, when I had to take responsibility for the killing of an animal.

Celestial Song

Forth flourish'd thick the clust'ring Vine, forth crept
The smelling Gourd, up stood the corny Reed
Embattl'd in her field: and the humble Shrub,
And Bush with frizzl'd hair implicit.

After spending roughly two years copying out *Paradise Lost* word for word, I am now far less sure about what constitutes a good line of poetry than I was before I started the project. Why is a certain conglomeration of words termed beautiful or ugly, silly or satirical, dull or impassioned? How do preconceptions about the aesthetics of language and what constitutes an acceptable style of expression influence my judgment?

As designated great art, *Paradise Lost* has received canonical tenure; it's been promoted to a mahogany case in a locked upstairs room. Criticism of the poem no longer involves crowing or complaint but has graduated to scholarly weightlifting. It's hard to remember that the poem may have existed in a present-tense world of muddled praise and jealousy and ignorance. It's hard to conceive that it ever had a plain, undemanding, ignorant new reader, a middle-aged man, perhaps, who opened the book by accident as he sat warming his feet by his cousin's fire, thoughtlessly picking up the epic lying next to him on the settle as I might pick up some *New York Times* bestseller left on a dentist's magazine table: twiddling it between my hands, examining the cover, randomly cracking it open at page 63, and dipping into unexpected waters.

Paradise Lost has no such readers today. High school teachers may assign a section or so to bewildered or uninterested college-prep students, and doctoral candidates may see it as relevant fodder for a dissertation or a journal article. An optimistic bookworm might tackle a few pages in hopes of assuaging some indefinite yearning for knowledge. But who finds it spread-eagled on a dentist's magazine table or bookmarked with a towel next to a public swimming pool? Though it once lived a physical life, the poem as an object has no free commerce with our daily world.

Because interactions with *Paradise Lost* have been reduced to either the rarefied commentary of specialized readers or slack-jawed student indifference, I find it difficult to trust my judgment of the work as a construction or my motives for liking or disliking it. I can respond like a high school sophomore, distilling my distrust of strangeness and complexity into eye rolling or "Yuck." I can retreat to an easy cosmopolitan cynicism, in which ridicule masquerades as world-weary cleverness ("The Epic Treadmill, or Famous Bores in History"). Like *Middlemarch*'s Mr. Casaubon, I can burrow away at obscure references and mythological minutiae, peering through my dusty microscope at "*Eden over Pontus, and the Pool / Maeotis,* up beyond the River *Ob.*" Like a half-baked literary evangelist, I can extol the poem's cosmic scope, its magnificent characterization of evil, of Satan "full of anguish driv'n," "bent / on Man's destruction, maugre what might hap / Of heavier on himself." But can I ask, "Is this line good? Is it bad? Is there a difference? Does it matter?"

There's the shyness I feel as an inferior artist, of course. For there's no question that *Paradise Lost* is a miracle, a shape-shifting behemoth, a universe; and like Adam before his maker, I'm overwhelmed by Milton, who "Surpassest far my naming":

How may I
Adore thee, Author of this Universe,
And all this good to man, for whose well being
So amply, and with hands so liberal
Thou hast provided all things.

But his epic is also littered with what contemporary poetry has coached me to believe
are verbal infelicities, including clunky repetitions ("And every creeping thing that
creeps the ground"), lack of variation (such as two lines in a row starting with "Or"),
ridiculous syntax ("*Adam,* from whose dear side I boast me sprung"), as well as numbers of
inadvertently comic descriptors ("Bush with frizzl'd hair implicit").

It may be counterintuitive, given Milton's reputation for stately grandeur and
labyrinthine syntax, to call these constructions unself-conscious; yet their clumsiness in
the midst of pomp strikes me as peculiarly innocent. "Forth crept / The smelling Gourd,
up stood the corny Reed": what could be sillier; what sweeter? Innocence is not a word
generally associated with Milton, yet how else can I account for such rambunctious verbal
sloppiness? It has the purity of youth, reckless as an elbowed glass of milk. And it charms
me. For in a poem the size of *Paradise Lost,* how could the poet avoid those moments
of tumbling invention, when words careened onto the page like screeching monkeys? I
picture him bouncing up from his chair and waving his arms around, while his secretary-
daughter hunches down on her stool in hopes of not getting slapped.

Milton's language is particularly impulsive in his long explanations of scientific wonders
and natural history, as in book 7, when he takes us through the six days of creation. Here
he describes the first birds hatched on earth (and apparently the egg came before the
chicken):

Meanwhile the tepid Caves, and Fens and shores
Thir Brood as numerous hatch, from th' Egg that soon
Bursting with kindly rupture forth disclos'd
Thir callow young.

I haven't forgotten the shifting inexactitudes of language. In the poet's time "callow
young" very likely connoted something substantially different from "pimple-faced kid."
But what about "bursting with kindly rupture"? Was that line ever not funny? What
possibly could have possessed Milton to pair "kindly" and "rupture"? The effect is jarring
and slapstick, with an aura of accident, as if he'd been playing with poetry magnets.

I suppose humor depends, to a large degree, on one's expectations of a work; and
it doesn't seem likely that anyone has ever expected a good laugh from a Bible-sized
poem about humanity's fall from divine grace. Milton himself certainly had somber
expectations: in the lugubrious opening lines of book 1, he glowers at his reader like a
dyspeptic schoolmaster, ready to smack the first giggler with a yardstick as he invokes
God's "aid to [his] advent'rous Song,"

That with no middle flight intends to soar
Above th' *Aonian* Mount, while it pursues
Things unattempted yet in Prose or Rhyme.

And the dense, portentous tone of much of *Paradise Lost*—"Those Notes to Tragic," as Milton terms his moody, heavy style—is enough to make most readers collapse into word coma, where every subject seems to be identically important and all the details of sound and language melt, "with long and tedious havoc," into a waste of gluey orange cheese sauce.

Yet even in word coma, how can you overlook this scene? Who knew that the first mammals exploded out of Eden's virgin soil like landmines?

The grassy Clods now Calv'd, now half appear'd
The Tawny Lion, pawing to get free
His hinder parts, then springs as broke from Bonds,
And Rampant shakes his Brinded mane; the Ounce,
The Libbard, and the Tiger, as the Mole
Rising, the crumbl'd Earth above them threw
In Hillocks; the swift Stag from under ground
Bore up his branching head; scarce from his mould
Behemoth biggest born of Earth upheav'd
His vastness: Fleec't the Flocks and bleating rose,
As Plants.

Nevertheless, I sometimes think I'm the only person in history who's evei laughed at *Paradise Lost*. In fact, I sometimes think I'm the only person in the world who's ever read it. Neither of these assertions is true, of course. Yet copying out the entire enormous, endless, complicated poem is a lonely task partly because living in Milton's mind is a lonely task. I ask myself, "Didn't he crack even a tiny smile after intoning 'The grassy Clods now Calv'd'?" And I think he didn't. I think he had no idea that any part of this scene was funny—not the "Tawny Lion" with his "hinder parts" stuck in the dirt, not the crowd of noisy woolly sheep sprouting "as Plants." Part of my tenderness toward the man arises from his solemn ignorance of the trivial powers of his tools: he oozed classical scholarship, forged an epic to rival Homer's, and in Satan created one of the greatest characters in literature. But he didn't comprehend that "the Tiger, as the Mole / Rising" deflates the tiger's nobility faster than a thumbtack on a queen's throne.

Of course, Milton isn't the only painfully serious poet in history. Virgil's *Aeneid* doesn't angle for laughter. Neither do *Beowulf* or the Bible, for that matter. By and large, the authors of epics are humorless. If comedy intrudes, it arrives accidentally and sometimes embarrassingly in snatches of "unpremeditated Verse." When we laugh at passages in *Great Expectations* and *Ulysses* and *Tristram Shandy*, we're fully aware that the writers expect us to laugh. There's nothing unpremeditated about the humor in *The Rape of the Lock*. But Milton doesn't expect me to laugh at him. He would be mortified, and also angry, to learn that some insouciant New World female had poked fun at his version of the sixth day of creation. So if I occasionally find myself imagining I've founded a Milton cult-of-one, I recognize, too, that I'm not so much an acolyte as a fond yet constantly exasperated daughter-in-law. That imagined familial bond loosens the reins of scholarship and respect: I can laugh at the poet but love him regardless. Yet I do so at the risk of offending his reputation, his earned greatness, his intentions. It is no small crime to belittle a life's work.

Thus, what I feel when faced with a clutch of young birds, who "soaring th' air sublime / With clang despis'd the ground," is a complicated admixture of amusement at the inappropriate "clang"; embarrassment for the poet, blithely dead to the issue for all these years; and shame at having been sidetracked from honoring a great poet to sneering at a single ugly word. This seems, on one level, considerable overreaction to "clang." Yet I think my squirmy doubts illustrate the way in which contemporary experts—critics, teachers, ambitious practitioners—tend to critique a poem as a conglomeration of aesthetic parts rather than a striving, searching, living, ambiguous whole. I don't say that a beetle-browed focus on minute aspects of rhythm or language is wrong. But art is great not because it is perfect but because it can override its own blunders; and in Milton's case the sheer torrent of words was the poem's propulsion, as if "clang" were a necessary station-stop en route to the sublime. For the lines continue:

> There the Eagle and the Stork
> On Cliffs and Cedar tops thir Eyries build:
> Part loosely wing the Region, part more wise
> In common, rang'd in figure wedge thir way,
> Intelligent of seasons, and set forth
> Thir Aery Caravan high over Seas
> Flying, and over Lands with mutual wing
> Easing thir flight; so steers the prudent Crane
> Her annual Voyage, borne on Winds; the Air
> Floats, as they pass, fann'd with unnumber'd plumes.

This glorious evocation of migration is itself akin to a flock of birds: the words join and take wing; "the Air / Floats as they pass, fann'd with unnumber'd plumes"; each syllable leaps unerringly into a pattern of sound that is also a pattern of sight and of meaning. If Milton had stopped to fuss over "clang," would he have maintained enough momentum to create such beauty?

The momentum of poetry is not something I hear much about, nor do I especially note it in the poems I come across in journals or classrooms, except insofar as it affects the basic structural klutziness of all new writers. The bonded momentum of sound, image, shape, and tale that so infects Coleridge's and Shakespeare's and Whitman's best work is not a modern poetic construct, partly because it requires a poet to ride out a riff that invites accident and error. Ginsberg aspired to such poetry and occasionally touched the hem of its garment; but like so many Whitman imitators, he was diverted into careless bluster rather than carried aloft by the rushing-river experience of writing as the concrete enactment of thought and emotion. Technically conscientious poets—those whom we might have expected to model themselves on Milton or Shakespeare or Coleridge—have in large part retreated to anxiety and bloodless perfectionism, where every word counts but no one knows exactly what it counts for.

There's a fine line between linguistic precision and fear of discovery, and a predilection for haiku or Williams-style compression may have little to do with verbal economy. Who invented that "less is more" catchphrase anyway? Not John Milton. And why do so many writers take it to heart? A lack of ambition or inspiration; the allure of aphoristic tidiness; boredom or dead ends or distraction or exhaustion. . . . Whatever the reason, under the guise of economy, too many poems ax the quest of poetry: to surprise ourselves into saying what we didn't know we knew. Verbal economy doesn't mean using the fewest words possible. It means writing everything you need to write as well as you can write it. This doesn't require honed perfection but relentless attention, and by that definition Milton was the most economical of writers. By sheer will and perseverance, he "calculate[d] the Stars, how they will wield / The mighty frame, how build, unbuild, contrive."

But as he himself noted,

> The skill of Artifice or Office mean,
> Not that which justly gives Heroic name
> To Person or to Poem. Mee of these
> Nor skill'd nor studious, higher Argument
> Remains, sufficient of itself to raise
> That name.

Milton's greatness relies on more than economy; for as a technician, he pushed poetry beyond beauty or storytelling into an active revelation of thought, with all its twists and turns and backsliding and discoveries.

Consider this passage, when Satan in the guise of a toad perverts Eve's innocent dreams,

> Assaying by his Devilish art to reach
> The Organs of her Fancy, and with them forge
> Illusions as he list, Phantasms and Dreams,
> Or if, inspiring venom, he might taint
> Th' animal spirits that from pure blood arise
> Like gentle breaths from Rivers pure, thence raise
> At least distemper'd, discontented thoughts,
> Vain hopes, vain aims, inordinate desires
> Blown up with high conceits ingend'ring pride.

Workshopped, the passage would suffer. "Pure blood" followed by "Rivers pure" may be a small matter, but some classroom complainer would surely point out that the repetition doesn't carry the rhythmic and sonic weight of "vain hopes, vain aims." Still, heaviest criticism would fall, I think, on Milton's easy deployment of undefined abstractions: those "discontented thoughts," those "high conceits ingend'ring pride."

Because I love this passage, I'm inclined to embrace these lines with a full heart and toss piddly infelicities to the wind. But I did notice "pure Blood" followed by "rivers Pure," and

I did question it. So does that make me a pedant? Or does it make me a philistine?
"Examples! examples!" we are taught. "Keep poetry in the world!" And so we should.
Yet there are worlds and there are worlds, and this is the land of "Phantasms and Dreams,"
where abstraction rules, where "inordinate desires" are as weighty and illusory as Satan's
coaxing voice. The passage reveals the "Organs of [Eve's] Fancy" with marvelous accuracy
because the poet relaxes into his language, ignores its fussy instructions, allows it to lift
him up, like water or air, and carry him on a ripple of syntax and image and adjective-
noun dreaminess into Eve's vulnerable sleeping brain.

At the beginning of book 7, Milton himself steps up from the shadows and sings a brief
bardic lay about his frustrations and desires as a poet. It's an odd digression, unexpected,
appearing in the middle of the poem, even in the middle of a conversation; and by the
time I realize this is Milton talking, he's already directed me to Raphael and Adam and the
story of creation. He addresses his lay to Urania, the Greek muse of astronomy, though he
calls on "the meaning, not the Name," instead reinventing her as "Heav'nly born," who

> Thou with Eternal Wisdom didst converse,
> Wisdom thy Sister, and with her didst play
> In presence of th' Almighty Father, pleas'd
> With thy Celestial Song.

A woman as representative of eternal wisdom? This is shocking enough, considering
Milton's crabby animadversions to Eve's powers of intellect. ("Not capable her ear / Of
what was high," and she'd rather prune her "Fruits and Flow'rs" than sit around listening
to Adam gab with the angels.) But Milton goes so far as to plead with this female, and
what he pleads for is the gift of pedestrian poetry:

> Up led by thee
> Into the Heav'n of Heav'ns I have presum'd,
> An Earthly Guest, and drawn Empyreal Air,
> Thy temp'ring; with like safety guided down
> Return me to my Native Element:
> Lest from this flying Steed unrein'd, (as once
> *Bellerephon,* though from a lower Clime)
> Dismounted, on th' Aleian Field I fall
> Erroneous there to wander and forlorn.

It's as if Milton, for all his self-confidence, has found himself forced to admit that
the sublime is not, after all, his natural element. "More safe I Sing with mortal voice,"
he tells the muse, though being Milton, he can't resist decorating his humility with a
trumpet blast. His voice may be mortal, but it's "unchang'd / To hoarse or mute." Don't
expect false modesty from a shaman, and who do you think taught Whitman how to sing?
Nevertheless, Milton does acknowledge that his talents are earthbound. Moreover, he's
not sorry about it. He may grumble and complain and demand a better crowd of admirers

("still govern thou my Song / *Urania,* and fit audience find, though few. / But drive far off the barbarous dissonance / Of *Bacchus* and his Revellers"), yet he begs her not to fail him "who thee implores."

Why did a return to everyday verse matter so much to the poet? And why did he decide this transitory invocation was important to include in the poem? As a segue between Raphael's story of heaven and his story of earthly creation, the passage allows Milton to brazenly position himself between heaven and earth. Yet he's homesick for earth; he's afraid of heaven; he's pleading to leave. He may be a Christian apologist in theme, but in poetic temperament he's a man, consumed with curiosity about geography and naked women and the composition of brimstone. And it's here—in his inquisitive, questing, flexible line; the foolish words that trip off his tongue; his eager adventuring into his own mind—that I discover some modicum of comfort. For I have a right to laugh at or linger over a poet who would rather be an ignorant artist than an angel. Ignorance may be the opposite of knowledge, but it's also innocence. What joy it must have been to know nothing, all the while unfurling *Paradise Lost,* that trove of nothing, from the shadows of his brain.

Killing Ruthie

Forth issuing on a Summer's Morn to breathe
Among the pleasant Villages and Farms
Adjoin'd, from each thing met conceives delight,
The smell of Grain, or tedded Grass, or Kine,
Or Dairy, each rural sight, each rural sound.

I asked my friend Steve to shoot my goat.

Steve is what his wife calls "a born-again redneck." His parents are genteel, well-educated, violin-playing Quakers, but Steve decided not to graduate from high school. He preferred to educate himself, and now he knows what ants taste like ("fruity") and how to turn raccoons into a couch blanket. Steve is a man who can efficiently pull a trigger but won't scorn you if you cry. Among men who handle guns, this is not a common trait.

He said he could shoot my goat on Sunday morning, though he wasn't in the mood to get tied up with butchering.

I said I would dig a hole.

My goat's name was Ruthie, a black and white American Alpine, eleven years old. She'd had breathing problems, an off-and-on panting snuffle, for six months or so. I called the vet, who said parasites might be migrating into her lungs. After I dosed her with wormer, she seemed maybe a little better, maybe the same. She ate as much as a Clydesdale, but she was thin and her hair was sloughing off in handfuls.

Eventually the vet dropped by and listened to the snuffle. Ruthie gobbled grain and snorted and bulged her eyes zestfully. The vet, muscle-bound and taciturn, said eleven was fairly old for a goat. She said maybe it was allergies but most likely not. The word *cancer* was not uttered. Sunlight seeped through the barn's grimy windows, flickered among the hanks of ancient spider webs dangling from the rafters. The barn smelled of dust and last summer's hay, vaguely of manure, more richly of repose, as a room in a house can smell of sleep.

Ruth licked the last grain flecks out of her plastic dish, tossed it upside down and rapped it with a black hoof, then snuffled and lurched onto my son's bare foot. He yelped. "Wear boots," I said to him.

"Prepare yourself," said the vet.

The moments before a catastrophe seem always, in retrospect, to be a fraught and melancholy prelude, a "Proem tun'd." But when a participant has contrived that portending disaster, the crowd's interactive ignorance may assume a formal and symbolic innocence, a point that Wisława Szymborska elucidates in her poem "The Terrorist, He's Watching." Her terrorist's omniscient eye stylizes the clueless actions of the bystanders, flattening them into a dancelike pattern that incorporates as well the man's own murderous intent.[5]

In *Paradise Lost,* the relationship between Satan and Eve has a similar stylized inevitability; and Satan, that elegant Nabokovian villain, expends considerable thought on the trembling pleasures and pangs of anticipated evil. Connoisseur that he is, he enjoys skating along the fragile icy crust between right and wrong; he looks forward to soiling

Eve's perfection even as he admires its beauty. He goes so far as to allow "her graceful Innocence" to disarm him—temporarily:

> Her every Air
> Of gesture or least action overaw'd
> His Malice, and with rapine sweet bereav'd
> His fierceness of the fierce intent it brought:
> That space the Evil one abstracted stood
> From his own evil, and for the time remain'd
> Stupidly good, or enmity disarm'd,
> Of guile, of hate, of envy, of revenge.

When one chooses to murder an animal, there is, in the hours and minutes preceding the act, a similar hiatus. On Sunday morning I was "stupidly good," weighed down by my bad intentions as well as by a calm patient kindness, both of them nailed to my conscience like Soviet posters on a plank fence. I considered the permutations of my wickedness and admired the shiny barrel of its gun. My conscience commented conversationally, "If you weren't going to Brooklyn in a week, you wouldn't dream of executing this goat today. It's a matter of convenience."

I replied, "No doubt she's suffering terrible pain," and sighed.

The artistic imagination—in this case, the simultaneous ability to experience grief and aesthetically reconfigure it—is both a marvelous distraction and a guilty torment, and one of Milton's great triumphs in his delineation of Satan is the way in which he guides the reader through the Fiend's coiling artistic intellect. In the final moments before Satan, in serpent guise, accosts Eve and cajoles her into betraying God's word and eating from the Tree of Knowledge, he meditates on his mind's vivid powers, the way in which his intellect detaches itself from the event and examines it clinically, aesthetically, with a ruthless clarity.

> Thoughts, whither have ye led me, with what sweet
> Compulsion thus transported to forget
> What hither brought us, hate, not love, nor hope
> Of Paradise for Hell, hope here to taste
> Of pleasure, but all pleasure to destroy,
> Save what is in destroying, other joy
> To me is lost.

He's not entirely happy with himself, certainly. Satan would prefer to be a single-minded villain, as God, "the Father infinite," is a single-minded king. Yet he recognizes his double bind: humans, "though of terrestrial mould," are, like gods, still exempt from suffering. The Fiend, a fallen angel, is not, "so much hath Hell debas'd, and pain / Infeebl'd me, to what I was in Heav'n." Evil he is, yet pitiable; for guile, "under show of Love well feign'd," distracts the deceiver from self-excoriation, doubt, and guilt. He tells Eve:

> The Gods are first, and that advantage use

On our belief, that all from them proceeds;
I question it, for this fair Earth I see,
Warm'd by the Sun, producing every kind,
Them nothing: If they all things, who enclos'd
Knowledge of Good and Evil in this Tree,
That so eats thereof, forthwith attains
Wisdom without their leave? and wherein lies
Th' offense, that Man should thus attain to know?
What can your knowledge hurt him, or this Tree
Impart against his will if all be his?
Or is it envy, and can envy dwell
In heav'nly breasts?

His questions are both honest and false. He may be asking them in order to delude his listener; but he's also a sufferer, and one who has no answers.

Before you kill a goat, you have to dig a grave, preferably close to the murder site so you don't have to drag the body too far. A full-grown dairy goat weighs as much as an average woman—Eve, for instance—but the grave can't be human-shaped. You need a square hole to accommodate those four skinny legs.

I fetched a spade from the chicken house and began scratching at likely patches of earth near the barn. Hand-digging a goat-sized hole in a New England forest is not a simple matter, and my choice of location was limited. In addition to harboring a tangle of spruce and pine roots, many as thick as my arm, the soil on the boundary of our clearing is dense with rock: wedges of slate, granite boulders, chunks of dirty luminous quartz. It's nigh on impossible to imagine a farmer plowing this ground, though once he did. He would weep to see it now, my rocky wilderness. Like scrub poplar and wild raspberries, stone reclaims.

The morning threatened storm. A silver fog hung over the trellised pea vines, heavy with rainwater and swelling fruit. The vines sagged like wet towels into the garden paths. On her side of the barnyard fence Ruthie snorted and coughed, lifting a foot now and then to shake off a fly as I scratched an estimated tomb pattern on the weedy verge. She wasn't exactly watching me. More, her presence radiated that combined interest-disinterest of familiars long penned up in the same garden. Affection is not the point in such cases. Trust stems from custom: you are always here; I am always here.

It is precisely this humdrum contiguity, this ordinary elbow rubbing, that Satan manipulates in his initial encounter with Eve. If he had appeared in all his Fiendish glory, brandishing his fiery trident, she would never have succumbed to his wiles. Instead,

                         With tract oblique
At first, as one who sought access, but fear'd
To interrupt, side-long, he works his way.
As when a Ship by skilful Steersman wrought
Nigh River's mouth or Foreland, where the Wind
Veers oft, as oft so steers, and shifts her Sail;

So varied hee, and of his tortuous Train
Curl'd many a wanton wreath in sight of *Eve*,
To lure her Eye; shee busied heard the sound
Of rustling Leaves, but minded not, as us'd
To such disport before her through the Field,
From every Beast, more duteous at her call,
Than at Circean call the Herd disguis'd.

Milton's allusion to Circe and her magicked swine is curious. Proper sex roles are always important matters to this poet, so aligning the tricksters Circe and Satan against Odysseus' enchanted seamen and "amaz'd unwary" Eve is a notable inversion. Yet even as he toys with this mythological parallel, he resists the comparison: it's Eve whose "Circean call" controls "the Herd disguis'd"; it's the "duteous" Fiend who "disport[s] before her through the Field." Guile and innocence flow and shift and mutate as the characters play out their fateful game.

His gentle dumb expression turn'd at length
The Eye of *Eve* to mark his play; he glad
Of her attention gain'd, with Serpent Tongue
Organic, or impulse of vocal Air,
His fraudulent temptation thus began.

Satan chooses, of course, that depressingly effective device, feminine temptation. Accustomed as she is to being Adam's obedient, not-too-bright helpmeet, Eve is encouraged to reimagine herself as "sole Wonder," "Beauty's heav'nly Ray," "Sov'ran of Creatures, universal Dame." "So gloz'd the Tempter," praising her "Celestial Beauty," declaring her "a Goddess among Gods" who should be "ador'd and serv'd / By Angels numberless." Yet his flattery delves deeper than mere "ravishment": he seizes her attention, and her trust, by speaking her language. Amazed, she asks the serpent:

What may this mean? Language of Man pronoun't
By Tongue of Brute, and human sense exprest?
The first at least of these I thought deni'd
To Beasts, whom God on thir Creation-Day
Created mute to all articulate sound.

Here, indeed, is the crux of our power over the lives of animals. Would I have planned Ruthie's killing if she had spoken the "Language of Man" through the barnyard gate? Would she have lived her entire life behind that fence? Would I have sold her children, arranged her fornications, and exhibited her publicly at county fairs? Where does slavery end and husbandry begin? Despite his malice, the serpent "with human voice endu'd" is a clarion for all "beasts that graze / The trodden Herb." He forces me, as he forces Eve, to reconsider "the rest / Of brutal kind, that daily are in sight."

The narrative of temptation drives book 9 of *Paradise Lost;* and because Milton is anxious to lure Eve to the Tree of Knowledge, he doesn't linger over the astonishments of a talking serpent. The humans—both poet and character—instantly habituate themselves to snaky conversation. But I find myself revisiting again and again this moment of revelation, "redoubl[ing] this miracle," the instant when a silent creature "cam'st . . . speakable of mute" and "human sense exprest." What if God had seen fit, from the beginning, to allow humans and beasts to speak freely to one another? What if I needed to *ask* Ruthie if she were ready to die?

I dreamed last night that my bathroom was full of hungry cats and kittens, perhaps twenty or thirty of them mewling and scratching and wailing. Gnawed toothbrushes and soap were overturned on the floor; towels were slashed and filthy. The room stank of cat urine, and the floor was littered with straw. I embraced an armful of cats; I tried to carry them away, but they slipped from my grasp, slick as eels: yet I knew they were desperate, desperate for my care.

The anxieties of animal rearing are legion. So much can go wrong. What about an enormous buck kid jammed in his mother's birth canal, his tongue squeezed in agony between his blunt teeth, as his mother screams and screams and screams? A shotgun to the head must surely be a release. These animals, "of abject thoughts and low," who "aught but food discern . . . / Or Sex," impel us, as caretakers, to manufacture the appropriate final solution. Or that is what the farmer schools herself to believe. "For in thir looks," as Eve affirms, "Much reason, and in thir actions oft appears." And their looks, though sometimes frightened, frenzied, morose, or belligerent, do not accuse us of treachery.

Ruthie's body was shrinking, withering. Her yellow eyes glittered. Her droppings were loose, sour, like a sick child's. She snorted and panted and left foamy traces of mucus in the water buckets. I believed that she was incurably ill, suffering at least constant discomfort if not actual pain, and was too weak to endure another Maine winter. She was not able to tell me otherwise. And I was able to arrange her death because I knew she would succumb to temptation.

> On a day roving the field, I chanc'd
> A goodly Tree far distant to behold
> Loaden with fruit of fairest colors mixt,
> Ruddy and Gold: I drew nearer to gaze;
> When from the boughs a savory odor blown,
> Grateful to appetite, more pleas'd my sense
> Than smell of sweetest Fennel, or the Teats
> Of Ewe or Goat dropping with Milk at Ev'n,
> Unsuckt of Lamb or Kid, that tend thir play.

Greed "urg'd . . . so keen" is not exclusively a human trait. The instinct of all living things is to consume as much as we can get, as fast as we can get it. The serpent tells Eve, "To satisfy the sharp desire I had / Of tasting those fair Apples, I resolv'd / Not to defer."

> About the mossy Trunk I wound me soon,
> For high from ground the branches would require
> Thy utmost reach or *Adam's:* Round the Tree

All other Beasts that saw, with like desire
Longing and envying stood, but could not reach.

The tale is false, of course. The incident Satan describes was concocted as trickery. But
Eve falls for the story: they *seem* real to her, "that alluring fruit," the animals "with like
desire." For instinctively we recognize the truth of seduction and desire; and if that
recognition is, perhaps, our deepest bond with the animal world, it is also, as Satan
proves, our locus of dominion.

Amid the Tree now got, where plenty hung
Tempting so nigh, to pluck and eat my fill
I spar'd not, for such pleasure till that hour
At Feed or Fountain never had I found.

I lured Ruthie to her death with a bowlful of grain. As soon as she heard the clank of the
grain-bin lid, she rushed to the gate, neck stretched, eyes popping. Eagerly, she watched
me scoop the sticky mix of pellets and oats and cracked corn into her green plastic dish.
Eagerly, she stamped her feet at the door—impatient, single-minded. I opened the gate,
held the dish high, out of her grasping, wriggling reach, and with the other hand snapped
a leash to her shabby collar.

But say, where grows the Tree, from hence how far?
For many are the Trees of God that grow
In Paradise, and various, yet unknown
To us, in such abundance lies our choice.

We tied her, Steve and I, to a steel barrel beside a tree, a common spruce tree, one of
a hundred, a thousand, spruce trees spearing our grey northern sky; these ordinary trees
whose roots writhe beneath our shallow acid soil; those tough, twisted roots I had so
lately been hacking with my sexton's spade.

Empress, the way is ready, and not long,
Beyond a row of Myrtles, on a Flat,
Fast by a Fountain, one small Thicket past
Of blowing Myrrh and Balm; if thou accept
My conduct, I can bring thee thither soon.

Ruthie yanked and tugged at the short leash in gluttonous desperation. Fog clung, like
comfort, to the lilacs, the dripping chokecherries, the serrated weeds along the forest
edge. I laid the dish of grain on the ground before the goat, and she ducked her head into
the bowl, gobbling fast, noisily, without thought or thanks.

Intent now wholly on her taste, naught else
Regarded, such delight till then, as seem'd,
In Fruit she never tasted, whether true

Or fancied so, through expectation high
Of knowledge, nor was God-head from her thought.
Greedily she ingorg'd without restraint,
And knew not eating Death.

I left her with Steve and walked away, into my garden.

Ideas for Writing

Choose one of the poetry exercises you worked on in chapters 1 through 8. Now imagine reading it aloud to the man who wrote book 7 of *Paradise Lost*. Write a page that details Milton's reactions to your draft as well your reactions to Milton. Quote your own work and Milton's poem at least once.

As you write, try very hard not to be funny. I love comedy as much as you do, but in these kinds of writing exercises it sometimes functions as an avoidance strategy. Strive for honesty; strive for vulnerability; strive for concentration. See where your curiosity, your pride, your humility can take you.

11

Brigit Pegeen Kelly: Pale Rider

Samuel Taylor Coleridge: The Rime of the Ancient Mariner

Now you see how things turn out.

—*Brigit Pegeen Kelly*

About the Poets and the Poems

The poetry of Brigit Pegeen Kelly (born 1951) is a striking amalgam of the physical and the surreal. Her poems come from a place of humility but also implacability. Their intensity can be unnerving, yet her language and pacing are elegant, restrained, even formal. Carl Phillips writes:

> To persuade the reader, poem after poem, that the surreal is no less real than what we call the real, to argue for—successfully—something akin to spiritual vision side by side with the more common suspicion of anything but the cold hard facts—this requires a rare authority, at the level of intellect, to be sure, but also in terms of language and, especially evident in Kelly's work, sheer beauty. Kelly has created a poem that often purports to be narrative, but turns out to work like a secular version of John Donne's sermons. . . . Her poems are like no one else's—hard and luminous, weird in the sense of making a thing strange, that we at last might see it.[1]

"Pale Rider," the poem in this chapter, is from her 2004 collection *The Orchard.* Writing of this collection, Fiona Sampson calls it "a dangerous grove where transformations happen." In the same vein, Pamela Hart writes, "What to make of this orchard, its old garden, dark pond, weird statues and shifting imagery of benevolent and malicious characters? That suffering and beauty go hand in hand, the foul and the fragrant, all the imaginings, the many arms of the mind, as Kelly writes of her orchard inhabitants—this is dangerous beauty."[2]

Samuel Taylor Coleridge (1772–1834) is a major figure of English poetry. With William Wordsworth, he collaborated on the groundbreaking collection *Lyrical Ballads* (1798), the first clarion cry of the Romantic poets. Although much of his work remained unfinished (thanks in large part to his opium addiction), he still left behind a formidable body of work, not only poetry but also lectures, literary criticism, and autobiography. Alfred Harbage called him "the greatest of Shakespearean critics": "Coleridge was a poet talking about a poet. . . . He applied ideas to a specific body of literature, in such a way as to illuminate that literature and to illustrate, test and modify the ideas."[3]

"The Rime of the Ancient Mariner," one of the featured poems in this chapter, appeared in the first edition of *Lyrical Ballads.* In his *Biographia Literaria* (1817), Coleridge recalled the genesis of the poem: "It was agreed, that my endeavours should be directed to persons and characters supernatural, or at least romantic; yet so as to transfer from our inward nature a human interest and a semblance of truth sufficient to procure for these shadows of imagination that willing suspension of disbelief for the moment, which constitutes poetic faith. . . . With this view I wrote the 'Ancient Mariner.'"[4]

Pale Rider
Brigit Pegeen Kelly

I found her beneath the fruiting honeysuckle,
The fallen doe. The hunter had cut her legs off,
And because the doe was so small, killed out of season,
The leg wounds looked huge, like neck wounds.
I found her in summer and then I forgot about her.
But many months later, on a day of cold rain,
And then unfallen snow, when I was tired because
I had not slept, and because I was tired, anxious,
I walked back to the grotto in the oldest part of the woods.
It is a dark unsettling place and I am drawn to it.
No sun finds its way through the trees, even in winter,
And, as if the place were cursed, birds pass through
Quickly or not at all, and they will not sing. Dusk
Had come early. The steep hill rose up black
Above the cave's blue walls, and from the water
Pooled on the rocks, the mist was already rising.
I could feel it before I saw it, stirring like the clouds
Of insects that sift through the swales in summer.
And then the mist took on weight and turned silver.
And then it grew heavier still and turned white.
I was having trouble seeing. I heard the call of a night bird,
Far off, perishable, and from the branches, high
And low, water dripped, a dull repeating sound,
Like the sound of many mute people flicking one
Finger slow and hard against their palms. And then
The sound fell off, and the mist turned warm,
As if it were coming not from the pools of water
But from deep within the ground, and in the mist
I smelled flowers. And I was confused. I thought
For a moment it must be summer and not winter,
And that I would see, if the mist suddenly thinned,
Not a stripped thorn, clinging to the grotto's rim,
But a blooming honeysuckle bush. I could taste
The honeysuckle on my tongue, a taste that was faint
At first, slightly rancid. But as the mist grew thicker
And thicker, golden now, softly vibrating, the taste
Grew stronger, and more sweet, like the taste of ether,
Until it seemed as if I were standing in a cloud,
Or a hive. I looked up: whiteness, milky, lit from within,
And, like mother-of-pearl, *something,* not clear, a shape,
The shape of an owl or a snowy hawk, hanging
Perfectly still, the way a hawk will hang for hours

In a stiff wind, but there was no wind. And the shape
Was not an owl, nor a hawk, but a shape my mind
At first resisted, the way my mind sometimes refuses
To make sense of words that are perfectly clear,
Simple words, spoken slowly with great care,
Because the words are so improbable, or will tell me,
Good or bad, the thing I most wish not to hear,
"He is dead," say, or, "Take up your bed and walk."
Below that shape I stood, a pointed shape, golden,
Not a hawk, nor a boot, nor a silk hat made of mist,
Yet still somehow indistinguishable from the mist,
But something else, until my mind gave in to my eyes,
And the thing I had not wanted to see, or thought
I could not see, hung suspended above me, a face,
The head on its long neck of the doe I had found
Beneath the honeysuckle—such a frail creature,
Too small to have been killed, so small the hunter
Could have carried her home on her back had he so desired,
But he had not so desired. And I knew it was *that* doe,
Though I cannot say how I knew, her narrow face small
And dark and shining, until the mist closed over it,
And it was gone. And then, almost at once, the face
Appeared in another place, and again the mist closed,
And again the face came back, as in a game,
Until I saw that the face was not one but two,
Not two faces, but four, a flock of small deer, but no,
Not a flock, and again my mind refused the shape
Taking on weight above me, four heads on four long necks,
Attached to one legless body, one golden swollen body
That smelled of fallen fruit splitting in the sun and shone
The way an image from dream will darkly shine,
Floating up from childhood, a hand holding out
A piece of torn bread that turns for no reason
Into a block of honeycomb filled not with honey
But with a marbled black and red substance,
Dense and sweet as charred flesh. She shone
The doe, her four heads, held high and perfectly still,
Facing in four different directions. And then I saw
Something else, darker, protruding from her breast.
It was a fifth neck and head, hanging upside down
In front, like the useless third leg of Siamese twins
Joined at the torso that hangs out of the spine,
And is amputated at birth, or like the water-darkened
Rudder of a ship. I heard the hot air sucking in and out
Of the doe's many nostrils, in and out. The mist

Grew darker, and I felt afraid, for I knew even before
My eyes confirmed it, that the fifth head was not
The doe's head at all, as I had thought, but the head
Of a grown child that the doe was trying to deliver
From her breast, and I knew that the child would never
Be born, but must ride always with her, his body
Embedded in hers, his head up to the sky. I wanted
To reach up and touch that head. But I did not do so.
I kept thinking that the doe would disappear, or that
She would say something, that her four mouths, five,
Would open and she would speak, but she did not disappear,
And she did not speak. A doe will never speak.
She will bark or cry out like a child if alarmed, but she
Will not speak. The mist smelled of warm milk,
And the doe's muteness grew loud, and louder still,
Until it was as dizzying as the sound of many trumpets
Blowing a single everlasting note. And I thought
Of the tongue, of how it is a wound, a pool of blood,
And of how you should bind a wound. And I thought
Of the earth covered with poor forked creatures
Walking around with broken faces, their substance
Pouring out in the form of words. And I thought of how
The mist would thicken further until it thinned,
All at once, to nothing, in the night air that smelled
Of sewage and poor man's roses, and of how the sound
Of the water dripping from the trees would return,
Tinnier, less insistent, as the water grew colder.
And I knew that soon on the high hill above the grotto
The fine dry snow would start to fall, and the field
Would draw silence to itself, and then as the air
Grew soft, the dry snow would turn to wet snow,
And the wet snow would lie heavy against the earth,
And the silence would multiply a dark mass of pulp
And wings stirring above a darker bed, until nothing
Was recognizable to itself, and things were as if dead,
Wrapped in sheets and soaked in spices and oil, and death
A great mercy. And the snow seemed to hiss softly,
Or the falling mist hissed softly, or the water sliding
Down the stones, and the doe's form became more ghostly—
Pale rider, lost in the woods where I was lost. And I stood
In the dark until I closed my eyes. And then I stood no more.

The Rime of the Ancient Mariner
Samuel Taylor Coleridge

I

It is an ancient Mariner,
And he stoppeth one of three.
"By thy long grey beard and glittering eye,
Now wherefore stopp'st thou me?

The Bridegroom's doors are opened wide,
And I am next of kin;
The guests are met, the feast is set:
May'st hear the merry din."

He holds him with his skinny hand,
"There was a ship," quoth he.
"Hold off! unhand me, grey-beard loon!"
Eftsoons his hand dropped he.

He holds him with his glittering eye—
The Wedding-Guest stood still,
And listens like a three years' child:
The Mariner hath his will.

The Wedding-Guest sat on a stone:
He cannot choose but hear;
And thus spake on that ancient man,
The bright-eyed Mariner.

"The ship was cheered, the harbour cleared,
Merrily did we drop
Below the kirk, below the hill,
Below the lighthouse top.

The Sun came up upon the left,
Out of the sea came he!
And he shone bright, and on the right
Went down into the sea.

Higher and higher every day,
Till over the mast at noon—"
The Wedding-Guest here beat his breast,
For he heard the loud bassoon.

The bride hath paced into the hall,
Red as a rose is she;
Nodding their heads before her goes
The merry minstrelsy.

The Wedding-Guest he beat his breast,
Yet he cannot choose but hear;
And thus spake on that ancient man,
The bright-eyed Mariner.

"And now the STORM-BLAST came, and he
Was tyrannous and strong;
He struck with his o'ertaking wings,
And chased us south along.

With sloping masts and dipping prow,
As who pursued with yell and blow
Still treads the shadow of his foe,
And forward bends his head,
The ship drove fast, loud roared the blast,
And southward aye we fled.

And now there came both mist and snow,
And it grew wondrous cold:
And ice, mast-high, came floating by,
As green as emerald.

And through the drifts the snowy clifts
Did send a dismal sheen:
Nor shapes of men nor beasts we ken—
The ice was all between.

The ice was here, the ice was there,
The ice was all around:
It cracked and growled, and roared and howled,
Like noises in a swound!

At length did cross an Albatross,
Thorough the fog it came;
As it had been a Christian soul,
We hailed it in God's name.

It ate the food it ne'er had eat,
And round and round it flew.
The ice did split with a thunder-fit;
The helmsman steered us through!

And a good south wind sprung up behind;
The Albatross did follow,
And every day, for food or play,
Came to the mariner's hollo!

In mist or cloud, on mast or shroud,
It perched for vespers nine;
Whiles all the night, through fog-smoke white,
Glimmered the white Moon-shine."

"God save thee, ancient Mariner!
From the fiends, that plague thee thus!—
Why look'st thou so?"—"With my cross-bow
I shot the ALBATROSS.

                    II
The Sun now rose upon the right:
Out of the sea came he,
Still hid in mist, and on the left
Went down into the sea.

And the good south wind still blew behind,
But no sweet bird did follow,
Nor any day for food or play
Came to the mariners' hollo!

And I had done a hellish thing,
And it would work 'em woe:
For all averred, I had killed the bird
That made the breeze to blow.
Ah wretch! said they, the bird to slay,
That made the breeze to blow!

Nor dim nor red, like God's own head,
The glorious sun uprist:
Then all averred, I had killed the bird
That brought the fog and mist.
'Twas right, said they, such birds to slay,
That bring the fog and mist.

The fair breeze blew, the white foam flew,
The furrow followed free;
We were the first that ever burst
Into that silent sea.

Down dropped the breeze, the sails dropt down,
'Twas sad as sad could be;
And we did speak only to break
The silence of the sea!

All in a hot and copper sky,
The bloody Sun, at noon,
Right up above the mast did stand,
No bigger than the Moon.

Day after day, day after day,
We stuck, nor breath nor motion;
As idle as a painted ship
Upon a painted ocean.

Water, water, every where,
And all the boards did shrink;
Water, water, every where,
Nor any drop to drink.

The very deep did rot: O Christ!
That ever this should be!
Yea, slimy things did crawl with legs
Upon the slimy sea.

About, about, in reel and rout
The death-fires danced at night;
The water, like a witch's oils,
Burnt green, and blue, and white.

And some in dreams assuréd were
Of the Spirit that plagued us so;
Nine fathom deep he had followed us
From the land of mist and snow.

And every tongue, through utter drought,
Was withered at the root;
We could not speak, no more than if
We had been choked with soot.

Ah! well a-day! what evil looks
Had I from old and young!
Instead of the cross, the Albatross
About my neck was hung.

III

There passed a weary time. Each throat
Was parched, and glazed each eye.
A weary time! a weary time!
How glazed each weary eye,
When looking westward, I beheld
A something in the sky.

At first it seemed a little speck,
And then it seemed a mist;
It moved and moved, and took at last
A certain shape, I wist.

A speck, a mist, a shape, I wist!
And still it neared and neared:
As if it dodged a water-sprite,
It plunged and tacked and veered.

With throats unslaked, with black lips baked,
We could nor laugh nor wail;
Through utter drought all dumb we stood!
I bit my arm, I sucked the blood,
And cried, A sail! a sail!

With throats unslaked, with black lips baked,
Agape they heard me call:
Gramercy! they for joy did grin,
And all at once their breath drew in,
As they were drinking all.

See! see! (I cried) she tacks no more!
Hither to work us weal;
Without a breeze, without a tide,
She steadies with upright keel!

The western wave was all a-flame,
The day was well nigh done!
Almost upon the western wave
Rested the broad bright Sun;

When that strange shape drove suddenly
Betwixt us and the Sun.

And straight the Sun was flecked with bars,
(Heaven's Mother send us grace!)
As if through a dungeon-grate he peered
With broad and burning face.

Alas! (thought I, and my heart beat loud)
How fast she nears and nears!
Are those *her* sails that glance in the Sun,
Like restless gossameres?

Are those *her* ribs through which the Sun
Did peer, as through a grate?
And is that Woman all her crew?
Is that a DEATH? and are there two?
Is DEATH that woman's mate?

Her lips were red, *her* looks were free,
Her locks were yellow as gold:
Her skin was as white as leprosy,
The Night-mare LIFE-IN-DEATH was she,
Who thicks man's blood with cold.

The naked hulk alongside came,
And the twain were casting dice;
'The game is done! I've won! I've won!'
Quoth she, and whistles thrice.

The Sun's rim dips; the stars rush out:
At one stride comes the dark;
With far-heard whisper, o'er the sea,
Off shot the spectre-bark.

We listened and looked sideways up!
Fear at my heart, as at a cup,
My life-blood seemed to sip!
The stars were dim, and thick the night,
The steersman's face by his lamp gleamed white;

From the sails the dew did drip—
Till clomb above the eastern bar
The hornéd Moon, with one bright star
Within the nether tip.

One after one, by the star-dogged Moon,
Too quick for groan or sigh,
Each turned his face with a ghastly pang,
And cursed me with his eye.

Four times fifty living men,
(And I heard nor sigh nor groan)
With heavy thump, a lifeless lump,
They dropped down one by one.

The souls did from their bodies fly,—
They fled to bliss or woe!
And every soul it passed me by,
Like the whizz of my cross-bow!"

IV

"I fear thee, ancient Mariner!
I fear thy skinny hand!
And thou art long, and lank, and brown,
As is the ribbed sea-sand.

I fear thee and thy glittering eye,
And thy skinny hand, so brown."—
"Fear not, fear not, thou Wedding-Guest!
This body dropt not down.

Alone, alone, all, all alone,
Alone on a wide wide sea!
And never a saint took pity on
My soul in agony.

The many men, so beautiful!
And they all dead did lie:
And a thousand thousand slimy things
Lived on; and so did I.

I looked upon the rotting sea,
And drew my eyes away;
I looked upon the rotting deck,
And there the dead men lay.

I looked to heaven, and tried to pray;
But or ever a prayer had gusht,
A wicked whisper came, and made

My heart as dry as dust.
I closed my lids, and kept them close,
And the balls like pulses beat;
For the sky and the sea, and the sea and the sky
Lay like a load on my weary eye,
And the dead were at my feet.

The cold sweat melted from their limbs,
Nor rot nor reek did they:
The look with which they looked on me
Had never passed away.

An orphan's curse would drag to hell
A spirit from on high;
But oh! more horrible than that
Is the curse in a dead man's eye!
Seven days, seven nights, I saw that curse,
And yet I could not die.

The moving Moon went up the sky,
And no where did abide:
Softly she was going up,
And a star or two beside—

Her beams bemocked the sultry main,
Like April hoar-frost spread;
But where the ship's huge shadow lay,
The charmèd water burnt alway
A still and awful red.

Beyond the shadow of the ship,
I watched the water-snakes:
They moved in tracks of shining white,
And when they reared, the elfish light
Fell off in hoary flakes.

Within the shadow of the ship
I watched their rich attire:
Blue, glossy green, and velvet black,
They coiled and swam; and every track
Was a flash of golden fire.

O happy living things! no tongue
Their beauty might declare:
A spring of love gushed from my heart,

And I blessed them unaware:
Sure my kind saint took pity on me,
And I blessed them unaware.

The selfsame moment I could pray;
And from my neck so free
The Albatross fell off, and sank
Like lead into the sea.

V

Oh sleep! it is a gentle thing,
Beloved from pole to pole!
To Mary Queen the praise be given!
She sent the gentle sleep from Heaven,
That slid into my soul.

The silly buckets on the deck,
That had so long remained,
I dreamt that they were filled with dew;
And when I awoke, it rained.

My lips were wet, my throat was cold,
My garments all were dank;
Sure I had drunken in my dreams,
And still my body drank.

I moved, and could not feel my limbs:
I was so light—almost
I thought that I had died in sleep,
And was a blesséd ghost.

And soon I heard a roaring wind:
It did not come anear;
But with its sound it shook the sails,
That were so thin and sere.

The upper air burst into life!
And a hundred fire-flags sheen,
To and fro they were hurried about!
And to and fro, and in and out,
The wan stars danced between.

And the coming wind did roar more loud,
And the sails did sigh like sedge;
And the rain poured down from one black cloud;
The Moon was at its edge.

The thick black cloud was cleft, and still
The Moon was at its side:
Like waters shot from some high crag,
The lightning fell with never a jag,
A river steep and wide.

The loud wind never reached the ship,
Yet now the ship moved on!
Beneath the lightning and the Moon
The dead men gave a groan.

They groaned, they stirred, they all uprose,
Nor spake, nor moved their eyes;
It had been strange, even in a dream,
To have seen those dead men rise.

The helmsman steered, the ship moved on;
Yet never a breeze up-blew;
The mariners all 'gan work the ropes,
Where they were wont to do;
They raised their limbs like lifeless tools—
We were a ghastly crew.

The body of my brother's son
Stood by me, knee to knee:
The body and I pulled at one rope,
But he said nought to me."

"I fear thee, ancient Mariner!"
"Be calm, thou Wedding-Guest!
'Twas not those souls that fled in pain,
Which to their corses came again,
But a troop of spirits blest:

For when it dawned—they dropped their arms,
And clustered round the mast;
Sweet sounds rose slowly through their mouths,
And from their bodies passed.

Around, around, flew each sweet sound,
Then darted to the Sun;
Slowly the sounds came back again,
Now mixed, now one by one.

Sometimes a-dropping from the sky
I heard the sky-lark sing;
Sometimes all little birds that are,
How they seemed to fill the sea and air
With their sweet jargoning!

And now 'twas like all instruments,
Now like a lonely flute;
And now it is an angel's song,
That makes the heavens be mute.

It ceased; yet still the sails made on
A pleasant noise till noon,
A noise like of a hidden brook
In the leafy month of June,
That to the sleeping woods all night
Singeth a quiet tune.

Till noon we quietly sailed on,
Yet never a breeze did breathe;
Slowly and smoothly went the ship,
Moved onward from beneath.

Under the keel nine fathom deep,
From the land of mist and snow,
The spirit slid: and it was he
That made the ship to go.
The sails at noon left off their tune,
And the ship stood still also.

The Sun, right up above the mast,
Had fixed her to the ocean:
But in a minute she 'gan stir,
With a short uneasy motion—
Backwards and forwards half her length
With a short uneasy motion.

Then like a pawing horse let go,
She made a sudden bound:
It flung the blood into my head,
And I fell down in a swound.

How long in that same fit I lay,
I have not to declare;
But ere my living life returned,
I heard and in my soul discerned
Two voices in the air.

'Is it he?' quoth one, 'Is this the man?
By him who died on cross,
With his cruel bow he laid full low
The harmless Albatross.

The spirit who bideth by himself
In the land of mist and snow,
He loved the bird that loved the man
Who shot him with his bow.'

The other was a softer voice,
As soft as honey-dew:
Quoth he, 'The man hath penance done,
And penance more will do.'

VI
FIRST VOICE

'But tell me, tell me! speak again,
Thy soft response renewing—
What makes that ship drive on so fast?
What is the ocean doing?'

SECOND VOICE

'Still as a slave before his lord,
The ocean hath no blast;
His great bright eye most silently
Up to the Moon is cast—

If he may know which way to go;
For she guides him smooth or grim.
See, brother, see! how graciously
She looketh down on him.'

FIRST VOICE
'But why drives on that ship so fast,
Without or wave or wind?'

SECOND VOICE
'The air is cut away before,
And closes from behind.

Fly, brother, fly! more high, more high!
Or we shall be belated:
For slow and slow that ship will go,
When the Mariner's trance is abated.'

I woke, and we were sailing on
As in a gentle weather:
'Twas night, calm night, the Moon was high;
The dead men stood together.

All stood together on the deck,
For a charnel-dungeon fitter:
All fixed on me their stony eyes,
That in the Moon did glitter.

The pang, the curse, with which they died,
Had never passed away:
I could not draw my eyes from theirs,
Nor turn them up to pray.

And now this spell was snapt: once more
I viewed the ocean green,
And looked far forth, yet little saw
Of what had else been seen—

Like one, that on a lonesome road
Doth walk in fear and dread,
And having once turned round walks on,
And turns no more his head;
Because he knows, a frightful fiend
Doth close behind him tread.

But soon there breathed a wind on me,
Nor sound nor motion made:
Its path was not upon the sea,
In ripple or in shade.

It raised my hair, it fanned my cheek
Like a meadow-gale of spring—
It mingled strangely with my fears,
Yet it felt like a welcoming.

Swiftly, swiftly flew the ship,
Yet she sailed softly too:
Sweetly, sweetly blew the breeze—
On me alone it blew.

Oh! dream of joy! is this indeed
The light-house top I see?
Is this the hill? is this the kirk?
Is this mine own countree?

We drifted o'er the harbour-bar,
And I with sobs did pray—
O let me be awake, my God!
Or let me sleep alway.

The harbour-bay was clear as glass,
So smoothly it was strewn!
And on the bay the moonlight lay,
And the shadow of the Moon.

The rock shone bright, the kirk no less,
That stands above the rock:
The moonlight steeped in silentness
The steady weathercock.

And the bay was white with silent light,
Till rising from the same,
Full many shapes, that shadows were,
In crimson colours came.

A little distance from the prow
Those crimson shadows were:
I turned my eyes upon the deck—
Oh, Christ! what saw I there!

Each corse lay flat, lifeless and flat,
And, by the holy rood!
A man all light, a seraph-man,
On every corse there stood.

This seraph-band, each waved his hand:
It was a heavenly sight!
They stood as signals to the land,
Each one a lovely light;

This seraph-band, each waved his hand,
No voice did they impart—
No voice; but oh! the silence sank
Like music on my heart.

But soon I heard the dash of oars,
I heard the Pilot's cheer;
My head was turned perforce away,
And I saw a boat appear.

The Pilot and the Pilot's boy,
I heard them coming fast:
Dear Lord in Heaven! it was a joy
The dead men could not blast.

I saw a third—I heard his voice:
It is the Hermit good!
He singeth loud his godly hymns
That he makes in the wood.
He'll shrieve my soul, he'll wash away
The Albatross's blood.

                VII
This Hermit good lives in that wood
Which slopes down to the sea.
How loudly his sweet voice he rears!
He loves to talk with mariners
That come from a far countree.

He kneels at morn, and noon, and eve—
He hath a cushion plump:
It is the moss that wholly hides
The rotted old oak-stump.

The skiff-boat neared: I heard them talk,
'Why, this is strange, I trow!
Where are those lights so many and fair,
That signal made but now?'

'Strange, by my faith!' the Hermit said—
'And they answered not our cheer!
The planks looked warped! and see those sails,
How thin they are and sere!
I never saw aught like to them,
Unless perchance it were

Brown skeletons of leaves that lag
My forest-brook along;
When the ivy-tod is heavy with snow,
And the owlet whoops to the wolf below,
That eats the she-wolf's young.'

'Dear Lord! it hath a fiendish look—
(The Pilot made reply)
I am a-feared'—'Push on, push on!'
Said the Hermit cheerily.

The boat came closer to the ship,
But I nor spake nor stirred;
The boat came close beneath the ship,
And straight a sound was heard.

Under the water it rumbled on,
Still louder and more dread:
It reached the ship, it split the bay;
The ship went down like lead.

Stunned by that loud and dreadful sound,
Which sky and ocean smote,
Like one that hath been seven days drowned
My body lay afloat;
But swift as dreams, myself I found
Within the Pilot's boat.

Upon the whirl where sank the ship
The boat spun round and round;
And all was still, save that the hill
Was telling of the sound.

I moved my lips—the Pilot shrieked
And fell down in a fit;
The holy Hermit raised his eyes,
And prayed where he did sit.

I took the oars: the Pilot's boy,
Who now doth crazy go,
Laughed loud and long, and all the while
His eyes went to and fro.
'Ha! ha!' quoth he, 'full plain I see,
The Devil knows how to row.'

And now, all in my own countree,
I stood on the firm land!
The Hermit stepped forth from the boat,
And scarcely he could stand.

'O shrieve me, shrieve me, holy man!'
The Hermit crossed his brow.
'Say quick,' quoth he, 'I bid thee say—
What manner of man art thou?'

Forthwith this frame of mine was wrenched
With a woful agony,
Which forced me to begin my tale;
And then it left me free.

Since then, at an uncertain hour,
That agony returns;
And till my ghastly tale is told,
This heart within me burns.

I pass, like night, from land to land;
I have strange power of speech;
That moment that his face I see,
I know the man that must hear me:
To him my tale I teach.

What loud uproar bursts from that door!
The wedding-guests are there:
But in the garden-bower the bride
And bride-maids singing are;
And hark the little vesper bell,
Which biddeth me to prayer!

O Wedding-Guest! this soul hath been
Alone on a wide wide sea:
So lonely 'twas, that God himself
Scarce seeméd there to be.

O sweeter than the marriage-feast,
'Tis sweeter far to me,
To walk together to the kirk
With a goodly company!—

To walk together to the kirk,
And all together pray,
While each to his great Father bends,
Old men, and babes, and loving friends,
And youths and maidens gay!

Farewell, farewell! but this I tell
To thee, thou Wedding-Guest!
He prayeth well, who loveth well
Both man and bird and beast.

He prayeth best, who loveth best
All things both great and small;
For the dear God who loveth us,
He made and loveth all."

The Mariner, whose eye is bright,
Whose beard with age is hoar,
Is gone; and now the Wedding-Guest
Turned from the bridegroom's door.

He went like one that hath been stunned,
And is of sense forlorn:
A sadder and a wiser man
He rose the morrow morn.

Ideas for Writing

In a previous chapter I mentioned how common, almost ubiquitous, the *I* point of view has become in poetry. So often our poems are outlets for the personal, the private, the spoken secret. Even when it is an outright fiction, a first-person poem can feel as raw as a diary entry.

Literary essays are a different story. While the *I* does rule over many forms of creative nonfiction, it is conspicuously absent in academic and critical prose. Its scarcity is puzzling because publishers, even scholarly ones, explicitly ask their authors to avoid wordy passive-voice constructions that mute the speaker's voice and opinions. "The book can be thought of as a waste of time" is a way to evade responsibility for announcing, "I think the book is a waste of time." Yet time and time again, authors retreat behind that cushion of words. In doing so, they may take themselves off the hot seat, but they also retreat into obscurity, anonymity, invisibility.

As you work to become a poet, you may find yourself in a position of needing, in some deep, personal way, to write about what you are reading. I urge to you to commit yourself to saying *I think*—not *we think,* not *people think.* Work hard to keep yourself from falling into convoluted grammatical "objectivity." The truth is that you should *not* be objective when you're writing a personal literary essay. You should push yourself to write subjectively about your own curiosity, your own reactions. The goal is to discover what you think about work of literature, not to create an essay that makes you look well read or professorially remote. Please understand that I am not deriding academic scholarship or theory. Simply I am saying that, like poetry, a personal literary essay comes from a different and far more vulnerable place in the author. It's important to push yourself to write in ways that cherish that vulnerability, not mask it.

If I sound bossy here, it's because I believe that for many years my own writing suffered from a timid unwillingness to face head-on some of the many issues I brought up in the Blake and Milton essays you read in the previous chapters. How does a contemporary poet speak to a poet of the past? How does an obscure woman speak to a canonized man? How can their speech be an actual conversation rather than rant, polemic, diatribe, or blind adoration? For creative writers who take reading seriously, these are fundamental questions that have never been easy to answer.

In the introduction I mentioned Countee Cullen's life-long, necessary conversation with the Romantic poets—and how some of his peers derided that need. Why, they asked, should a twentieth-century African American poet waste his time talking to nineteenth-century English white men? The question I ask is, why shouldn't he? Easier said than done, however . . . especially if every writer around you seems to be engaged in a more politically topical or aesthetically fashionable pursuit. But if you persevere with your own necessary conversations, you honor both your deepest influences and your own questing mind. As Teresa Carson writes in her essay "The Temple of Delight: John Keats and Jack Wiler,"

> Soul-level influence is not a simple pass-the-baton process; we do not read
> our poetic ancestors and then just pick up the conversation where they left
> off. Rather, we are, by nature, related to particular poetic ancestors but not to
> others. As J. D. Salinger said, "The true poet has no choice of material." We and

our influences cannot help but work the same vein of the Underneath, however dissimilar our surfaces may appear. If we are persistent, honest, and loyal to that vein, then we participate in and continue the conversation of poetry—a conversation that transcends time, place, and style.[5]

But who are these soul-level influences? How do we discover them? Writing a personal literary essay is one way to begin to track your own patterns of inspiration and resonance, of fear and distraction. We are all imperfect. We make flippant judgments about serious poems. We revere famous writers who spoil us as poets, sometimes even as human beings. We obediently admire what a teacher tells us to admire and are embarrassed to admit that we return again and again to a poet that this same teacher has publicly derided. None of these reactions helps us grow as a poet. You may have a flamboyant voice and a facile ear. You may be a formal genius or the best-read person in town. But if you don't engage honestly with your own thoughts, feelings, and reactions, you are treading in the shallows.

I chose this chapter's two featured poems because both are complex and ambitious while remaining distinctly different from one another. Moreover, I have never written an essay about either of them—meaning that you and I are both staring at a blank page wondering what we might possibly have to say. To jumpstart our thoughts, I'm going to suggest some open-ended questions that might help us begin to feel our way into a personal literary essay about the two poems. Mix and match the questions as you wish. Focus on just one, or try to address all of them. Follow your own curiosity into new questions. Just make sure that what you write matters to *you*.

DIFFERENCES IN TIME

How does time pass differently in each of these poems? Which approach attracts and/or repels you? Why? How? Point out some examples.

How do you tend to handle the passage of time in your own poems? Do you find your approach timid or limiting? Uncontrolled or dangerous? Why? How? Show some examples. What might Kelly or Coleridge have to say about time in your poems? What might they have to say about time in each other's poems?

Does variation in sentence length have any relationship to the time differences in these poems? What about stanza or line style? Why? How?

Where does time become confusing in these poems? Are you the only one who's confused? Are the characters also confused? Is the speaker confused? Are the poets confused? Why? How?

A SHARED UNWILLINGNESS

It seems to me that the characters and/or speakers in both of these poems go out of their way to avoid facing up to something. What are they trying to avoid? Is that avoidance part of the storyline? Is it revealed in the language? How? Where?

Is avoidance something you struggle with in your own writing? What do you veer away from saying? How do your language choices reflect that avoidance?

Is avoidance always a bad thing? Do poets really have to say everything? What does it mean to be vulnerable and honest in a poem?

Are Kelly and Coleridge vulnerable and honest in their poems? How can you tell?

DIFFERENCES IN TIME, A SHARED UNWILLINGNESS

Can a poet's approach to time have anything to do with avoidance? Do you think these issues are related in Kelly's and/or Coleridge's poem? How? Why?

Do you prefer to write in past tense or present tense? How does the difference in tense change your sense of time? How does it change your ability to avoid a topic or an emotion?

Which of these poems do you wish you'd written yourself? Why? Or why are you relieved not to have written either one?

Does the length of these poems play into any of your feelings about avoidance? Do you avoid reading or writing long poems? Why or why not?

Meeting a Poem in Its Context

12

Gray Jacobik
Ten Poems from *Little Boy Blue*

nothing is ever remembered with enough
precision & no one is ever a keeper
                                        —*Gray Jacobik*

About the Poet and the Poems

Gray Jacobik (born 1944) is both a poet and a painter. In a 2009 interview she spoke about the way in which these pursuits conflict with one another in her creative life:

> I began my life as a painter, but stopped for more than two decades and devoted myself to writing poems and teaching. It was only after my third book was accepted, that I permitted myself to paint again. A few years ago, I thought I'd made the transition to painter completely and would not return to writing. I find painting and writing conflict with one another because I have limited time to devote to either and certainly not enough to devote to both. When I attempt both, I do neither well, and feel torn apart continuously. Right now, I'm not painting, although I miss it very much. A few years ago, I wasn't writing. A part of me would like to put this conflict to rest, but I love both ways of expressing myself creatively.[1]

Yet certainly this tension contributes to the visual power of Jacobik's writing. In "Sylvia Plimack Mangold Paints," a poem from her 1998 collection *The Double Task,* she writes, "No art without a frame, Magritte said, only the long / considered game of division."[2] Her poems frame and consider—and divide. Always she is thinking her way into her work: "I don't care for poems that carry only impressions or sensations and little or no thought. I try to make sure there's at least one line that aims at what I like to think of as the intellectual underpinning of the poem."[3]

Little Boy Blue (2011) is Jacobik's sixth poetry collection. Subtitled "A Memoir in Verse," the book is an autobiographical retelling of Jacobik's fraught relationship with her son. She recalls, "At the time I was writing *Little Boy Blue,* my son had asked me not to communicate with him; I hadn't heard his voice in two years. The poems wrote themselves, of necessity."[4]

Ten Poems from *Little Boy Blue*
Gray Jacobik

1

Three days passed before you found your
    way to the crook of my arm;
that's why Marilyn Monroe was a part of it.

Two days because you were born jaundiced,
    so they transfused your blood, kept
you in the nursery—that era when any woman

could get lost for the tease she was & the power
    it gave here—when Presidents could,
at the swankiest hotels, order call girls brought up

on service elevators. Roe vs. Wade hadn't
    happened or you'd not have been
born. I did try to find & couldn't, a back-alley

abortionist in the Negro district of Newport News,
    then took thirty pills of quinine
your father's football coach gave him to give me,

leaving me in a coma for three days, pills that
    didn't chase you from my body,
although years later I'd learn the tooth buds that

failed to grow in your mouth were caused by the quinine,
    & who knows, maybe your bipolar disorder,
maybe your ADHD, & back then doctors thought

nothing of keeping a mother from her newborn
    or a newborn from his mother; besides,
the spinal block I'd finally gotten, when I needed

surgery, three hundred stitches to sew up
    a ruptured womb (for the labor was induced
before either of us was ready), meant that I was flat out

with lightning pain across my scalp, spasms ruling
    my back, plus the soreness of labor,
delivery, surgery, I woke angry, crying, jealous

of the mother in the next bed over, her son
    born the day you were, white trash
your grandmother had called her, a girl, as I was,

from one of the Eastern Shore's backwater towns.
    Her baby came for the twenty minutes as scheduled
eight times a day. The radio between our two beds

said Marilyn Monroe was dead, an apparent suicide.
    August 5th, 1962. Kennedy was President.
I was eighteen. Nobody breastfed babies back then,

especially the poor who aspired to imitate the well-off
    as they still do. You had a cut at the back
of your neck, & all I wanted was to unwrap you,

look at you whole although I was awash with
    the desire, that first time, but often thereafter,
to shove you back up inside me as if you were

an homunculus, a little man & not an infant;
    for there, in the empty doubt
of my body, no one could hurt you. But you

cried & didn't stop crying for six months,
    & the travesties, those injurious acts
that ravel & twist the heart, had just begun.

2

Not quite two years since you sat in your white truck

in my driveway, your two toast-brown dogs
in the seat beside you, eager to go, & you
telling me your girlfriend is a good person,
& you love her, news which gladdens me

though you won't believe that, for how seldom
have you loved anyone? Way back behind
the heavy green dazzle of late September light,
somewhere in the sadness I felt at your leaving,

I knew I'd never see you again, you & the truck
& the dogs & the woman, who is not here
but who's said you cannot ever speak to me
again, for she won some game of her design,

you the prize, me the loser, some struggle she sees
between good, aligned with her, evil, aligned
with me, & you, there, compliant, ready
to go; although I see you are sick with the pain

of it, your face wincing before you harden yourself
once more, your head bowed as if you'd been
sentenced. I hear again, that awkward, tuning-fork
hum of the silence that's always been between us.

Pussy-whipped, your stepfather says of you
as if that might explain what has taken you away
this time. A vagina opening within the dusty-rose
folds, or purple-red folds, or ivory-rose folds

of the vulva, or stretched to the brink of tearing,
or tearing jaggedly, or closed together, withering
to slime in the casket, or burning to a half ounce
of ash in the crematorium, the vagina, the clitoris,

vulva, only a woman's genitals, not a force
of division & yet division begins at this site.
After the moment of crowning comes the head,
the pressed-tight little face, rounded shoulders,

slick bulb of the buttocks, thighs, feet, cord, blood.
But this is a bloodless separation: you are going
into your own life, late, in your forties, to struggle
& suffer as you will, to try, to succeed or fail

to separate yourself again from someone who sees
her survival dependent on yours, & and you on hers.
Because distortion is here & betrayal, disbelief
on my part has nothing to do with it. An imperative

as fierce as any we humans know, what belief
can do when it is painstakingly encoded as thought,
what we cannot know or know we do not know—
the fate we make of what we say, not the one born to.

3

Channel surfing I find one of those nanny-knows-best
shows. Nanny takes over & mommy & daddy &

three towheaded brats begin to see slight flickerings
of a possible ordered existence; then the insistent

screams & wide-flung limbs of the boy who's three
remind me of how you'd hurl yourself against any wall

at daycare when I'd try to leave, or in our tiny apartment
whenever you felt frustrated or thwarted—or who

knows why?—neighbors banging on the floor above
or pounding the hall door yelling they'd call the landlord

if I didn't shut that kid up. You'd hurl yourself
as if you intended to shatter your body, then you'd

slide down & pinwheel kick, screaming, flailing,
spinning on your back, your face blood-red,

tear-soaked, gasping for breath that, once caught,
fueled still louder screams. I'd straddle you

with my feet or on all fours doing a kind of war jig
above you to block your head or a leg or hand

from coming down hard on the edge of something.
But not to stop you. I couldn't stop you.

Such fury dazed me, &, later, holding
your spent & hot body, rocking you to sleep,

singing *Hush, Little Baby* or *Tura-Lura-Lural,*
entranced by the scent of your soft hair,

I'd pretend we were a tribe of two, confused
mother & furious child, two who couldn't see

the tragedy or the comedy of it—that our torment
didn't mean anything, anymore than our happiness did.

4

The wake the ferry's engines
churned up widening into
lacework, that plume of white

on a pewter sea, that's what
tempted me. I was riding
a Trailways back to school,

the bus having wound its way
through the six flat snow-dusted
corn-stubble counties & now

stood car-bound below deck crossing
the wide mouth of the Chesapeake,
Cape Charles to Old Point Comfort.

Hours before, as your grandmother
stood at the sink & I by the stove
in that weakly framed house

once used by tenant farmers—
now rented to a school nurse
& a printer & their five children—

I told her I was pregnant.
That mouth of hers so often
pinched around a menthol,

fell open to a blank hole &
she sunk down to a kitchen
chair. Then—not a whisper,

not a cry—but slowly & tightly
enunciated, *How could you do
this to us? How could you*

*shame us like this? Have you
no self-respect? No decency?*
I was at the rail thinking

about how to climb onto it
& hurl myself into the wake.
No "right to life" on my mind.

Not yours. Not mine. Only
the need to no longer be.
A passion to obliterate.

The wind shoved my coat
or the ferry jerked—
a sudden forward surge.

I slammed into the rail.
The dream broke & I
went down below deck

& climbed back into
the high dark bus riding
the bay's cold waves.

Twice more in the years ahead
I came close, but this is the one
I still feel, that shove, that jerk,

it wakes me from sleep
with a start, my guardian
body leaping in front of me.

5
A few months before you left for good, your girlfriend
called & said I had abandoned you seventeen times,
didn't deserve a son. You'd told her this. Seventeen?

Such perceptions are not to be quarreled with, but when
the night won't let my sorrow go, I begin to count:
I forgot you once at Precious Cargo Daycare—the irate

worker, your joy at climbing into our car, a fall evening,
the ground wet. And when you were ten, although you'd
spent the spring with me, I sent you back to your grandparents.

You were shuffled back & forth after your first father
abandoned us, after I left your second father, & when
the neighborhood became too dangerous; when

my housemates said the kid went or I did, & I didn't.
It is true, mostly, I didn't want you—didn't want to be
a mother. Had I been less ignorant, less restless,

had I led a life before your life became the one I was
supposed to put first, but couldn't; had you not been
the tormented typhoon you were, bed-wetter,

toy-breaker, food-thrower, scrapper, kicker, screamer,
a day & night fury. My doing—the bed I'd made . . .
Not a bed. The front seat of a 1956 Chevrolet sedan,

two-toned green, my grandmother's car, borrowed
one night for a date when your father-to-be came
looking for me in Virginia after he'd hitch-hiked

for sixty-three hours from Fort Bliss, Texas, where
he'd just finished boot camp, at seventeen, having
lied to get in, poor Army-brat kid trying to make his

Colonel Daddy proud of him, & I his only solace,
he mine. It was November & still the crickets sang.
We'd parked where couples always parked in that

town, Chesapeake Avenue, across from the lights
of Norfolk. But all the harm done to you afterwards,
yes, my selfishness as you say. I can't explain the

force in me I couldn't suppress. I wanted more
than I'd ever had, experiences I'd caught hints
of in books. That's putting it simply & it wasn't simple.

O little boy in your orange & blue-striped shirt
& khaki shorts, your blue Keds—I see you shrinking
in my rearview—your brave half-wave, that big-sad

hurt in rubbed-red eyes. You turn & walk off
holding someone's hand. Or I tuck you in & leave
to cross town to a lover's bed, come back by morning,

or not, sometimes not before you'd had breakfast
or gone to school. Although I never left you alone,
I left, alone, & left you behind, & yes, sent you

away to a boarding school, finally, relieved & free,
the only place that would have you without Ritalin
in your bloodstream, the neuron-slowing "speed" that

killed your spirit with its ever-higher dosages needed
to stupefy you—demanded of me or you weren't
allowed in second grade, third, fourth, fifth . . .

But it was me, my fantastic offer to be better, learn more,
be richer, smarter, outshine anyone & everyone
who'd ever said I was to blame for getting pregnant

in the first place. Seventeen. You think it only seventeen . . .

6

I hate the facts as much as you do: our just-another-
    American-story strewn
throughout with the usual mass-produced consumer
    cheapness. All true, the over-
whelming melodramatic tackiness, the *de-crap-itude,*
    including your aunt's
thirty-six-day coma, her brain damage that's wrought
    one family tragedy after
another such that your cousin, right now, with no
    sense of remorse, is in
an Orlando prison for selling meth & grand larceny,
    the last of your grandfather's
life savings having gone to pay restitution to his victims.

Divorces, foreclosures, accidents, lawsuits, abortions,
    & seven thousand other
dramatic occasions—poverty's ravishments. And on it goes.
    One moves as far away
as possible, holds it at arm's length. Your second father's
    icy heart nearly killed me.
As it turned out, he was gay, & after *aversion hypnosis*
    ("when you desire a man
you will feel nauseous") failed to work, other *lifestyle
    choices* were called for,
but I'd left by then & taken you & your sister,
    moved to a commune.

He brought all of his stupidities into our marriage, & I made
    fancy cakes and puddings
out of them since I was still my mother's daughter,
    living out her dream
to marry into White Southern Aristocracy (instead of the
    Brooklyn-Jewish
hoypoloi she got). Thoroughly sexist, of course, &
    his racism, well, call it
anti-whiteism. He'd rather have been a Black man than
    the white homosexual
he turned out to be, perhaps because the only true
    compassion he'd known
came to him from the men & women who worked
    for his family on that
decaying antebellum estate in Carloville, Alabama, that
    red-clayed, pecan-treed,
fire-ant haven of malignant neglect & ossified traditions.
    Thus his move to the slums
of Baltimore to be near his true folk, & the ex-con drug
    addict who's beaten
him nearly to death repeatedly, gone back to prison
    for it, been forgiven by him
& given him AIDS, & who, of late, bought smack with
    every cent of your &
your sister's inheritance—well, that's accounted for in some
    theory of just-recompense
that may or may not relate to an individual life. But what
    does this have to do with you, with me?

He came into your life when you were four & you began
    to stutter. He'd scream at you,
Get it out! Get it out of your goddamn mouth! walking away
    from you whenever
you tried to talk to him, & then I'd scream at him
    for screaming at you, &
that only made matters worse. We lived in post-war
    temporary housing,
still temporary twenty years after the war. You may
    remember the neighborhood—
a school across from us, playground on the corner, where,
    once, on your blue bike
you were hit by a car. I remember the long Western
    vest your second father liked
to wear. It was dyed purple & he'd get high on a few tokes
    & swing the leather fringe

back and forth, rocking in his boots, swishing his long
    brown hair across his face,
blissed-out, grinning. The only time he ever looked free.

He was the third man that year, the year I was twenty-two,
    to propose to me,
& my mother wanted us out of the house, so I married
    him, knowing him only
six weeks. He was a virgin, I was, well, promiscuous.
    Little Boy Blue, sweet,
wild, little child. I see you trying to block the door when
    we were leaving on our honey-
moon, November 1966 & we drove to New Orleans.
    I wore a silk-&-lace peignoir
that night, pretending to be a real bride, but the cheap try
    wasn't lost on me.
Still, out of this, we got your good & loving sister.

7

You were a funny kid though, kept us in stitches.
You made up little rituals. Your grandfather
likes to tell of how you'd begin a left-right face,
arm-swinging goose-step march from wherever
you were into the bathroom, crying out *hep-two,
hep-two.* Once there you'd square off, click heels,
center yourself before the toilet, then bark out,
lid up! pants down! underpants down! then *squirt!*
reversing the order of your commands after the act
was done, your aim the usual aim of a four-year-
old. If your aunts & I were still laughing or
struggling not to when you marched back in,
you'd take umbrage and withdraw, for we were
to understand the seriousness of this. How I wish
I could, just once, kneel down before that boy,
as I would then, & apologize for laughing,
take you in my arms, kiss your cheek or forehead,
& hold your little body against mine.
No one was supposed to laugh at you,
               but, my god, you were funny.

8

The day Picasso dies, April & the cherry trees
are pink as pink chiffon skirts, the sunlight shade-

mottled, grass dandelion-dotted. Whenever I imagine
an afterlife & that old cliché about some saint

stepping up & saying you can have one day back
to live again on Earth, this is the one I choose—

just the three of us—you're eleven, your sister's five.
Your way of telling me you're tired of living

with your grandparents is to say, "I'm not needed
there anymore," but today we're on the farm in

Linden, Virginia, the foothills of the Shenandoahs.
Fiery Run is the name of the stream that zigzags

through the front pasture, where the two chestnut
horses, Nosey & Pokey, usually graze, & Fiery

Run is what *we* call the farm—the communards
& I who live in the city & rent this country

place for a year. You & your sister play house
in a tiny unused chicken coop we've swept out

& hosed down. You are content & absorbed,
fixing that little house up & pretending an orderly,

safe life of small domestic tasks. She is her usual
pacific self, bustling to do what you ask of her,

& I spend my day sitting under an apple tree
watching & listening to the two of you, or running

into the house or barn to find some item you
think is needed to make your house more homey.

I love you both so absolutely at that moment
I keep feeling betaken or transfixed, something

on that order—swayed out of time. For that day,
at least, we live in the peaceable kingdom

of fairytales. Once, at midday, you poke your
head through a glassless window & say,

"Mom, you're most like a zebra—calm & flashy."

9

You'd run from driveway
to corner, &, if not retrieved
(kicking, screaming), cross

the street to the playground,
then scamper into the woods
as if summoned or compelled.

Hyperactive was the diagnosis.
What, in the ancient world,
would they have said of you?

Or in Charlotte Brontë's? Spawn
of Dionysus? Imp? Hellion?
And yet such a sweetness

in you too, a tender-heartedness
& sympathy. You were, I think
now, hypersensitive, living

in a culture that had to brutalize
you. I know I had a part in that.
By the time you were five

you'd begun speaking for the dogs,
cats, birds, any small creature—
from falsetto to bass you'd

create voices: Bonnie,
our Dalmatian—*Ruff. Ruff.*
We gotta move back to our

old house. Ruff. I gotta dig up
the bone—ruff—I buried
by the big tree. Or for the cat—

I want a G.I. Joe for my birthday
even though I'm a girl. Then,
in your voice—*Mehitabel's*

birthday is <u>*tomorrow*</u>*, not next*
week. My birthday is <u>*next*</u> *week.*
You'd orchestrate animal

morality plays, voicing conflicts,
fears, desires, the rule each
creature was to abide by, end

with a kiss-&-make-up scene.
How astonishing it was, at times,
just to behold you—*the shapes*

a bright container can contain.
I have a sketch I made of you
at four—down-turned mouth,

eyebrows pinched, the angle you
hold your head—by then you
were sorrowful, wistful, already

Little Boy Blue on speed, running.

10

When you came home again, after a decade,
    in California, age forty, your marriage over,

your girlfriend chasing you out with the dogs
    while she sold the house, bedraggled

& frightened after four days & nights
    in your truck crossing the country—

I showed you the room I'd prepared for you
    & you said, *Mom, this is too nice for me.*

A few days later, burrowing in, you hung
    sheets as makeshift walls, drew the blinds,

blackened the skylight, preferring, as always,
    the compact, dark, & cordoned-off,

the tiniest & untidiest of places. Twenty years
    earlier, you'd made your bed in the laundry

room, next to the furnace & water tank.
    When I'd do the wash, I'd find empties

of DeKuyser's Peppermint Schnappes, cheap,
    one hundred proof. Self-medicating

on liquor or dope, as you had since fifteen,
    you now had the will-to-oblivion once mine

& if I tried to stop you, you weren't beyond
    shoving me or taking a swing. Your next

move, when you worked for a plumber,
    was to a rooming house in Leominster,

a triple-decker with rambling additions
    where welfare mothers, their kids, &

a few neglected elderly lived. One January night,
    your cigarette ignited your mattress.

A smoke alarm woke the man across the hall
    who got you out. Fire trucks, sirens,

woke everyone else. When I arrived, driving
    through a blizzard, your smoking mattress

lay on the snow, ice-edged even as it smoldered.
    Still smashed, stumbling, weeping & rocking,

hair singed, arms swinging—you punch-hit
    the red flares & revolving lights—

refused to come back home with me.
    I saw it was true—you didn't want to live.

The first time you burrowed, you were nine,
    living in a house I rented with another woman

& two men. You staked out a closet, maybe
     three-by-eight, would sleep nowhere else,

made a cocoon, one thing piled on another.
     So many small spaces I've seen you build

over the years—self-designed Murphy beds,
     collapsible desks, cubbyholes. Your first

website video-clipped the marijuana factory
     you'd created in a closet: silver-lined walls,

full-spectrum around-the-clock lights, automatic
     misting, closed-circuit camera on the plants.

This was the rooming house in Ukiah,
     where cokeheads & dealers lived, where

through a corner window, lured by your budgie,
     Netanyahu, Western jays & pigeons flew

into your room. You'd trained Net to shower on
     your shoulder & whistle the theme from

The Andy Griffith Show. Hermit, yes, easily,
     enclaved in disarray & neglected smells.

I've not seen where you live these days, in southeastern
     Georgia, with your girlfriend, four dogs,

three cats, an aggressive parrot named Hector
     whom she talks to in a high-pitched squeaky voice,

and in a high-pitched squeaky voice,
     the parrot talks back. I dream you are happy

& at peace, tucked in, unbothered by those
     who would, easily, given the slightest

provocation, commit you to hospital or prison.
     Oh wary malcontent, recluse at ease when

your world is small enough to ignore, be safe.
     May you have, near at hand, whatever you need.

An Interview with Gray Jacobik

In October 2013 I sent Gray Jacobik a series of interview questions about the first ten poems in her collection *Little Boy Blue*. Her responses address many of the central topics of this book, which was my hope when I formulated the questions. Serendipitously, they also refer specifically to poet-teachers Walt Whitman, Baron Wormser, and Robert Frost, who have been my touchstones throughout. It would be hard for me to overstate the pleasure I take in this unintentional overlap between our separate conversations—or in the fact that Gray chooses that word herself when she says, "My brain was formed in English: every thought I've ever had, my entire internal and external conversation has been framed by the grammatical conventions of English."

Dawn

As I read these poems, I kept thinking about the precision of your word choice. For instance, in poem 2, I couldn't stop thinking about the words *separation* and *separate,* which to me feel central not only to that particular poem but also to the collection as a whole. As you were writing these poems, did certain words persist in your mind? Did they guide or inhibit your intentions as you wrote? Perhaps you could talk a bit about how the pressure of words affects you as a poet.

Gray

Well, I love words, of course . . . words, phrases, clauses, sentences, paragraphs. But I wrote these poems as an outpouring; thus, they came too fast for me to stop to feel or think about individual words. I did very little revision, and then only the sort I think of as "mopping up." When I did revise, it was primarily shaping that consisted of line lengths, imposing end-stopped or enjambed lines, determining stanza patterns, and so on. So my revisions were formal rather than content-related: that's what comes with amassing forty years of emotional pressure, especially when you've spent (as I did) the previous thirty years writing poems and mastering craft.

Dawn

To my ear, your sentences have a very coherent sound in all ten of these poems. What I mean is that your approach to syntax and grammar doesn't radically change from poem to poem. In addition, your line length is relatively consistent: it doesn't shift from very long to very short, although sometimes you do indent lines. Other than those indents, the greatest visual difference among the poems lies in the stanza breaks. Could you talk about how you decided where to break the stanzas? Did you generally make those choices as you wrote the first drafts, or did you do most of that decision making as you revised?

Gray

The content of the poems arrived whole cloth. I remember having the practice of two contemporary poets in mind when I was shaping stanzas: C. K. Williams (whose models are Whitman and Ginsberg) and W. S. Merwin. I borrowed Williams's verse-paragraph pattern: every other line indented, each stanza functioning as a prose paragraph functions, except not always (that is, sometimes the enjambment carries over the stanza break). By *prose paragraph* I mean a topic sentence and supporting sentences—the understanding that a whole action has been accomplished and the focus is going to shift now (announced by the blank space of the stanza break).

Merwin has written many poems *sans* punctuation, in a headlong, on-rushing, intensely enjambed style, and I used his pattern for several of the poems (although none that you're including here). For the concluding poem, number 23, I had Allen Ginsberg's "Howl" in mind. I wanted a sense of breathlessness and a compiling and a jumbling up until all the particulars spun out of control. I was aiming for an epiphany.

Dawn

In general, these poems use traditional spelling and punctuation, but you have made one noticeable break from standard usage: you consistently insert an ampersand instead of the word *and*. Why did you decide to employ such powerful visual repetition in these poems?

Gray

I remember deciding to change all the *ands* to ampersands after all the poems were written, an unusual choice for me because I had never used an ampersand before. I remember being critical of any poet who did because I believe poems are made of words, not symbols, but of course words are symbols too. I wish I had a better reply to your question other than that the ampersand just looks better to me in the context of these particular poems. *Context,* I'd define as the gestalt of the poem, the whole of it, the world from which it derives and to which it returns, and, I hope, contributes. That's a big elusive abstraction, I know, but it is something a poet begins to feel at some point, particularly with a long poem or a long sequence of related poems, as in *Little Boy Blue.*

Dawn

The poems in this collection are filled with specific, vivid details of actual places, people, events, and things. As you were writing, did you ever find yourself replacing factual details with fictional ones because you wanted to intensify, for instance, the drama or cadence or imagery? What are your thoughts about the relationship between truth and lies in a poet's choice of details?

Gray

My commitment to myself when I began writing these poems was that I would tell only the truth: I would not add or embellish or exaggerate. I don't hesitate to "replace factual details with fictional ones" for "drama or cadence or imagery" in the normal course of writing lyrical or narrative poems; but these are dramatic poems. More importantly, the whole is a memoir. There would have been no point in writing the poems if I were going to tell anything less than the truth as I knew it to be, not that personal memory cannot be faulty at times. We all know it is, but there is nothing in *Little Boy Blue* that I know to be false.

Let me just say that the context in which I wrote these poems was entirely personal. I hadn't seen or spoken to my son in two years. I was not sure I would ever see or talk with him again. I was in a state of grief, and writing the poems became a way of speaking to him in a literary way because I could not speak to him in a literal way. I'd never told him the story of our life together as I knew it, and under the circumstances of our estrangement and separation, I wanted to tell him. There was a pressure that built up in me, an imperative force that caused the poems to come forth. They are essential poems, necessary poems, written under duress. I needed to write them whether or not he'd ever read them, and I didn't write them to publish them or even necessarily to keep them. However, a part of me no doubt wanted them in the world because I read some of them in public a few times—testing the waters, so to speak—and it was the intense and enthusiastic response of friends and others poets— two particular poets, Baron Wormser and Robert Cording—that led me to seek publication.

Even so, I sat on them for two years and did not submit them to CavanKerry Press until 2008. A period of five years went by between the time of composition (the first six months of 2006) and the time of publication. During those years I came to see the poems as something other than personal. While they come from my personal history, they comprise as well just another American story, the story of a girl and then a woman; a baby, a child, and then a man; mother and son, immersed in white, working-class, North American life in the mid- to late twentieth century. I no longer relate to the poems as personal. I consider them to be transpersonal.

Dawn

Writers are constantly faced with the painful dilemma of whether or not to use close acquaintances as characters in their creative work. Even in the best of situations, this can feel terribly ruthless. Do you have any advice for poets who are struggling with the moral and emotional ramifications of using close acquaintances as characters in their work?

Gray

I don't use my son's name, and he has a different surname from mine. I changed the proper names (or nicknames) of anyone I mentioned who was associated with him, and I also changed one place name. Other characters are identified by their role only. These are minor protections against privacy, the very least someone can do and probably insufficient as safeguards in this Internet world. After we were reconciled and he was back in my life again, I gave the manuscript to my son and asked for his permission to publish, and was given it, before I signed a publishing agreement (but not before I sought publication). I do not know what I would have done if he'd asked me not to publish it. Because he had suffered so much in life, I think he wanted his story told, but I'm speculating, I don't know for certain, and he may change his mind someday.

Advice? Every situation is different, but I think it is one of those "greater good" issues. Does it serve the greater good of the cultural moment to a sufficient degree that jeopardizing another's privacy is worth the risk? That's going to be a calculated guess under even the best circumstances. The writer knows the people or person he or she is writing about and on that knowledge has to honestly judge the potential impact. Sit on the poem or manuscript or memoir for a time if the subjects are still living and haven't given overt permission to disclose what's being disclosed. Try to get one's own ego out of the way. That's easier to do if one's a poet because there's no chance any money or fame will ever be earned as a consequence. I'm sure it's a lot more complicated if a financial motive is involved. Of course the privacy of each of us is at risk all the time now, so the dynamic is changing. Who knows what privacy even means? There is only, ever, now, relative privacy.

Dawn

These ten poems from *Little Boy Blue* are all written in free verse, and on first listen, they sound much like plain, informal speech. Some critics find fault with contemporary free verse precisely because it imitates the everyday meters of prose. What's your reaction to that point of view? How much importance did the sounds of words, the rhythm of lines, the stresses of grammar and syntax play in your construction of these particular poems?

Gray

I am so deeply immersed in *language as language,* so sensitive to sound, whether or not that pertains to the cadence of a line or a sentence or to smaller-frame sounds such as alliteration, assonance, chiming, rhyming, and so on. Thus, it is impossible for me not to be extremely conscious of how a thing (as small as a phoneme, as long as an entire poem) sounds. Those critics who find fault with free verse because it sounds too much like everyday prose are stick-in-the-mud traditionalists, and nothing will ever change their points of view.

When a poem sounds like prose or too much like prose, other elements of poetic composition come to the fore: metaphor, metonym, compression, the dance of contraries, the dramatic element, as Frost talks about it—dozens, if not hundreds of other variables, all factoring into what it takes to lift a particular bit of writing up off the flat ground and into the realm to which we give the honorific title *poem*. Besides, why besmirch prose as inferior to poetry when some prose sounds quite amazing and lyrical? That very fact belies the contrarian's argument.

Dawn

Robert Frost once wrote, "A poem should be a set of sentences." Do you agree with him? Do the grammatical conventions of English influence the way in which you puzzle your way into a poem you writing? Do you think of your poems as being sets of sentences rather than sets of words, or sets of stanzas, or sets of images?

Gray

Well, I don't think in terms of "sets." My brain was formed in English: every thought I've ever had, my entire internal and external conversation has been framed by the grammatical conventions of English. There's no "outside" to that "inside" box, at least not for me.

Earlier you asked about the pressure of individual words. For me, I feel the *force* of a sentence forming. It has a momentum; the beginning of a sentence seems to long for its end to come, and I like to vary the length and types of sentences I use. I think of sentences as musical instruments: sometimes one wants to listen to a quartet, at other

times an orchestra. I've never cottoned to poems that have a monotonous sentence
structure . . . over and over again the same sentence type (for example, all active voice,
nary a passive voice to be heard). The only poet I've ever read who I thought could get
away with like-sentences piled upon like-sentences is Whitman, but then his sentences
are so long the reader forgets that here comes another one just like the other one: thus,
his genius.

Dawn
Finally, I want to ask you about the way in which you organize time in this collection.
In one poem, the son might be in his forties; in the next he might be a four-year-old;
in the next he might not have been born yet; in the next he might suddenly be middle-
aged again. Why did you decide to organize the poems out of chronological order?
Were you envisioning a different sort of order?

Gray
There are twenty-three poems altogether, of which you've selected ten; and, yes,
you're correct: the chronology is all mixed up. The poems appear in the order in which
I wrote them. I spoke of the poems as being necessary, essential, born out of duress.
What I did was acquiesce to the order those forces chose. After long consideration,
trying them this way and that, I realized that a mixed-up chronology required the
reader to participate more in shaping the narrative, and I wanted each reader to put the
parts together in whatever way his or her mind makes the connections.

Ideas for Writing
In the opening chapters of this book, I asked a series of questions about poetic elements.
In my chapter on Kelly's and Coleridge's poems, I asked a series of questions about what
was going on in both their work and my own. In this chapter, I asked a poet a series of
questions about how she wrote a poetry collection that I deeply admire.

It's valuable to push myself to ask these kinds of questions. As those of you who are
teachers may already know, the act of creating a question requires you to concentrate on
the work at hand, to imagine a broad or precise response, to frame words that allow the
responder to speak in her own voice and reveal her own knowledge. Creating a question
can be as instructive for the questioner as it is for the listener.

In this chapter I offered you a sheaf of poems from a single collection with the hope
of showing you that poems are more than individual entities. They are pieces within a
larger, coherent body of work. A poet doesn't just jumble the poems into any old order.
She creates an arc, consciously or intuitively. She constructs a work of art composed of
smaller works of art.

So I'm going to suggest that you give yourself the chance to spend time with an entire
collection of poetry. Choose a collection you know very well, or open a new collection
for the first time. Read the book from beginning to end, and then make a list of at
least five questions to ask the poet. It doesn't matter if the poet is dead or living: the
conversation you are creating will stay alive in you, and in your poems.

Now reread the collection and try to answer your own questions. To do this, you'll need to put yourself into the poet's mind. Imagine what she would say to you: try to use your own words to follow the pathways of her thought. This is a tremendously difficult exercise. I guarantee you will be exhausted. But I think you will also have learned something about concentration and intellectual empathy. For as Jorge Luis Borges writes, "every time I read an article about me . . . I am generally amazed and very grateful for the deep meanings that have been read into those quite haphazard jottings of mine. Of course, I am grateful to them, for I think of writing as being a kind of collaboration. That is to say, the reader does his part of the work; he is enriching the book."[5]

Afterword
A Few Thoughts about Publication

"The line of words fingers your own heart," writes Annie Dillard. "It invades arteries, and enters the heart on a flood of breath."[1] But when I reach the end of a draft, suddenly the aloneness of writing becomes intolerable. Someone, somewhere, must need my poem. Where can I send it? I don't have a moment to waste! I've moved from concentrating on the poem to drifting into the daydream that Natalia Ginzburg describes so well:

> I used to think that one day some famous poet would discover [my poems] and have them published and write long articles about me; I imagined the words and phrases of those articles and I composed them from beginning to end, in my head. I imagined that I would win the Fracchia prize. I had heard that there was such a prize for writers. As I was unable to publish my poems in a book, since I didn't know any famous poets, I copied them neatly into an exercise book and drew a little flower on the title page and made an index and everything.[2]

Ginzburg's words capture the goofy sweetness of a writer's hopes. They remind me of my own silly dreams, not to mention the sheaves of bad poetry I've written over the course of my life. Still, I believe it's important to cherish ambition in its innocence, not only in our students and friends but in ourselves. Even Milton, that canonical heavyweight, once whispered, "Listen, . . . but in secret, lest I blush; and let me talk to you grandiloquently for a while. You ask what I am thinking of? So help me God, an immortality of fame. What am I doing? Growing my wings and practicing flight. But my Pegasus still raises himself on very tender wings."[3]

Writers yearn for readers. They are the other half of the conversation, the one we idealize in our minds as we struggle with the unwieldy materials of our art. It's natural and right to feel this way. Our ongoing imaginary conversations not only help us frame and dramatize our thoughts, but they also remind us of the heavy moral obligations of speech. Nonetheless, you've no doubt read plenty of interviews in which some famous writer snarls her version of "publication is a soul-sucking waste." Cynically, you note that this particular writer has published stacks of books and shows no signs of abandoning ship. Yet it's hard to forget her words, for they seem to deride your own dreams.

Ginzburg reminds us that there are reasons to sympathize with the predicament of writers who have succeeded in making their art the center of their lives:

> As a vocation [writing] is no joke. . . . We are constantly threatened with dangers whenever we write a page. . . . The days and houses of our life, the days and houses of the people with whom we are involved, books and images and thoughts and conversations—all these things feed it, and it grows within us. It is a vocation which also feeds on terrible things, it swallows the best and worst in our lives and our evil feelings flow in its blood just as much as our benevolent feelings.[4]

Commitment to a vocation changes an artist. Suddenly the daydreams that sustained her as an apprentice retreat into the shadows. As she becomes more entangled in her art, she often becomes less able to endure the business side of writing: submissions, self-promotion, interviews. If she is earning enough money from her work, she can hire a publicist or an agent to help manage that rift. But this is rarely the case with poets, most of whom earn almost nothing from their books. A cranky, dismissive writer may in truth be desperately overwhelmed by the dangers of her art.

As far as I can tell, there's no easy way to negotiate the problematic relationship between writing and publishing poetry. Even poets who are writing at a very high level struggle to publish their manuscripts. Midsized and large presses are market-driven, and poetry doesn't pay their bills. Small presses try to manage their cash troubles by relying on contests with hefty submissions fees. As a result, thousands of hopeful poets write checks and submit manuscripts to contests that they have little chance of winning. Many of these unsuccessful manuscripts are truly not ready for publication. But some of them are, and they still remain unpublished.

It is easy to become cynical about the publishing world. Conspiracy theories are rife: "Such-and-such a contest judge is choosing his own students for prizes!" "Anyone without a degree from such-and-such a program has no chance!" Some of these suspicions are founded on fact. But many honest, idealistic publishers are simply overwhelmed. With tiny staffs and limited resources, they cannot print more than a few books a year.

I'm not suggesting that you stop dreaming about publishing a book of poems. But as Ginzburg reminds us, much of the dream's charm is its vast separation from real life. It's important to learn to be patient with your poems, both in their creation and their dissemination. Literary journals are good place to start, but some of the famous ones are even more exclusive than book publishers are. Many journals have content preferences: for instance, one might prefer metrical poetry, while another is looking for experimental prose poems. The Internet glut is daunting. Every day someone founds a new online literary journal, but many of these journals last for only an issue or so. It's not much comfort to publish a poem and then discover that the journal has vanished into the aether.

Another option is to self-publish, either in print or on a blog or other online platform. This gives you the option to release your work quickly, but it also has many pitfalls. The first, and greatest, is the unscrupulous vanity press market, which you should avoid entirely. Although there are some honest presses that will help you self-publish, you must be vigilant in your research.

If you choose to publish on a blog, you avoid the issue of fees, but you risk falling into a different sort of trap. When publishing becomes so easy and immediate, you are likely to begin posting work that isn't ready for publication. And this leads me back to the topic of patience. In *Letters to a Young Poet,* Rilke writes to Franz Kappus:

> You ask whether your verses are good. You ask me. You have asked others before. You send them to magazines. You compare them with other poems, and you are disturbed when certain editors reject your efforts. Now (since you have allowed me to advise you) I beg you to give up all that. . . . Nobody can counsel you and help you, nobody. There is only one single way. Go into yourself. Search for the reason that bids you write.[5]

Given the pleasure that Rilke took in sharing his thoughts and advice with Kappus, I don't entirely believe his statement. We all have individual paths into our vocation. Some of us require strict isolation. Some of us benefit enormously from mentors or classes or reading groups. But when Rilke says, "There is only one single way. Go into yourself. Search for the reason that bids you write," I think, as much as anything, he's reminding Kappus to be patient about his apprenticeship. It takes a great deal of time to learn any craft. And craft is not the end of the story. Learning to transform those artisan techniques into art requires many more layers of patience and concentration.

When you write a poem draft and immediately post it on online, you imply a state of completion: "This poem is done. Want to read it?" Your mind is no longer absorbed by the potentials of creation and revision. It has moved into a state of hope and anxiety; it has forgotten the intensities of immersion in the work. Sometimes that is exactly the right place for your mind to be. But the lure of quick publication can blind you to the actual condition of the poem itself. What if you revised the draft another ten or fifteen times? What would you discover? What would the poem become?

There's another, more down-to-earth ramification of publishing poems on blogs or discussion forums: you no longer have the option to submit them to a literary journal. Most journals will not consider previously published work, which includes anything published online, even on your own blog. You can get around this situation by only publishing on unsearchable blogs or private forums, but that strictly limits your readership. Many school blogs are set up like this, and it's also a good way to create an online reading or workshop group. But if your goal is wide dissemination, then you're caught in a bind.

In the end, all you can do is "search for the reason that bids you write" . . . and then write. Make sure that the vocation itself is calling you, not the dream of praise. But honor the conversation as well. It may arise where you least expect it, not from publication or a prize but from a student, a stranger, a poet long dead, the sparrow that alights on your hand—the life that hears you, and answers—that you hear; that you answer. In the words of Zbigniew Herbert,

> what would the world be
> were it not filled with
> the incessant bustling of the poet
> among the birds and stones[6]

Recommended Resources

There are thousands of useful and eloquent craft manuals, biographies, letter collections, and anthologies. Here I list a few of my own favorite resources—books I return to again and again for advice, explanation, inspiration, and support.

Aldington, Richard, ed. *The Viking Book of Poetry of the English-Speaking World.* 2 vols. New York: Viking, 1958.
> Don't give away old anthologies just because they're old. As survey anthologies go, Richard Aldington's is completely out of date, but I've always liked it because he offers an unusually rich assortment of Elizabethan and Victorian poetry. Recently I discovered that Aldington was a spokesman for the Imagist movement in poetry (a group that included Ezra Pound, H. D., and Amy Lowell). From the contents of these volumes, I never would have guessed.

Atwood, Margaret, ed. *The Oxford Book of Canadian Verse in English.* Toronto: Oxford University Press, 1982.
> This anthology chronicles, as the back cover explains, "the emergence of poetic expression in a developing country." Beginning with sixteenth-century poets and ending with poets born in the 1950s, Margaret Atwood's anthology coheres into a complex portrait of a population coming to grips with itself and its landscape. It's one of my favorite poetry books.

Bate, Walter Jackson. *John Keats.* Cambridge, Mass.: Belknap/Harvard University Press, 1964.
> This is the best poet's biography I have ever read. As he traces John Keats's growth as a poet, Walter Jackson Bate manages to make me feel as if he is simultaneously tracing the expansion of my own mind. It is not only a wondrous achievement but a tremendous source of encouragement for any apprentice poet.

Borges, Jorge Luis. *This Craft of Verse,* edited by Călin-Andrei Mihăilescu. Cambridge, Mass.: Harvard University Press, 2000.
> I always like to find out what other people read and listened to before they began to think of themselves as writers, and that's much of what Jorge Luis Borges does in this collection of lectures. He entwines these memories with beautifully articulated explanations of the way in which craft intersects passion.

Byatt, A. S. *Passions of the Mind.* New York: Vintage International, 1993.
> A. S. Byatt is primarily known as a novelist, but she is also a literary scholar and a skilled and complex personal essayist. This collection focuses on a number of her favorite writers, including poets such as Robert Browning, Sylvia Plath, and Samuel Taylor Coleridge. It is an excellent model for anyone who is striving to write prose about literature.

Carruth, Hayden. *Letters to Jane.* Keene, N.Y.: Ausable, 2004.
> In 1994, Hayden Carruth learned that fellow poet and friend Jane Kenyon had been diagnosed with leukemia. His first instinct was to write her a letter, though he told her, "Don't think about answering this." She never was able to answer him, but he continued to write to her regularly until she died in 1995. This book collects that one-sided correspondence, a moving example of the way in which a conversation endures despite silence. Teacher Ruth Harlow writes, "*Letters to Jane* is more than a resource. It speaks to that power of friendship and communication that is simply so human."[1]

Frost, Robert. *The Notebooks of Robert Frost,* edited by Robert Faggen. Cambridge, Mass.: Belknap/ Harvard University Press, 2006.
> Robert Frost's notebooks are a mishmash of drafts, cranky polemic, opinions about poetry, and his teaching philosophy. Spanning nearly seventy years, they are an unparalleled window into the thought process of a poet who was also a committed teacher of poetry. This is one of our touchstone texts at the Frost Place Conference on Poetry and Teaching.

Lopate, Phillip, ed. *The Art of the Personal Essay: An Anthology from the Classical Era to the Present.* New York: Anchor/Doubleday, 1994.
> If you're interested in writing personal essays about what you've been reading, Phillip Lopate's anthology is one of the best resources available. Not only does the book offer numerous models, but his detailed introduction illuminates many facets of the genre, which, "unlike the formal essay, . . . depends less on airtight reasoning than on style and personality, what Elizabeth Hardwick called 'the soloist's personal signature flowing through the text.'"

Miłosz, Czesław. *The Witness of Poetry.* Cambridge, Mass.: Harvard University Press, 1983.
> Polish poetry occupies a unique niche in the history of European literature. Since at least the Middle Ages, Polish poets have aligned themselves with the traditions of classical Greek and Roman literature. Yet the nation itself has been in almost constant political turmoil—a pawn in every invasion, its borders altered, its government usurped, its people murdered. Miłosz was one of several twentieth-century Polish poets who brought their art to an extraordinarily high level in this atmosphere. His lectures consider how external events and aesthetic history influence the art of both an individual and a generation.

Nims, John Frederick. *Western Wind: An Introduction to Poetry.* New York: Random House, 1983.
> I bought this poetry guide when I was a college student, and I have never found a better one. Not only will it teach you everything you need to know about form, meter, figurative language, and other technicalities, but it also includes poems, writing exercises, philosophical talk, and even physics demonstrations.

Reynolds, David S. *Walt Whitman's America.* New York: Knopf, 1995.
> This biography of Whitman is also a biography of his times. Reynolds explores the busy, shifting world of nineteenth-century American politics, culture, and society as it influenced Whitman's transformation from hack journalist to poet-sage. It's a wonderful portrait, overflowing with details and color.

Rilke, Rainer Maria. *Letters to a Young Poet* (1929), translated by M. D. Herter Norton. New York: Norton, 1954.
> These are among the sweetest, most patient, most sensible letters every written. Whether you are a mentor or an apprentice (or both), Rilke's words will be sustenance.

Rukeyser, Muriel. *The Life of Poetry* (1949). Reprint. Ashfield, Mass: Paris Press, 1996
> I opened this book having no idea what I would find; but in the brief time that I've owned it, the book has become one of the most valuable volumes on my shelf. Rukeyer's observations are both bardic and intimate, and the ground she covers is astonishing. The book is a manifesto for poets, for readers, for listeners.

Sternburg, Janet, ed. *The Writer on Her Work*. Vol. 2, *New Essays in New Territory*. New York: Norton, 1991.

In this volume Janet Sternburg collects twenty personal essays by women writers who talk about how they found their way into their art. Covering a broad range of genres, the book includes pieces by several poets, including Rita Dove, Linda Hogan, Maxine Kumin, and Carolyn Forché.

Woolf, Virginia. *The Common Reader*. 1st and 2nd series. New York: 1948.

Virginia Woolf is, without a doubt, my primary influence as an essayist. Although she was a voracious and wide-ranging reader, she had no formal schooling. As a result, her essays are extraordinarily personal, revealing their author's obsessions, excitements, snobberies, shyness, anxieties, and brilliance. I love them dearly.

Wormser, Baron, and David Cappella. *A Surge of Language: Teaching Poetry Day by Day*. Portsmouth, N.H.: Heinemann, 2004.

_____.*Teaching the Art of Poetry: The Moves*. Mahwah, N.J.: Erlbaum, 2000.

Baron Wormser founded the Frost Place Conference on Poetry and Teaching. In these two books, he and his colleague David Cappella lay out a blueprint for a poetry-centered classroom. *A Surge of Language* is the diary of a fictional teacher, whereas *Teaching the Art of Poetry* is a guide to teaching specific poetic elements. Both, however, offer innumerable ideas for making poetry a regular part of the school day. The books are invaluable for teachers working at all levels, kindergarten through university.

Notes

Opening epigraph: Robert Frost, notebook 13 (1919), in *The Notebooks of Robert Frost*, ed. Robert Faggen (Cambridge, Mass.: Belknap/Harvard University Press, 2006), 180.

Introduction: Fellow Feeling and Common Experience

1. Robert Frost, notebook 4 (1909–50), in *The Notebooks of Robert Frost*, ed. Robert Faggen (Cambridge, Mass.: Belknap/Harvard University Press, 2006), 54.
2. Frost, notebook 6 (1910), in ibid., 87.
3. Countee Cullen, "To John Keats, Poet, at Springtime" (1925), in *The Book of American Negro Poetry*, ed. James Weldon Johnson (New York: Harcourt, Brace, and World, 1931), 227–28.
4. James Weldon Johnson, "Countee Cullen," in ibid., 220.
5. Francis Bacon, "Of Studies," in *The Essayes or Counsels, Civill and Morall, of Francis Lo. Verulam, Viscount St. Alban* (London, 1625), http://andromeda.rutgers.edu/~jlynch/Texts/studies.html.
6. Baron Wormser and David Cappella, *A Surge of Language: Teaching Poetry Day by Day* (Portsmouth, N.H.: Heinemann, 2004), 7.
7. Rainer Maria Rilke, *Letters to a Young Poet* (1929), trans. M. D. Herter Norton (New York: Norton, 1954), 52–53.
8. All quotations are from my blog, http://dlpotter.blogspot.com.
9. Gretel Ehrlich, "Life at Close Range," in *The Writer on Her Work*, vol. 2, *New Essays in New Territory*, ed. Janet Sternburg (New York: Norton, 1991), 178.
10. Muriel Rukeyser, *The Life of Poetry* (1949; reprint, Ashfield, Mass.: Paris Press, 1996), 175.
11. Philip Levine, "The Poet in New York in Detroit" (1994), in *A Poet's Sourcebook: Writings about Poetry, from the Ancient World to the Present*, ed. Dawn Potter (Autumn House Press, 2013), 226.
12. Jorge Luis Borges, "The Telling of the Tale," in *This Craft of Verse*, ed. Călin-Andrei Mihăilescu (Cambridge, Mass.: Harvard University Press, 2000), 43.
13. Jorge Luis Borges, "A Poet's Creed," in ibid., 115.
14. M. H. Abrams, "Criticism," in *A Glossary of Literary Terms*, 4th ed. (New York: Holt, Rinehart, and Winston, 1981), 35.
15. Rukeyser, *The Life of Poetry*, 11.
16. Ibid., 132.

1 William Shakespeare: Sonnet 81

Epigraphs: Virginia Woolf, "Indiscretions," *Vogue* (November 1924), in *The Essays of Virginia Woolf*, ed. Andrew McNeillie (San Diego: Harcourt Brace Jovanovich, 1988), 3:463; Hayden Carruth, *Letters to Jane* (Keene, N.Y.: Ausable Press, 2004), 38–39.

1. Samuel Taylor Coleridge, "Shakespeare's Poetry" (1808), in *The Portable Coleridge*, ed. I. A. Richards (New York: Penguin, 1950), 413.
2. Horace, "To Virgil" (23 B.C.E.), in *The Odes of Horace*, trans. David Ferry (New York: Noonday, 1997), 65.
3. Adrienne Rich, "Images for Godard" (1970), in *Adrienne Rich's Poetry*, ed. Barbara Charlesworth Gelpi and Albert Gelpi (New York: Norton, 1975), 53.
4. Wisława Szymborska, "The Railroad Station" (1967), in *View with a Grain of Sand: Selected Poems*, trans. Stanisław Barańczak and Clare Cavanagh (San Diego: Harcourt Brace, 1995), 41.
5. John Keats, "On First Looking into Chapman's Homer" (1816), in *Selected Poems and Letters by John Keats*, ed. Douglas Bush (Boston: Houghton Mifflin, 1959), 18.
6. William Shakespeare, *The Tragedy of Hamlet* (1603, 1604, 1623), in *The Riverside Shakespeare*, ed. G. Blakemore Evans (Boston: Houghton Mifflin, 1974), I.iv: l. 90.
7. Sylvia Plath, "Words," in *Ariel* (New York: Harper and Row, 1961), 85.

8. Pablo Neruda, poem 44, in *The Book of Questions* (1973), trans. William O'Daly (Port Townsend, Wash.: Copper Canyon Press, 1991), 44.

9. Robert Frost, notebook 17 (1924–25), in *The Notebooks of Robert Frost*, ed. Robert Faggen (Cambridge, Mass.: Belknap/Harvard University Press, 2006), 234.

10. Jorge Luis Borges, "Thought and Poetry," in *This Craft of Verse*, ed. Călin-Andrei Mihăilescu (Cambridge, Mass.: Harvard University Press, 2000), 84.

2 Emily Dickinson: "He put the Belt around my life"
Epigraphs: Mabel Loomis Todd, journal entry (September 15, 1882), in Polly Longsworth, *Austin and Mabel: The Amherst Affair and Love Letters of Austin Dickinson and Mabel Loomis Todd* (Amherst: University of Massachusetts Press, 1984), 4; Stanley Kunitz, "Foreword" (1972), in *Obscenities*, by Michael Casey (Pittsburgh: Carnegie Mellon University Press, 2002), xiii.

1. Christopher Benfey, "Emily Dickinson and the American South," in *The Cambridge Companion to Emily Dickinson*, ed. Wendy Martin (Cambridge, U.K.: Cambridge University Press, 2002), 31, 32.

2. Ibid., 30.

3. Baron Wormser and David Cappella, *Teaching the Art of Poetry: The Moves* (Mahwah, N.J.: Erlbaum, 2000), 41.

4. David S. Reynolds, *Walt Whitman's America* (New York: Knopf, 1995), 314.

5. Amy Clampitt, "Amherst" (1990), in *The Collected Poems of Amy Clampitt* (New York: Knopf, 1999), 319.

6. Federico García Lorca, "Deep Song" (1922), in *In Search of Duende*, ed. and trans. Christopher Maurer (New York: New Directions Publishing, 1998), 13.

7. Ruth Stone, "Lines," in *In the Next Galaxy* (Port Townsend, Wash.: Copper Canyon Press, 2002), 86.

8. Robert Pinsky, *The Sounds of Poetry* (New York: Farrar, Straus, and Giroux, 1998), 14.

9. William Blake, "A Pretty Epigram from the Entertainment of those who have Paid Great Sums in the Venetian & Flemish Ooze" (n.d.), in *The Prose and Poetry of William Blake*, ed. David V. Erdman (New York: Doubleday, 1970), 505.

10. Betsy Sholl, "Reading," in *Late Psalm* (Madison: University of Wisconsin Press, 2004), 77.

11. Walt Whitman, *Song of Myself*, part 1 (1891–92), in *Complete Poetry and Selected Prose by Walt Whitman*, ed. James E. Miller, Jr. (Boston: Houghton Mifflin, 1959), 25.

12. John Keats, "On First Looking into Chapman's Homer" (1816), in *Selected Poems and Letters by John Keats*, ed. Douglas Bush (Boston: Houghton Mifflin, 1959), 18; William Shakespeare, *The Tragedy of Hamlet* (1603, 1604, 1623), in *The Riverside Shakespeare*, ed. G. Blakemore Evans (Boston: Houghton Mifflin, 1974), III.i: l. 78; Samuel Taylor Coleridge, "Kubla Khan, or, A Vision in a Dream" (1798), in *The Portable Coleridge*, ed. I. A. Richards (New York: Penguin, 1950), 157; Langston Hughes, "Dream Dust" (n.d.), in *Selected Poems of Langston Hughes* (New York: Knopf, 1959), 75.

13. Allen Ginsburg, "Transcription of Organ Music," in *Howl and Other Poems* (San Francisco: City Lights Books, 1956), 31.

14. Linda Pastan, "snow shower" (2009), in *The Autumn House Anthology of Contemporary Poetry*, 2d ed., ed. Michael Simms (Pittsburgh: Autumn House Press, 2011), 296.

15. Barbara Anderson, "Deuce: 12:23 a.m." (1991), in *New American Poets of the '90s*, ed. Jack Myers and Roger Weingarten (Lincoln, Mass.: Godine, 1991), 3.

16. Octavio Paz, "The Other Voice" (1989), in *The Other Voice: Essays on Modern Poetry*, trans. Helen Lane (Orlando, Fla.: Harcourt Brace Jovanovich, 1990), 158.

17. Emily Dickinson, "Going to Him! Happy letter!" and "Going—to—Her!" (c. 1862), in *The Complete Poems of Emily Dickinson*, ed. Thomas H. Johnson (Boston: Little, Brown, 1976), 238–39.

---

3 Percy Bysshe Shelley: To a Skylark

Epigraphs: Richard Holmes, *Shelley: The Pursuit* (New York: New York Review Books, 1994), 730; Tim Seibles, "Ice Cold: Tim Seibles on Teaching, Privacy, and His National Book Award Nominated *Fast Animal,*" an interview by Alan W. King, *Bomblog* (December 6, 2012), http://bombsite.com/issues/1000/articles/6949.

1. Mary Shelley, "Preface," in *The Poetical Works of Percy Bysshe Shelley*, ed. Mary Shelley (Boston: Little, Brown, 1855), x.

2. Jane Welsh Carlyle, letter to Mrs. Welsh (September 5, 1836), in *I Too Am Here: Selections from the Letters of Jane Welsh Carlyle,* ed. Alan Simpson and Mary McQueen Simpson (Cambridge, U.K.: Cambridge University Press, 1977), 164.

3. T. S. Eliot, "Shelley and Keats," in *The Use of Poetry and the Use of Criticism: The Charles Eliot Norton Lectures* (1932–33), cited in Neil Arditi, "T. S. Eliot and *The Triumph of Life,*" *Keats-Shelley Journal* 50 (2001): 124; W. H. Auden, "Introduction," *Nineteenth-Century British Minor Poets* (1966), cited in John Ashbery, "John Clare," in *Other Traditions: The Charles Eliot Norton Lectures* (Cambridge, Mass.: Harvard University Press, 2000), 7.

4. Mary Shelley, cited in Holmes, *Shelley,* 599. Holmes doesn't identify the source of this quotation.

5. Gwendolyn Brooks, "The Rites for Cousin Vit" (1949), in *Western Wind: An Introduction to Poetry,* by John Frederick Nims (New York: Random House, 1983), 337.

6. John Berryman, poem 54 of *Sonnets to Chris* (1947, 1966), in *Collected Poems, 1937–1971,* ed. Charles Thornbury (New York: Noonday, 1989), 97.

7. Mary Austin, "The Grass on the Mountain" (1923), in *American Poetry: The Twentieth Century* (New York: Library of America, 2000), 1:24.

8. W. H. Auden, "Writing," in *The Dyer's Hand and Other Essays* (New York: Random House, 1962), 22, 26.

9. Aphra Behn, "The Willing Mistress" (1673), in *The Viking Book of Poetry of the English-Speaking World,* ed. Richard Aldington (New York: Viking, 1958), 1:501.

10. Holmes, *Shelley,* xiii–xiv.

11. Richard Hugo, "The Triggering Town," in *The Triggering Town: Lectures and Essays on Poetry and Writing* (New York: Norton, 1979), 11.

12. Ibid., 12.

13. André Breton, quoted in *Western Wind,* 22. The author, Nims, doesn't identify the source of this quotation.

14. Robert Browning, "An Essay on Percy Bysshe Shelley" (1852), in *Essays on Poetry: Peacock, Shelley, Browning,* ed. H. F. B. Brett-Smith (Boston: Houghton Mifflin, 1921), 82.

15. William O'Daly, "Introduction," in *The Book of Questions,* by Pablo Neruda (1974), trans. William O'Daly (Port Townsend, Wash.: Copper Canyon Press, 1991), xi.

16. Gjertrud Schnackenberg, "Darwin in 1881," in *Supernatural Love: Poems, 1979–1992* (New York: Farrar, Straus, and Giroux, 2000), 27.

17. Rainer Maria Rilke, *Letters to a Young Poet* (1929), trans. M. D. Herter Norton (New York: Norton, 1954), 34–35.

18. Robert Frost, notebook 23 (1938–51), in *The Notebooks of Robert Frost,* ed. Robert Faggen (Cambridge, Mass.: Belknap/Harvard University Press, 2006), 328.

19. Percy Bysshe Shelley, "A Defence of Poetry" (1821), in *A Poet's Sourcebook: Writings about Poetry, from the Ancient World to the Present,* ed. Dawn Potter (Autumn House Press, 2013), 112.

20. Margaret Atwood, "Nine Beginnings," in *The Writer on Her Work,* vol. 2, *New Essays in New Territory,* ed. Janet Sternburg (New York: Norton, 1991), 152.

NOTES

4 Gerard Manley Hopkins: The Soldier

Epigraphs: Elizabeth Bishop, "Gerard Manley Hopkins: Notes on Timing in His Poetry" (1934), in Brett C. Millier, *Elizabeth Bishop: Life and the Memory of It* (Berkeley: University of California Press, 1993), 53; Gerard Manley Hopkins, letter to Robert Bridges (1885), cited in Robert Bridges, "Editor's Preface to Notes," in *Poems*, by Gerard Manley Hopkins (1918), reprinted by *Bartleby*, http://www.bartleby.com/122/101.html.

1. Gerard Manley Hopkins, letter to R. W. Dixon (October 5, 1878), in *Hopkins: Poems and Prose*, ed. Peter Washington (New York, Everyman, 1995), 143–44.

2. Bridges, "Editor's Preface to Notes."

3. Baron Wormser and David Cappella, *Teaching the Art of Poetry: The Moves* (Mahwah, N.J.: Erlbaum, 2000), 85, 84.

4. Philip Larkin, "The Art of Poetry No. 30," an interview by Robert Phillips, *The Paris Review* 84 (summer 1982), http://www.theparisreview.org/interviews/3153/the-art-of-poetry-no-30-philip-larkin. Thanks to Thomas Rayfiel for sharing this interview with me.

5. bill bissett, "th wundrfulness uv th mountees our secret police" (1978), in *The New Oxford Book of Canadian Verse*, ed. Margaret Atwood (Toronto: Oxford University Press, 1982), 361.

6. Sonia Sanchez, "Song No. 3" (1987), in *A Formal Feeling Comes: Poems in Form by Contemporary Women*, ed. Annie Finch (Ashland, Ore.: Story Line Press, 1994), 198.

7. Melissa Stein, "So deeply that it is not heard at all, but," *Green Mountains Review* 23, no. 1 (2010): 114.

8. Russell Edson, "Out of Whack" (1977), in *The Longman Anthology of Contemporary Poetry, 1950–1980*, ed. Stuart Friebert and David Young (New York: Longman, 1983), 386.

9. Richard Hugo, "Nuts and Bolts," in *The Triggering Town: Lectures and Essays on Poetry and Writing* (New York: Norton, 1979), 40.

10. Derek Walcott, *The Prodigal* (New York: Farrar, Straus, and Giroux, 2004), 38.

11. Thomas M. Bernstein, *The Careful Writer: A Modern Guide to English Usage* (New York: Atheneum, 1977), 370; William Strunk, Jr., and E. B. White, *The Elements of Style*, 3d ed. (New York: Macmillan, 1979), 7.

12. Robert Frost, notebook 44 (n.d.), in *The Notebooks of Robert Frost*, ed. Robert Faggen (Cambridge, Mass.: Belknap/Harvard University Press, 2006), 640.

13. Carlene Gadapee, personal communication, April 24, 2013.

14. Robert Pinsky, *The Sounds of Poetry* (New York: Farrar, Straus, and Giroux, 1998), 63.

15. Gerard Manley Hopkins, letter to Robert Bridges (February 15, 1879), in *Hopkins: Poems and Prose*, 62.

16. John Cheever, *The Wapshot Chronicle* (New York: Harper and Row, 1957), 111. Thanks to Ruth Harlow for reminding me of this mention.

17. Ange Mlinko, "Gerard Manley Hopkins: 'The Windhover'" (n.d.), *Poetry Foundation*, http://www.poetryfoundation.org/learning/guide/182786#guide.

18. Anne Sexton, "With Mercy for the Greedy," in *All My Pretty Ones* (Boston: Houghton Mifflin, 1961), 23.

5 Amy Lowell: Thompson's Lunch Room—Grand Central Station

Epigraphs: Amy Lowell, "Preface," in *Sword Blades and Poppy Seed* (1914), reprinted by *Project Gutenberg*, http://www.gutenberg.org/files/1020/1020-h/1020-h.htm; Joe-Anne McLaughlin, "A Brood of Critics; A Mischief of Poets," in *Jam* (Rochester, N.Y.: BOA Editions, 2001), 66.

1. David Perkins, *A History of Modern Poetry: From the 1890s to the High Modernist Mode* (Cambridge, Mass: Belknap/Harvard University Press, 1976), 343.

2. Ibid., 327.

3. Mark Jarman, "Astragaloi" (1998), in *The Autumn House Anthology of Contemporary Poetry*, 2d ed.,

ed. Michael Simms (Pittsburgh: Autumn House Press, 2011), 171.

4. Theodore Roethke, "Words for Young Writers" (1948–49), in *On Poetry and Craft* (Port Townsend, Wash.: Copper Canyon Press, 2001), 89.

5. H. D. [Hilda Doolittle], *The Gift* (1941, 1943; reprint, New York: New Directions, 1982), 72.

6. Terry Blackhawk, "The Burn," in *The Light Between* (Detroit: Wayne State University Press, 2012), 29.

7. Jessie Redmon Fauset, "Christmas Eve in France" (n.d.), in *The Book of American Negro Poetry,* ed. James Weldon Johnson (New York: Harcourt, Brace, and World, 1931), 206.

8. Ted Hughes, "Sketching a Thatcher" (1989), in *Selected Poems, 1957–1994* (New York: Farrar, Straus, and Giroux, 2002), 182.

9. Baron Wormser and David Cappella, *Teaching the Art of Poetry: The Moves* (Mahwah, N.J.: Erlbaum, 2000), 111.

10. Siegfried Sassoon, "The rank stench of those bodies haunts me still" (1916), in *The Penguin Book of First World War Poetry,* 2d ed., ed. Jon Silkin (London: Penguin, 1979), 124–25.

11. Adrienne Rich, "Ghazals: Homage to Ghalib," in *Leaflets: Poems, 1965–1968* (New York: Norton, 1969), 75.

12. Mona Van Duyn, "The Talker" (1973), in *Poetry in Motion: 100 Poems from the Subways and Buses,* ed. Molly Peacock, Elise Paschen, and Neil Neches (New York: Norton, 1996), 88.

13. Seamus Heaney, "The Government of the Tongue," in *The Government of the Tongue: The 1986 T. S. Eliot Memorial Lectures and Other Critical Writings* (London: Faber and Faber, 1988), 102, 106, 108.

14. Perkins, *A History of Modern Poetry,* 327.

15. Denise Levertov, "Sojourns in the Parallel World" (1994), in *The Life Around Us: Selected Poems on Nature* (New York: New Directions, 1997), 75–76.

16. John Berryman, "Poetry Chronicle, 1948: Waiting for the End, Boys," in *The Freedom of the Poet* (New York: Farrar, Straus, and Giroux, 1976), 297.

17. William Dunbar, "Done is a battle" (c. 1500), *Poetry Foundation,* http://www.poetryfoundation. org/poem/180331; Rodney Jones, "Mule" (1989), in *New American Poets of the '90s,* ed. Jack Myers and Roger Weingarten (Lincoln, Mass.: Godine, 1991), 189.

6 *Robert Hayden: Aunt Jemima of the Ocean Waves*

Epigraphs: Pontheolla T. Williams, *Robert Hayden: A Critical Analysis of His Poetry* (Champaign: University of Illinois Press, 1987), 54; Ruth L. Schwartz, "Photograph of the Child," in *Dear Good Naked Morning* (Pittsburgh: Autumn House Press, 2005), 5.

1. Stuart Friebert, "Robert Hayden," in *The Longman Anthology of Contemporary Poetry, 1950–1980,* ed. Stuart Friebert and David Young (New York: Longman, 1983), 65.

2. Ibid; David Perkins, *A History of Modern Poetry: Modernism and After* (Cambridge, Mass: Belknap/ Harvard University Press, 1987), 607.

3. Sharon Olds, "The Quest" (1987), in *New American Poets of the '90s,* ed. Jack Myers and Roger Weingarten (Lincoln, Mass.: Godine, 1991), 275.

4. Peter Cooley, "Self-Portrait as Van Gogh" (1987), in ibid., 36.

5. W. H. Auden, "The Globe," in *The Dyer's Hand and Other Essays* (New York: Random House, 1962), 181.

6. D. H. Lawrence, "When I Read Shakespeare" (1929), in ibid., 177.

7. Julia Alvarez, "Against Cinderella" (1984), in *The Poets' Grimm,* ed. Jeanne Marie Beaumont and Claudia Carlson (Ashland, Ore.: Story Line Press, 2003), 172.

8. Robert Cording, "For Primo Levy," in *Against Consolation* (Fort Lee, N.J.: CavanKerry Press, 2002), 35.

9. Annie Boutelle, "Puppeteer," in *This Caravaggio* (Amherst, Mass.: Hedgerow Books, 2012), 30.

10. Richard Wilbur, "Fabrications," in *Mayflies: New Poems and Translations* (New York: Harcourt,

2000), 21.

11. Charles Webb, "The Death of Santa Claus" (2001), in *Poetry 180,* ed. Billy Collins (New York: Random House, 2003), 231.

12. Tim Seibles, "What Bugs Bunny Said to Red Riding Hood" (1999), in *The Poets' Grimm,* 53.

13. Joe-Anne McLaughlin, "Abishag's Brag," in *Jam* (Rochester, N.Y.: BOA Editions, 2001), 13.

14. Czesław Miłosz, "Allen Ginsberg," in *Facing the River,* trans. Czesław Miłosz and Robert Hass (Hopewell, N.J.: Ecco, 1995), 38.

7 Joe Bolton: In Memory of the Boys of Dexter, Kentucky
Epigraphs: Baron Wormser, "Mr. Unpleasant and Mr. Pleasant," *Manhattan Review* (fall/ winter 2007–2008), http://baronwormser.com/pdfs/Wormser_Pleasant.pdf; A. E. Stallings, "Recitative," in "The Long Poem," *Beloit Poetry Journal Blog* (March 4, 2013), http://blog.bpj.org/ search?updated-max=2013-06-06T19:54:00-04:00&max-results=2.

1. Donald Justice, "Introduction," in *The Last Nostalgia: Poems, 1982–1990* (Fayetteville: University of Arkansas Press, 1999), xiii–xiv.

2. Robert Pinsky, *The Sounds of Poetry* (New York: Farrar, Straus, and Giroux, 1998), 5.

3. "The Hymn to Earth" (c. 650 B.C.), in *The Homeric Hymns,* trans. Charles Boer (Dallas: Spring Publications, 1970), 2. Because these poems are traditionally associated with Homer, I've used the pronoun *his* in my conversation, but their actual authorship is unknown.

4. Donald Justice, "Psalm and Lament" (1987), in *New and Selected Poems* (New York: Knopf, 1995), 149.

5. Edna St. Vincent Millay, "Recuerdo" (1919), in *American Poetry: The Twentieth Century* (New York: Library of America, 2000), 1:857.

6. David Perkins, *A History of Modern Poetry: From the 1890s to the High Modernist Mode* (Cambridge, Mass: Belknap/Harvard University Press, 1976), 333, 334.

7. "Cadence," in *The Harvard Brief Dictionary of Music,* by Willi Apel and Ralph T. Daniel (Cambridge, Mass.: Harvard University Press, 1960), 39.

8. Robert Frost, notebook 44 (undated), in *The Notebooks of Robert Frost,* ed. Robert Faggen (Cambridge, Mass.: Belknap/Harvard University Press, 2006), 640.

9. John Frederick Nims, *Western Wind: An Introduction to Poetry* (New York: Random House, 1983), 162.

8 John Donne: The Triple Foole
Epigraphs: A. S. Byatt, "Introduction," in *Passions of the Mind* (New York: Vintage, 1991), xiv; Alexander Pope, letter to Lady Mary Wortley Montagu (August 18, 1716), in *The Letters and Works of Lady Mary Wortley Montagu,* edited by Lord Wharncliffe and W. Moy Thomas (London: Bell, 1898), 1:282.

1. M. H. Abrams, "Metaphysical Poets," in *A Glossary of Literary Terms,* 4th ed. (New York: Holt, Rinehart, and Winston, 1981), 101.

2. Charles M. Coffin, "A Note on the Text," in *The Complete Poetry and Selected Prose of John Donne* (New York: Modern Library, 1952), xxxvii.

3. Theodore Roethke, "A Psychic Janitor" (1959–63), in *On Poetry and Craft* (Port Townsend, Wash.: Copper Canyon Press, 2001), 179.

4. Carolyn Forché, "The Province of Radical Solitude," in *The Writer on Her Work,* vol. 2, *New Essays in New Territory,* ed. Janet Sternburg (New York: Norton, 1991), 185.

5. "Sentence," in *The New Shorter Oxford English Dictionary* (Oxford: Oxford University Press, 1993), 2:2777.

6. Jeanne Marie Beaumont, "Afraid So," in *Curious Conduct* (Rochester, N.Y.: BOA Editions, 2004), 48.

7. Maxine Kumin, "Rehearsing for the Final Reckoning in Boston," in *Connecting the Dots* (New York: Norton, 1996), 29.

8. Alexander Pope, "Ode on Solitude" (1700), in *The Viking Book of Poetry of the English-Speaking World,* ed. Richard Aldington (New York: Viking, 1958), 1:529.

9. Lynn Emmanuel, "Dressing the Part," in *The Breath of Parted Lips: Voices from the Frost Place,* vol. 2, ed. Sydney Lea (Fort Lee, N.J.: CavanKerry Press, 2004), 109.

10. Robert Frost, letter to John Bartlett (1913), in *Robert Frost: A Life,* by Jay Parini (New York: Holt, 1999), 133.

11. Lucille Clifton, "sorrows," *Poetry* (September 2007), http://www.poetryfoundation.org/poetrymagazine/poem/180005.

12. Walt Whitman, "Preface to the 1855 Edition of *Leaves of Grass,*" in *A Poet's Sourcebook: Writings about Poetry, from the Ancient World to the Present,* ed. Dawn Potter (Autumn House Press, 2013), 139.

13. Walt Whitman, "Crossing Brooklyn Ferry" (1891–92), in *Complete Poetry and Selected Prose by Walt Whitman,* ed. James E. Miller, Jr. (Boston: Houghton Mifflin, 1959), 116.

14. Virginia Woolf, "Romance and the Heart" (May 1923), in *The Essays of Virginia Woolf,* ed. Andrew McNeillie (San Diego: Harcourt Brace Jovanovich, 1988), 3:367.

9 William Blake: America: A Prophecy

Epigraph: Nancy Willard, "The Tiger Asks Blake for a Bedtime Story," in *A Visit to William Blake's Inn: Poems for Innocent and Experienced Travelers* (San Diego: Harcourt Brace Jovanovich, 1981), 40.

1. Peter Ackroyd, *Blake: A Biography* (New York: Knopf, 1995), 21.

2. Mary Lynn Johnson and John E. Grant, introduction to "America: A Prophecy," by William Blake (1793), in *Blake's Poetry and Designs,* ed. Mary Lynn Johnson and John E. Grant (New York: Norton, 1979), 103.

3. The title of this essay is borrowed from William Blake, "The Mental Traveller," in *The Pickering Manuscript* (c. 1807), in *Blake's Poetry and Designs,* 201.

4. William Blake, annotations to Johann Caspar Lavater's *Aphorisms on Man* (1788), items 54 and 36, reprinted in *The Poetry and Prose of William Blake,* ed. David V. Erdman (New York: Anchor/Doubleday, 1970), 574.

5. Evan S. Connell, *Son of the Morning Star: Custer and the Little Bighorn* (New York: North Point, 1984), 128–32.

6. Blake, "The Little Vagabond," in *Songs of Innocence and of Experience* (1789–94), in *Blake's Poetry and Designs,* 52.

7. Blake, annotations to Lavater, item 409, in *Poetry and Prose,* 581.

8. Blake, annotations to Francis Bacon's *Essays Moral, Economical and Political* (1798), in *Poetry and Prose,* 618.

9. Blake, annotations to Henry Boyd's *A Translation of the Inferno in English verse, with Historical Notes, and the Life of Dante* (1785), in *Poetry and Prose,* 623.

10. Blake, annotations to Lavater, item 244, in *Poetry and Prose,* 577.

11. Blake, "The Mental Traveller," 205.

12. Blake, *The Marriage of Heaven and Hell* (1790), in *Blake's Poetry and Designs,* 88.

13. Ibid., 89.

14. Blake, "The Lamb," in *Songs of Innocence and of Experience,* 21–22.

15. Ackroyd, *Blake,* 121.

16. Blake, "The Tyger," in *Songs of Innocence and of Experience,* 49–50.

17. Blake, *The Marriage of Heaven and Hell,* 89.

18. Ibid., 91, 90.

10 John Milton: Paradise Lost, Book 7
Epigraph: A. R. Orage [R. H. Congreve], "A Fourth Tale for Men Only," *New Age* (May 2–June 6, 1912), quoted in *The Life of Katherine Mansfield,* by Antony Alpers (New York: Viking, 1980), 142. According to Alpers, the fictional woman ridiculed in the quotation was a thinly veiled stand-in for Mansfield.
1. All of the *Paradise Lost* quotations in this chapter are from John Milton, *Paradise Lost* (1667), ed. Merritt Y. Hughes (Indianapolis: Odyssey, 1962).
2. Andrew Marvell, "On Mr. Milton's 'Paradise Lost'" (1674), in *The Complete Poems,* ed. Elizabeth Story Donno (London: Penguin, 1972), 193.
3. C. S. Lewis, *A Preface to "Paradise Lost"* (London: Oxford University Press, 1942), 2–3.
4. Dawn Potter, *Tracing Paradise: Two Years in Harmony with John Milton* (Amherst: University of Massachusetts Press, 2009), 135–36.
5. Wisława Szymborska, "The Terrorist, He's Watching" (1976), in *View with a Grain of Sand: Selected Poems,* trans. Stanisław Barańczak and Clare Cavanagh (San Diego: Harcourt Brace, 1995), 108–9.

11 Brigit Pegeen Kelly: Pale Rider Samuel Taylor Coleridge: The Rime of the Ancient Mariner
Epigraph: Brigit Pegeen Kelly, "The Valiant," *Poetry* (September 1984): 335.
1. Carl Phillips, "The Surreal Is No Less Real: Brigit Pegeen Kelley," *American Poet* 36 (2009), http://www.poets.org/viewmedia.php/prmMID/20963.
2. Fiona Sampson, "The Transforming Soul," *The Guardian* (February 23, 2008), http://www.theguardian.com/books/2008/feb/23/featuresreviews.guardianreview24; Pamela Hart, "*The Orchard* by Brigit Pegeen Kelly," *Galatea Resurrects #10* (July 20, 2008), http://galatearesurrection10.blogspot.com/2008/07/orchard-by-brigit-pegeen-kelly.html.
3. Alfred Harbage, "Introduction," in *Coleridge's Writings on Shakespeare,* ed. Terence Hawkes (New York: Putnam, 1959), 25, 16.
4. Samuel Taylor Coleridge, *Biographia Literaria,* in *A Poet's Sourcebook: Writings about Poetry, from the Ancient World to the Present,* ed. Dawn Potter (Autumn House Press, 2013), 85.
5. Teresa Carson, "The Temple of Delight: John Keats and Jack Wiler," in ibid., 301.

12 Gray Jacobik: Ten Poems from Little Boy Blue
Epigraph: Gray Jacobik, poem 13, in *Little Boy Blue* (Fort Lee, N.J.: CavanKerry Press, 2011), 37.
1. Melanie Greenhouse, interview with Gray Jacobik, *New London Day* (September 6, 2009), http://grayjacobik.com/page4/page4.html.
2. Gray Jacobik, "Sylvia Plimack Mangold Paints," in *The Double Task* (Amherst: University of Massachusetts Press, 1998), 32.
3. Brian Brodeur, interview with Gray Jacobik, *How a Poem Happens* (April 8, 2011), http://howapoemhappens.blogspot.com/2011/04/gray-jacobik.html.
4. Greenhouse, interview.
5. Jorge Luis Borges, "A Poet's Creed," in *This Craft of Verse,* ed. Călin-Andrei Mihăilescu (Cambridge, Mass.: Harvard University Press, 2000), 119.

Afterword: A Few Thoughts about Publication
1. Annie Dillard, *The Writing Life* (New York: Harper Perennial, 1989), 20.
2. Natalia Ginzburg, "My Vocation" (1949), in *The Little Virtues,* trans. Dick Davis (New York: Arcade, 1985), 54.
3. John Milton, letter to Charles Diodati, November 23, 1637, in Barbara K. Lewalski, *The Life of John Milton* (Oxford: Blackwell, 2000), 70.

4. Ginzburg, "My Vocation," 68.

5. Rainer Maria Rilke, *Letters to a Young Poet* (1929), trans. M. D. Herter Norton (New York: Norton, 1954), 18.

6. Zbigniew Herbert, "A Tale" (1957), in *The Collected Poems, 1956–1998,* trans. Alissa Valles (New York: Harper Collins, 2007), 77.

Recommended Resources
1. Ruth Harlow, personal communication, October 3, 2013.

Reprint Acknowledgments

Following is a list of sources and credit lines for all of the reprinted poems. Briefer extracts within the chapters meet U.S. Copyright Office guidelines for fair use.

1 William Shakespeare: Sonnet 81
William Shakespeare, Sonnet 81 (1609), in *The Riverside Shakespeare,* ed. G. Blakemore Evans (Boston: Houghton Mifflin, 1974), 1764; Robert Frost, "Range-Finding" (1916), in *The Poetry of Robert Frost,* ed. Edward Connery Lathem (New York: Holt, Rinehart, and Winston, 1969), 126; Catherine Doty, "The Hungry Child," in *Momentum.* ©2004 by Catherine Doty. Reprinted by permission of CavanKerry Press, LLC; Ben Jonson, "On My First Son" (1616), in *The Complete Poems,* ed. George Parfitt (New Haven, Conn.: Yale University Press, 1975), 48; Hayden Carruth, "Adolf Eichmann," from *Collected Shorter Poems, 1946–1991.* Copyright ©1991 by Hayden Carruth. Reprinted with the permission of The Permissions Company, Inc., on behalf of Copper Canyon Press, www.coppercanyonpress.org; William Wordsworth, "Composed Upon Westminster Bridge, September 3, 1802, in *Selected Poems and Prefaces,* ed. Jack Stillinger (Boston: Houghton Mifflin, 1965), 170.

2 Emily Dickinson: "He put the Belt around my life"
Emily Dickinson, "He put the Belt around my life." Reprinted by permission of the publishers and the Trustees of Amherst College from THE POEMS OF EMILY DICKINSON, Thomas H. Johnson, ed., Cambridge, Mass.: The Belknap Press of Harvard University Press, ©1951, 1955, 1979, 1983 by the President and Fellows of Harvard College; "'See it was like this when' (#9)," by Lawrence Ferlinghetti, from A CONEY ISLAND OF THE MIND, copyright ©1958 by Lawrence Ferlinghetti. Reprinted by permission of New Directions Publishing Corp.; George Gordon Byron, "So, we'll go no more a roving" (1830), in *The Portable Romantic Poets,* ed. W. H. Auden and Norman Holmes Pearson (New York: Penguin, 1950), 254; Baron Wormser, "Jerry Lee Lewis at Nuremberg," *New World Writing* (spring 2013). Reprinted by permission of the author; John Keats, "To Autumn" (1820), in *Selected Poems and Letters,* ed. Douglas Bush (Boston: Houghton Mifflin, 1959), 247–48; Michael Casey, "break room," in *Millrat,* ©1999 by Michael Casey. Reprinted by permission of Adastra Press.

3 Percy Bysshe Shelley: To a Skylark
Percy Bysshe Shelley, "To a Skylark," in *The Poetical Works of Percy Bysshe Shelley,* ed. Mrs. [Mary] Shelley (1839; reprint, Boston: Little, Brown, 1855), 3:29–34; Thomas Hardy, "The Self-Unseeing" (1902), in *Western Wind: An Introduction to Poetry,* by John Frederick Nims (New York: Random House, 1983), 492; Sara Teasdale, "Summer Night, Riverside" (1915), in *American Poetry: The Twentieth Century* (New York: Library of America, 2000), 1:499; Christina Rossetti, "Twice" (1866), in *The Viking Book of Poetry of the English-Speaking World,* ed. Richard Aldington (New York: Viking, 1958), 2:999–1000; Jane Kenyon, "Having It Out with Melancholy," from *Collected Poems.* Copyright ©2005 by the Estate of Jane Kenyon. Reprinted with the permission of The Permissions Company, Inc., on behalf of Graywolf Press, Minneapolis, Minnesota, www.graywolfpress.org; Tim Seibles, "Trying for Fire," from *Hurdy-Gurdy.* Copyright ©1992 by Tim Seibles. Used with the permission of Cleveland State University Poetry Center, http://csuohio.edu/poetrycenter/.

4 Gerard Manley Hopkins: The Soldier
Gerard Manley Hopkins, "The Soldier" (1885), in *Hopkins: Poems and Prose,* ed. Peter Washington (New York, Everyman, 1995), 62; Andrea Hollander, "Question," from *Landscape with Female*

Figure: New and Selected Poems, 1982–2012. ©2013 by Andrea Hollander. Reprinted by permission of the author and Autumn House Press; Teresa Carson, "Fill in the [Blanks] for July 3–25, 1986," in *Elegy for the Floater.* ©2008 by Teresa Carson. Reprinted by permission of CavanKerry Press, LLC; Robert Francis, "The Base Stealer," from *The Orb Weaver* ©1960 by Robert Francis. Reprinted with permission of Wesleyan University Press, www.wesleyan.edu/wespress; Li-Young Lee, "The Hammock," from *The City in Which I Love You.* Copyright ©1990 by Li-Young Lee. Reprinted with the permission of The Permissions Company, Inc., on behalf of BOA Editions, Ltd., www.boaeditions.org; Meg Kearney, "Living in the Volcano," from *Home by Now.* ©2009 by Meg Kearney. Reprinted with permission of Four Way Books. All rights reserved; Sir Philip Sidney, "My Muse may well grudge at my heav'nly joy" (c. 1582), in *Selected Poems* (London: Penguin, 1994), 135.

5 Amy Lowell: Thompson's Lunch Room—Grand Central Station
Amy Lowell, "Thompson's Lunch Room—Grand Central Station" (1916), in *American Poetry: The Twentieth Century* (New York: Library of America, 2000), 1:166–67; Jonathan Swift, "A Description of the Morning" (1709), in *Western Wind: An Introduction to Poetry,* by John Frederick Nims (New York: Random House, 1983), 434; Kim Addonizio, "Garbage," from *Tell Me.* Copyright ©2000 by Kim Addonizio. Reprinted with the permission of The Permissions Company, Inc., on behalf of BOA Editions, Ltd., www.boaeditions.org; Joe-Anne McLaughlin, "Evening Star," from *JAM.* Copyright © by Joe-Anne McLaughlin. Reprinted with the permission of The Permissions Company, Inc., on behalf of BOA Editions, Ltd., www.boaeditions.org; Edward Thomas, "Gone, Gone Again" (1917), in *The Penguin Book of First World War Poetry,* 2d ed., ed. Jon Silkin (London: Penguin, 1981), 100; Walt Whitman, "There Was a Child Went Forth" (1891–92), in *Complete Poetry and Selected Prose,* ed. James E. Miller, Jr. (Boston: Houghton Mifflin, 1959), 258–59.

6 Robert Hayden: Aunt Jemima of the Ocean Waves
Robert Hayden, "Aunt Jemima of the Ocean Waves." Copyright ©1970 by Robert Hayden, from COLLECTED POEMS OF ROBERT HAYDEN by Robert Hayden, edited by Frederick Glaysher. Used by permission of Liveright Publishing Corporation; Joan Arden [Milly Jourdain], "Watching the Meet," in *Unfulfilment* (Oxford: Blackwell, 1924), 40; William Butler Yeats, "Easter 1916" (1921), in *The Collected Poems of W. B. Yeats* (New York: Macmillan, 1953), 177–80; Gary Snyder, "Why Log Truck Drivers Rise Earlier Than Students of Zen," from TURTLE ISLAND, copyright ©1974 by Gary Snyder. Reprinted by permission of New Directions Publishing Corp.; Robert Browning, "My Last Duchess" (1842), in *Robert Browning's Poetry,* ed. James F. Loucks (New York: Norton, 1979), 58–59; Ruth L. Schwartz, "Highway Five Love Poem," *Dear Good Naked Morning.* ©2005 by Ruth L. Schwartz. Reprinted by permission of the author and Autumn House Press.

7 Joe Bolton: In Memory of the Boys of Dexter, Kentucky
Joe Bolton, "In Memory of the Boys of Dexter, Kentucky," from *The Last Nostalgia: Poems, 1982–1990.* Copyright ©1999 by Ed Bolton. Reprinted with the permission of The Permissions Company, Inc., on behalf of the University of Arkansas Press, www.uapress.com; [Emily] Pauline Johnson, "Marshlands" (1912), in *The New Oxford Book of Canadian Verse,* ed. Margaret Atwood (Toronto: Oxford University Press, 1982), 60; Christopher Marlowe, "The Passionate Shepherd to His Love" (1599), in *The Viking Book of Poetry of the English-Speaking World,* ed. Richard Aldington (New York: Viking, 1958), 1:168–69; A. E. Stallings, "An Ancient Dog Grave, Unearthed During Construction of the Athens Metro." Copyright ©2006 by A. E. Stallings. Published 2006 by Triquarterly Books/Northwestern University Press. All rights reserved;

Alfred Tennyson, "The Charge of the Light Brigade" (1855), in *The Complete Poetical Works of Tennyson,* ed. W. J. Rolfe (Boston: Houghton Mifflin, 1898), 226–27; William Carlos Williams, "Paterson: The Falls," from THE COLLECTED POEMS: VOLUME II, 1939–1962, copyright ©1944 by William Carlos Williams. Reprinted by permission of New Directions Publishing Corp.; Anonymous, "The Demon Lover" (c. 16th century), in *Western Wind: An Introduction to Poetry,* by John Frederick Nims (New York: Random House, 1983), 401–2.

8 John Donne: The Triple Foole
John Donne, "The Triple Foole" (1650), in *The Complete Poetry and Selected Prose of John Donne,* ed. Charles M. Coffin (New York: Modern Library, 1952), 14–15; George Herbert, "Sinne" (1633), in *The Poems of George Herbert,* ed. Helen Gardner (Oxford: Oxford University Press, 1961), 38–39; Howard Levy, "Polish Prism," in *A Day This Lit..* ©2000 by Howard Levy. Reprinted by permission of CavanKerry Press, LLC; Lady Mary Wortley Montagu: "Epistle from Mrs. Yonge to Her Husband" (1724), *Poetry Foundation,* http://www.poetryfoundation.org/poem/180948; John Clare, "Badger" (written c. 1835), in *The Portable Romantic Poets,* ed. W. H. Auden and Norman Holmes Pearson (New York: Penguin, 1950), 450–52; Lucille Clifton, "sleeping beauty," from *The Collected Poems of Lucille Clifton.* Copyright ©1991 by Lucille Clifton. Reprinted with the permission of The Permissions Company, Inc., on behalf of BOA Editions, Ltd., www.boaeditions.org.

9 William Blake: America: A Prophecy
William Blake, *America: A Prophecy* (1793), in *Blake's Poetry and Designs,* ed. Mary Lynn Johnson and John E. Grant (New York: Norton, 1979), 107–21; Dawn Potter, "For the Eye altering alters all," *Sewanee Review* (spring 2013): 236–41; Dawn Potter, "Blake the Terrible," *New Walk* (autumn/winter 2011–12): 19–21.

10 John Milton: Paradise Lost, Book 7
John Milton, *Paradise Lost,* ed. Merritt Y. Hughes (Indianapolis: Odyssey, 1962), book 7, pp. 163–83; Dawn Potter, "Celestial Song" and "Killing Ruthie." Reprinted from *Tracing Paradise: Two Years in Harmony with John Milton.* Copyright ©2009 by Dawn Potter and published by the University of Massachusetts Press.

11 Brigit Pegeen Kelly: Pale Rider   Samuel Taylor Coleridge: The Rime of the Ancient Mariner
Brigit Pegeen Kelly, "Pale Rider," from *The Orchard.* Copyright ©2004 by Brigit Pegeen Kelly. Reprinted with the permission of The Permissions Company, Inc., on behalf of BOA Editions, Ltd., www.boaeditions.org; Samuel Taylor Coleridge, "The Rime of the Ancient Mariner" (1798), in *The Portable Coleridge,* ed. I. A. Richards (New York: Penguin, 1983), 80–105.

12 Gray Jacobik: Ten Poems from Little Boy Blue
Gray Jacobik, poems 1–10, in *Little Boy Blue.* ©2011 by Gray Jacobik. Reprinted by permission of CavanKerry Press, LLC; Gray Jacobik's interview responses. ©2013 by Gray Jacobik. Reprinted by permission of the author.

Index of Authors and Titles